LAWS OF TRANSGRESSION

The Return of Judge Schreber

Laws of Transgression

The Return of Judge Schreber

EDITED BY PETER GOODRICH
AND KATRIN TRÜSTEDT

UNIVERSITY OF TORONTO PRESS
Toronto Buffalo London

Toronto Buffalo London
utorontopress.com

ISBN 978-1-4875-0915-6 (cloth)
ISBN 978-1-4875-3982-5 (EPUB)
ISBN 978-1-4875-3981-8 (PDF)

Library and Archives Canada Cataloguing in Publication

Title: Laws of transgression : the return of judge Schreber / edited by Peter Goodrich and Katrin Trüstedt.
Names: Goodrich, Peter, 1954– editor. | Trüstedt, Katrin, editor.
Description: Includes bibliographical references and index.
Identifiers: Canadiana (print) 2022013510X | Canadiana (ebook) 20220135142 | ISBN 9781487509156 (cloth) | ISBN 9781487539825 (EPUB) | ISBN 9781487539818 (PDF)
Subjects: LCSH: Schreber, Daniel Paul, 1842–1911. | LCSH: Schreber, Daniel Paul, 1842–1911. Denkwürdigkeiten eines Nervenkranken. | LCSH: Judges – Germany – 19th century – Biography. | LCSH: Jurisprudence – Germany. | LCGFT: Biographies.
Classification: LCC KK185.S368 L39 2022 | DDC 347/.014092 – dc23

We wish to acknowledge the land on which the University of Toronto Press operates. This land is the traditional territory of the Wendat, the Anishnaabeg, the Haudenosaunee, the Métis, and the Mississaugas of the Credit First Nation.

University of Toronto Press acknowledges the financial support of the Government of Canada, the Canada Council for the Arts, and the Ontario Arts Council, an agency of the Government of Ontario, for its publishing activities.

Funded by the Government of Canada
Financé par le gouvernement du Canada
Canada

Contents

Acknowledgments

Fulsome thanks to the contributors for their commitment and patience over the *longue durée* of this project, from speech to writing, conference to text, law to transgression. Zvi Lothane's unbending commitment to proving Schreber's sanity was an important initiatory rite. McKenzie Wark's tweets on the absent core of identity gave us confidence at low ebbs. Swethaa Ballakrishnen focused her laser eye of doubt upon transitions in the text and provided directions on fluidity of theme and consistency of diction. Linda Mills proffered the insights of a therapist and the unbounded madness of support. As is appropriate to an endeavour such as the present, the contributions express internal struggle, crises of experience, conflicting pathways, and healthy moments of anxiety. A final note of thanks to Daniel Quinlan for his commitment to the idea, and for an unflagging and impeccable attention to detail. We acknowledge here, and with apposite gratitude, that he caught ambiguities, a nuance or two that we both missed.

Peter Goodrich
Katrin Trüstedt

LAWS OF TRANSGRESSION

The Return of Judge Schreber

Introduction

PETER GOODRICH AND KATRIN TRÜSTEDT

One of the most commented upon texts in psychiatric literature, Daniel Paul Schreber's *Memoirs of My Nervous Illness*, has received surprisingly short shrift in legal studies.[1] This remarkable work documents the gender dysphoria and transitional desires of a senior judicial office holder, but far from ending his legal investments it rather manifests an intensification of his engagement with the law during the course of an existentially disorienting and socially disapprobated experience of turning into a woman. The present study focuses upon the connection between these two seemingly antithetical features of the autobiography – the body writing of transition and the coercive lure of propriety – so as to argue that his life, in its plurality and positivity, as a judge, a transitional being, and bellowing, tormented, exiled, laughing, litigating subject, embodied an as yet unexplored nexus between law and gender, normativity and sexuality. To acknowledge the depth of Schreber's contribution means to return to him *as a judge* and consider the turbulent ties and troubled tensions between law and gender, normativity and sexuality in the ontography of his autobiography.

Famously appointed to the presidency of one chamber of the German Supreme Court, it was as a successful judicial office holder and decision maker that Schreber entered the asylum. His time of incarceration and his account of his interior life have been the subject of over a century of psychoanalytic and medical scrutiny. With the contemporary trans turn, the wave of transgender and transsexual modalities of jouissance, the dissipating materiality of the body and the instability of identities, interest in the judge's desire to become a woman has intensified, and a plethora of studies acknowledge Schreber's ownership and right to gender variance and desire for difference.[2] The *Memoirs of My Nervous Illness* are gaining renewed attention and are coming to be seen to have something novel to say. Even well over a century after their initial publication, still in print, the diagnosis of psychosis, common to Freud and Lacan, has morphed into a paean of gender fluidity and transitional desire.[3] The transgression of categories, the collapse of binaries, the hesitant and blurred edges of gender performance and ascription of sex allow a challenge to law and analysis alike. The argument simply insists upon respect for choice and indecision of sex and role. Take it further and the argument can be made that "as both high court judge and certified lunatic, Schreber embodies – and his text mirrors – a profound uncertainty about the Law through which his words make sense, and not only or most importantly to himself."[4] Why not let Schreber also be a woman, bearer of an X passport, a cross-dressing trans, a feminine judge? It is peculiarly significant, we will argue, and a primary instigation of the present volume, that, lost in the ocean of diagnoses and determinations, is the paradoxical fact that the judge's juridical career continued, that the *Memoirs* are also a *legal* text, the ontological reflections of a jurist in torrid and conflicted transition. Schreber proffers a jurisprudence of sexual difference that formed a key part of a surprisingly successful litigation in a historical and legal era that was inexorably hostile to even recognizing sexual ambivalence as anything other than madness tout court.[5] Yet Schreber's legal career did not end; rather, it took a radical turn when he abandoned the bench and sought to open new bodily spaces, as well as challenging the founding principle of law: the harsh and increasingly untenable binary distinction of sex.

The judge's challenge to the first rules of legal personality, settled since the tripartite division of law into persons, things and actions in the *Institutes of Gaius*, and to the social grammar that follows from it, was arguably good reason for lawyers to give the *Memoirs* short shrift. If the judge was a woman, by late nineteenth-century legal criteria she could not, as Schreber acknowledged, be either a lawyer or *a fortiori* a judge. To allow recognition of transition, to elide male and female and permit a crossing of the borders of gender performance and sexual designation disqualified the troubled erstwhile practitioner from reason and law alike. It would be a subversion of the axioms of the jurist, and the world as lawyers then knew it would be turned upside down. The transitional spaces that Schreber experienced and expressed, the fluidity and transgression of foundational boundaries, opened up spaces interior to legality and to the laws of thought that in the late nineteenth century were literally unthinkable and remain deeply problematic or perhaps simply opaque today.[6] It is the unique and productive tension of Schreber's account, written in a fully juristic and yet intensively committed corporeal and desiring vein that disorders the cultural and legal definitions of sex and opens them up, in proleptic and radical fashion, to the questions of identity and gender that the next century was so painfully to explore and that only in recent years have been partially addressed through rights of choice.[7] Where his contemporary, lawyer and social theorist Max Weber, sought beauty in reason, and the neo-Kantian jurist Hans Kelsen advocated for purification of legal thought, the judge proleptically bucked the trend and argued for the beauty and comedy of the body beyond its normatively shaped masculine form.[8] Tensile, erogenous, and most importantly constantly shifting shape, expanding, contracting, ingesting, expelling, retaining, exploding the body of the judge, the *corpus iuris*, is the datum and the avenue of change, of opening to new imaginings and novel discourses, to corporeal spaces and discursive ventures that law had historically sought rigorously to exclude. The phenomenological body of the judge unfolded, expanded, and retracted as the site of alternately hedonic and suicidal ideations, as the paradoxical motor of dignity and abjection. It is worth sitting with the fact, the text, of a judge who struggles to shit, who describes being fucked by the divinity, who develops breasts, experiences multiple orgasms, and variously embodies a plural identity, a shifting, cross-dressing gender, and a fecund and plural instability of sex. The judge's world collapses, changes, opens, is rife with desire, raw with law, while at the very same time the jurist is appearing judiciously as a litigant, manipulating a technical vocabulary, and persuading the German Supreme Court that nothing in this affective maelstrom, this miraculous interior mutation and bodily transformation, is a threat to the sobriety of mores and manners or indicative in any way of legal incompetence or social incontinence. The *Memoirs* begin indeed by celebrating a legal victory, by waving the certificate validating legal personality and competence in exultation and in the face of the narrative that follows. The judge did not just leave the law for its supposed other – madness, femininity, corporeality, jouissance; he was also not just a victim of an "investiture crisis."[9] Through his legal case in which the *Memoirs* played such a significant part, he managed to incorporate the supposed other of the law into the law, expanding it in the paradoxical form of resistance and acceptance of a mobile identity and shifting persona that nonetheless remained a subject of juridical rights.

How was it then that the law got left out? Why is the shifting identity of the judge, the changing shape of the lawyer, ignored? The answer requires a brief return to the history and reception of the *Memoirs*. Freud, it seems, who wrote what Lacan dubbed his best essay on the judge as a case of "dementia praecox," managed to make Schreber's *Memoirs* famous, yet thereby inadvertently colonized its legacy and blocked actual readings of his complex text outside of psychoanalytic, medical, and psychiatric discourses determined to find a subject in need of a cure.[10] Labelling him psychotic, pathologizing her non-normative behaviour,[11] diverted attention from the original text to the secondary literature. Against Freud's own notion of the importance of close and attentive reading – be it of dreams, texts, symptoms or slips – his analysis of Schreber, who was incidentally alive while the essay was being conjured, is based on the records of the warden of the asylum, on theoretical presuppositions that confirm the emergent discipline of psychoanalysis, and on very selective statements of Schreber's, rather than on any confrontation or close reading of the actual, much more complex, text. The details, the viscera, the play, and the transgression are not simply lost, but his discourse obliterated, suppressed, consigned to the dustbin of perversions, the refuse tip of obsolescent ideas. The judge's judgment is ignored in favour of diagnosis and definition, a defining out, that is brilliant in its own right but also silences the subject's language and substitutes the label of homosexuality for erotic plasticity, hallucination for feminine self-fashioning, and psychosis for the affect of law's literary desire. Any open and imaginative encounter with the discourses of so-labelled psychosis will understand such ontography as also being a creative aesthetic and inventive intellective system. The brilliant madness or mad brilliance of the *Memoirs* that Cornelius Castoriadis, and Tom Mitchell in this volume, recognize and expound, shows that much of the transgressive character of the discourse and of the performance is bodily, unconscious, and that the euphoric elaborations are poetic or matterphorical rather than simply and abstractly reasoned.[12] It is precisely the violence of law, the force and pain of the asylum's interpretation of Schreber's corporeal condition that the judge so brilliantly describes and so bravely fights. The judge, it would seem, was in reality to be discounted for veering too far off the straight and cis, the *via regia*, of Freud's Man of Law.[13]

Much-quoted though the Schreber case may be, however, the tradition following Freud's fantastical essay continued to use the judge's vivid *Memoirs* as a psychiatric exemplum, domesticating the more radical aspects of Schreber's *Memoirs* and their transgressions of norms and boundaries, splits and subjectivities. Against the grain of such "monologues by reason *about* madness,"[14] Schreber's *Memoirs* can be rediscovered and reread in the strong sense of the term,[15] not only in their political implications,[16] but as a transitional and transgressional text that challenges law and normativity on many levels while simultaneously demanding recognition for a right to plasticity and the legal competence of the transitional subject. Schreber's vision of transitioning from man to woman, from a highly esteemed judge to God's only object of desire, from a subject of rationality to a being of excessive jouissance, and all the complex entanglements along the way, continue today, perhaps more than ever, to pose a challenge to the normative "Order of the World." Miss Schreber is best thought of as the subject's own unique creation. Such respects their desire and allows them, albeit posthumously, to speak. This leaves us with the paradox of a legal and scientific account full of juridical terminology, citations to the German Civil Code, nuanced jurisprudential descriptions, and carefully crafted technical arguments on the one hand, and grandiose visions of a voluptuous God, talking rays, automatic writing machines, fleeting-improvised-men, and in summation, at the heart of this vivid critical analysis, Miss Schreber on the other.

Turning from passive patient deemed unfit to speak for himself to successful suitor for agency in court, Schreber ultimately forced the judges to accept his lunacy and her critique of the legal system. In the verdict of the case, this tension can even inadvertently be seen. The Royal Court of Appeal praises the rationality and high earnestness (*hoher Ernst*) of the *Memoirs* and Schreber's "logical and juridical operations" that ultimately lead to his reinstatement and recognition of hir capacity as one capable of "dealing with the demands of life … the orderly regulation of which is the object of the law."[17] In one and the same stroke, the court extols Schreber's carefully crafted and restrainedly rational argumentation while simultaneously also praising the passionate character of his response. The occurrence of obscenity throughout the text, the coprophilia, excretions, and ejaculations are brilliantly explained by the court through adopting the judge's own discourse, which in Freud's designation is that of psychosis, acceding that the obscenities cannot be attributed to Schreber himself, man and judge, as they are only the reproduction of the ghost voices (*Geisterstimmen*) talking at him. In an ironic contrast to Freud, the Royal Court of Dresden was closer to the judge's discourse and to "psychosis," than it was to lawful speech as understood in psychoanalytic diction. It ruled that statements by an author can actually be attributed to other sources beyond the author's intention, that one individual can thus include several voices and instances, and that what ultimately counts are not statements, but *the way in which they are written*. The cracks and the openings, the plasticity and instability of material forms that Schreber experiences and enunciates at length, reappear in the judgment of the Royal Court, as if, despite themselves, the judges seem strangely attracted, uncannily compelled by the miracles, eerily persuaded by the visions, the sights and smells, the world view that gains such stylishly weird expression, such aesthetic form in juridical pleadings and in the well-tempered, meticulously orchestrated adversarial disposition of the judge as litigant.

Laws of Transgression: The Return of Judge Schreber sets out to revisit Schreber's text with an intense attentiveness to detail, style, diction, and form, so as to hear what is said, and in particular to unfold Schreber's complex relation to the law. The judge's continuing use of law in hir war against law, the jurist's retention of and deference to legal technicality and proper form, while at the same time exploding the interior boundaries of such forms can only be approached by way of diverse perspectives. The chapters that follow variously explore the figure of Schreber as the Other of the Law, as sick from the law, as messianic transsexual legal reformer, as a mutable transitional body within legality, as subject-object of juridical scrutiny, as a poet jurist, a philosopher of law, a theologian concerned with higher norms and hierarchies, or a modern Antigone exposing the irreducible collision of law with itself. The texts turn to the *Memoirs* as the quasi-judicial writing of an enigmatic lawyer who radically changed his legal path and desires, as a judge who judged judging and found it wanting, and so too as a revolutionary text *avant la lettre*, one that created a disturbance in the symbolic order and a challenge to secularized law. The stream of consciousness, wild associations, anguish and ecstasy are forms of struggling with, translating, and exposing the tensions inherent to legality, its mechanisms, authority, and legitimacy in vivid and brilliant anticipation of the changes in bodily consciousness and juristic perception that really began to gain recognition only some three quarters of a century later.

A key element of Schreber's "minor jurisprudence"[18] is thus that of how the *Memoirs* relate not mainly to sexual orientation, but to the plasticity of gender identity, to variant and shifting gender roles, plural and playful performances, and the instability of all juridical attempts at binary demarcations of gender and sex. In Schreber's time – and the judge had early in his career worked on drafting the positivistic German Civil Code that was eventually promulgated in 1900 – the legal was tied directly and explicitly to the rational, the abstract, the deliberately and deadeningly masculine.[19] It was in the judge's own expression, a virile profession, a masculinist enterprise. Femininity served in many ways as law's other and was explicitly understood to be less than the juridical, as inferior in reason and prone to the infantile and to madness.[20] The *Memoirs* themselves take up this topos and offer a reworking of the classical juridical distribution of values, most vividly by exposing the judge's interior sensibility and imagery as a being becoming feminine, as a body developing voluptuous surfaces, as an unfolding of libidinal tensors expressive of a subject transitioning. The variability and plasticity of gender and the polymorphous character of sex is obviously complex in this text. As the judge struggles to articulate and describe dreams, visions, and experiences, disparate elements appear in excessive, deeply ambivalent, painful and entangled, challenging and ultimately unstable forms that leave binary gender norms behind, wrecked on the shoals of difference, distant splits in the rear-view mirror of an anomic art of pursuing the ethics of desire. In simple yet still novel terms, especially in the legal world, Freud's diagnostic category was homosexuality, and the repression of this then-deviant inclination was the motivating factor and drive in diagnosing Schreber. As the homosexual is no longer viewed mainly as a distorted and distorting figure organizing the norms of sexuality,[21] or the lure of the lunatic, and transitional desire and identity is no longer being treated as madness,[22] it is time to return to Judge Schreber's work and conceive it also as a contribution to a theory of law and the law's conflicted relation to identity, gender, desire, and sex. The judge's experience and the record of transition sit at the dawn of transgender theory as that of an embodied performativity, an enactment of the plurality of identities and the mobility of sexual subjectivity.

Schreber's self-fashioning of the body, and ownership of desire, the aesthetics of appearance, the beauty of style and form as lived and experienced in materiality are key features of the theatre of legality and the drama of trial, in however repressed form they manifest themselves in the political and juridical culture of late nineteenth-century Germany. The *in vivo* requirement of appearance before the law, in court, propels the body into the juridical dominion of the dead bodies of textuality, but also the materiality, and performance of litigation. The comedy of manners and the theatre of the self, of body, mask and expression, play crucial roles, not just in Schreber's *Memoirs,* but also in the law, and particularly in the legal office of the judge, which happened, of course, to be Schreber's own office. On the one hand, the judge, enacting the supposedly lucid, rational, and abstract text of the law, is traditionally – and not without significant paradox – invested in hiding the particularity of their subjectivity, their body, behind the monumental architecture and hierarchy of the legal forum, and on the other hand the judicial persona emerges theatrically transformed by wig and robes, and the other dramatic contexts, costumes, and regalia of civilian trial.[23]

The image and affect, the vestments of legal rationality as performed, show law to be intrinsically theatrical, on occasion transvestite and dramatically dependent upon the thespian skills of the dramatis personae who appear, if not in the "Gods," at least well above the subjects on trial.

For lawyers, and however disavowed, *age officium tuum*, perform your office was ever the role.[24] It is precisely such theatricality, usually put under narrow constraints, that Schreber's narrative excessively extends and expands, deconstructs and exposes. While successfully demonstrating his legal capacity and clarity of judgment so as to have his tutelage rescinded, in dressing up as a woman, in mutating physically, in owning both art and desire, in the narrative of "Miss Schreber," the jurist at the same time puts on a performance of spectacular theatrical quality. The advocacy not only transgresses the boundaries of legal reason while proving that Schreber is rational, but plays out for the judges the visceral and physical roots of affect that "the bench" simultaneously embodies and denies in their corporeal embrace and material inhabitation of *ratio iuris*, of the purity and abstraction of juridical judgment.

In pursuit of this paradox, the present volume aims to bring out how Schreber's *Memoirs* are also a textual experiment reflecting on and redrafting law. Reading and rereading the *ipsissima verba*, paying close attention to its unique complexity, inherent tension, tropes and creative rhetoric, highlighting its dynamic and transitional nature, discloses the text as a complex, painful, and comedic challenge to the law. The *Memoirs*, the thoughts worth thinking, are here understood and interpreted as a radical work of philosophical and juridical advocacy, and as a political theology of law. The immediate claim of the text argues for the right of the lawyer to hir desires and seeks to expose the contradictions of the juristic form as bearer of its own genre of madness, and as the disordering of a more expansive theory of being. Possessed by embodied thoughts, a gesticulating and bellowing intellect, Schreber devised a jurisprudence of transition, conceived and lived as an anomic corporeal transgression of the static ontological basis of law itself. *Elegantior iuris* gained a wholly new expression in the sartorial armamentarium of Miss Schreber.

Laws of Transgression: The Return of Judge Schreber brings together leading scholars in legal theory, literary studies, and psychoanalysis, practitioners and academics, to attend to the legal sources and the juristic impetus and implications of the judge's writings. Schreber not only wanted to revise the "Order of the World," the dominion and scope of law, the nomos of the earth, but also to rewrite the subject of law. Incarcerated against his will in the Sonnenstein Asylum, alleging that God was turning him into a woman, the judge left the law and, in her own words, nailed her flag to femininity, to change himself, but at the same time also to expose and change the law. Schreber's *Memoirs* continue to challenge and potentially transform its implicitly gendered hidden foundations.

In the opening chapter, "Schreber's Cases: Escaping from Rational Law," the artist and lawyer Werner Gephart, founder of the Centre for Law and Culture at the University of Bonn's law faculty, where Max Weber made his last institutional home, pursues the context – historical and juridical – of the judge's work. Surprisingly there has been no analysis of Judge Schreber's judgments, or of his doctoral studies, or of his work on the German Civil Code during his time as a civil servant. This chapter places Schreber in the context of turn of the century German social and legal science, paying particular attention to another key iconoclastic figure, Max Weber, a lawyer who fought, in his own fashion, against the iron cage of science as experienced in that century. Following the trajectory of nineteenth-century rationalism as it affected law, and most forcefully in Weber's ideal type of rational law as gapless, completely logical, and operative according to hierarchical subsumption, the lawscape or environment against which Schreber rebelled is vividly depicted. Schreber reacts against a jurisprudence that denies emotion and reduces law to its rational dimension. In contestation of this iron cage of legal rationality, the Cartesian dominion of an abstract *cogito*, Schreber embarks upon a thorough revision of the image of law, turning the negative indictment of femininity and desire into a florid and feminist imagination of a breakout from the crystal palace, a shattering of the ideal type, an aesthetic challenge to the theory of formal rational law by plunging into real law, matter and *mater*, the body and its torrid emotions. Gephart offers glimpses of beginnings and examines one of the last lawsuits that Schreber decided, a case ironically in which a litigant incarcerated in an asylum pleaded for release but was denied by the very judge who was soon to be litigating the same case, but on his own behalf. A facsimile of the judgment, and a translation, are appended to this volume.

The epistemic and juristic background to Schreber's journey is taken up in the Lacanian terms of the symbolic Law and the mirror stage of subject formation by Mark Sanders in "Primal Scene." One of the principal claims made by Jacques Lacan in his *Psychoses* (1955–56) is that, in Schreber, as with psychosis generally, we observe a *Verwerfung* (rejection) by the subject of a "primordial" or "fundamental signifier." Because this signifier organizes signification more generally – it is a condition of possibility for signification – its resulting lack or absence has profound consequences for the subject's relation to language. And because signification is linked to what Lacan calls the "Symbolic" and "Law," to which the subject accedes through the Oedipus complex, and *Verwerfung* of the primordial signifier is also thought to be a *Verwerfung* of the idea of castration, this lack or absence leads not only to the psychotic unmooring of language and thought from a common frame of reference – what has always been a sign of madness – but also an unmooring of sex/gender. The "imaginary disturbance" that Lacan identifies when the Law and the Symbolic Other (with a capital *O*) are short-circuited is that, literally – although Lacan does not refer to the relevant passages – Schreber looks in the mirror and sees not a man but a woman. Revising Lacan's interpretation of the judge as a comedic object of the psychoanalyst's own desire, Sanders takes a first bold step towards acknowledging the choice to pass through the mirror and to treat both body and sex as real choices. The law of persons, the complex social encoding of gender performances that law encapsulates, also totters towards instability. If I recognize myself as another, that other may in time recognize me.

The transitions of the trial, the advocacy of a delinquent desire as proof of rationality and legal competence because of the style of its performance, is addressed at the level of jurisprudence by Rajgopal Saikumar in "The Office of Pleasure: The Place of God in Schreber's Minor Jurisprudence." Throughout the trial, representing himself as the antagonistic vanquisher of the divine, Schreber banishes the implicit theology and religious justification of law and judging. The tradition, a major jurisprudence – school, tradition, inveterate practice – one could say, is here confronted by an alternative jurisprudence and deterritorialized language that debates, contests, and contends with the secularization of modern law. He asks whether Schreber's rationalization of his breakdown and his efforts at self-healing hint at a "minor jurisprudence" that speaks directly to certain aporias that plague questions of legitimacy and authority in a positive law that is predicated upon the absence of God. Whereas Schreber initially conceived of his un-manning as a conspiratorial persecution, over time he started to see it as a moral duty to God. Examining this shift, Saikumar argues that Schreber invokes some notion of the "miracle," understood as a state of exception, in order to justify the eroticization of his behaviour as being sane, legitimate, and obligatory, and legally as well as morally valid. A minor jurisprudence is also in this sense a subaltern language, a marginal set of corporeal and discursive practices, a series of repressed enthusiasms – wild forms of thought – that challenge the bases of their exclusion and the epistemology of their non-recognition. The minor, as Schreber evinces, is often greater and longer lived than the major.

Katrin Trüstedt, in "Schreber's Double Process: Legal and Literary Transformations of the *Memoirs of My Nervous Illness*," reads the *Memoirs* from the perspective of the transitional processes at work in the various layers of the text. Constituted by two main levels of proceedings, Schreber's *Denkwürdigkeiten* manifest a tension between two similar, yet opposed, processes of transition: while the process *described by* the text is a transformation from a male judge defined by a formalistic type of rationality to a female body aligned with excess, desire, and sexuality, the process of *describing* this transformation is itself a transition now from the excessive, otherworldly, and supposedly mad material into a coherent legal and scientific argument that ultimately succeeded in court. Making use of legal and literary techniques and using them against their grain, the *Memoirs* ultimately offer another use of legal procedure, of writing, and of bodily transformations, opening up new and other potentials, of the law, of literature, of gender roles. By relating this double-edged process to theories of legal procedure and other processes, this chapter reveals the complexity of the way Schreber's texts work as an original contribution to a theory of process and procedure, advancing and complicating our understanding of the legitimizing effects of legal practices, bodily use, and textual performances. That a transitional poet jurist, a self-defrocked – and re-frocked – judge could use the legal process quite properly and successfully to deride and transform its jurisprudential bases, the static automatism of legal bodies and juridical discourse, suggests a certain *Aufhebung*, an overcoming of legal corporeality and the binaries of sex and law. What evolves is what matters, what is material: the wild legalism of becoming other, the surreal dynamics of real change, the plurality of contradicting processes that make us who we are.

A minor jurisprudence is also an argument for a space of indetermination, an opportunity to open up the thought of law to foreign presences, alien languages, excluded and abnormal others. For Ludwig Schmitz, in "Address without Signature: Schreber's *Memoirs* and the *Manning-Lamo Chat Logs*," the canonized, thoroughly interpreted and psychoanalyzed case of Daniel Paul Schreber is read in light of another document of paranoia, the *Manning-Lamo Chat Logs*. The purpose of this juxtaposition is to suggest that the paranoid position could be construed as a contradictory insistence on simultaneously refusing a particular subjectivation and requesting to become recognized as such a symbolically valid subject. Schreber's and Manning's texts can then be read not so much as paranoid texts, but as in the first case a response to, and in the second case a reaction against, a process of subjectivation that is intrinsically paranoid – structured upon a constitutive suspicion that is conditioned not on the presence of corresponding experiences but on their absence: not knowing what is normal, or who is determining the norm, is what coerces one to act normal.

For Daniela Gandorfer in "Thoughts Worthy of Being Thought," the *Denkwürdigkeiten* bears the potential to rethink the past and future of law and legal thought. Actualizing a different (legal) future, one that doesn't thoughtlessly reiterate structures oblivious to bodies and embodiment, requires reconsidering what it means to read a text and a commitment to attend to these bodies, constantly struggling, transforming, expressing, unfolding, hurting. Gandorfer takes her cue from Goodrich's argument in *Schreber's Law,* according to which Schreber fell ill of law, and the title of the *Denkwürdigkeiten,* already stating that there are indeed things worthy of being thought. The question, however, is not simply what is *worthy*, but even more importantly, what it means to *think*. Schreber struggles to think, fears losing his mind as he is constantly he suspects to exhaust his thoughts. As a response, the judge, who, as Gephart also traces, was sick of law, expresses the need for embodied thought, that is, for the body to become expressive of a different law, one that resists Cartesianism and is, as such, becoming-woman. In other words, for Gandorfer, Schreber, and the *Denkwürdigkeiten* reveal a crisis in legal thought, which has, building on the Cartesian mind and matter dualism and on the Enlightenment subject, created a notion of law that is best suited for bodiless minds. In showing how the *Denkwürdigkeiten* can be mobilized to read different possible legal futures — namely, transhuman and posthuman(ist) — Gandorfer makes a case for embodied legal thought and a mode of reading that breaks with the authority of the text and its interpretations.

Schreber turns the tables, reverses the logic of cause and effect, and rather than using the law to judge the body of the subject, uses the body to judge the law. In "Schreber's *Grande Bellezza,*" psychoanalyst, theorist, and transgender activist Patricia Gherovici returns to Freud's reading of the *Memoirs* so as to draw out a further aspect of the judge's style. President Schreber wanted to become a woman for aesthetic reasons. A dream revealed this to him: "It must be very beautiful (*recht schön*) to be a woman succumbing to the act of copulation." The preoccupation with beauty ran deeply in Schreber's family. His father, Dr. Daniel Gottlieb Moritz Schreber, was not only a famous physician but an athlete who proselytized for the benefits of exercise and physical fitness. The elder Schreber popularized the pursuit of a beautiful, healthy body. His preoccupation with a perfectly erect posture, even during sleep, was combined with the use of constraining straps and belts as part of his crusade against children's masturbation. At the age of fifty, Schreber's father, still a body-builder and winner of several fitness contests, used his body as the model for the illustrations in his book *Pangymnasticom.* His biographer observes that "constant training had given his body perfect beauty," a beauty foregrounded by the title of one of his books, *Callipedia or Education towards Beauty through the Natural and Progressive Production of a Normal Body.* Schreber's father's pedagogical method exposes an aesthetic preoccupation based on the classical ideals of beauty condensed in the German word *Plastik.*

Daniel Paul Schreber, who thought that he was becoming a woman because God wanted to copulate with him so as to recreate a human race about to be wiped out, was also concerned with the "beauty" of his transformation. Lacan pointed out the role played by aesthetics in Schreber's purported transsexual delusion in which the most repulsive excrement co-exists with the most beautiful image. Schreber twists and parodies the normative concept of beauty promoted by his father, who naively believed he could embody the classical ideals of male beauty in his own body. Daniel Paul twists his father's posture by feminizing it and rewriting it in the superlative model of beauty as being a woman having sex.

Using Paolo Sorrentino's movie *La Grande Bellezza*, Gherovici shows how Schreber's debunking of the father's law is similar to Sorrentino's satire of Catholicism. Schreber's father embodied a Law that was also a model of aesthetics. In Sorrentino's film, satirical moments making fun of Catholicism and its mixture of aestheticism and perversity question the source of beauty, asking whether it can be divorced from the theology that perpetuated it for centuries. Beauty in *La Grande Bellezza* is what remains when you have lost your religious faith, a thin, last veil before death. Similarly, Schreber's beauty is buttressed on an apocalyptic sense of destruction of human beings compensated by regeneration through children he will bear with God. The beauty of being transformed into a woman was for Schreber a strategy of survival in the face of an impossible law and an insane world.

The life-and-death issues surrounding transition, the issue of survival, of making life liveable, are taken up by W.J.T. Mitchell in "On Gifted Schizophrenia." The idea is to perform a comparative diagnosis of the psychoses of five well-known cases: Schreber, Aby Warburg, John Nash, Elyn Saks, and William Blake. Mitchell reframes these cases inside one that is unknown to the world, but very well-known to him: his son, Gabriel Mitchell, an artist and filmmaker who left a large archive of work documenting his struggle with schizophrenia. The relation to law and the state of exception is fairly simple. The link is our model of the "sovereign subject" who is simultaneously "above the law" (as the sovereign who "decides on the exception") and below the law, as an abject victim of forces beyond his control (the "tumult"). The sovereign form of psychosis tends toward monomania, grandiosity, and solipsism (a phenomenon sometimes observed in political sovereigns – especially in present times). The abject form of psychosis experiences the self as shattered into a quarrelling multitude and beset on all sides by delusions and hallucinations. All of these cases become intelligible as variations on this theme: Schreber as messianic transsexual; Warburg as Herculean Atlas surrogate; Nash as discoverer of the mathematical laws justifying free market capitalism; Saks as fantasized mass murderer tormented by a guilt complex; Blake as a world-building poet/ prophet visionary who heard voices and saw things; and Gabriel as a combination of these roles, building world-models out of diagrams and structures, and planning a cinematic atlas of madness as the fundamental human condition. The desire to be king, so often noted in the registers, the "law books" of the asylum, gains its quintessence in the arche-angelological project of Gabriel.[25]

The prevalence of suicide, the experience of life as unliveable if pathologized, if refused the right to self-identification engenders a world of pain and suffering. Davide Tarizzo, in "The Delusional Metaphor: On Schreber's Anathema," takes up this theme, addressing the Schreber case as a criminal trial in which it is the father – and by extension the *nom du père* – that is the culpable cause of the judge's unease, dislocation, madness, and transition. If it were a matter of legal procedure, if one were looking for the culprit who did wrong in this case, one should interrogate Daniel Paul's father sooner or later. In fact, Daniel Gottlieb Moritz Schreber cannot be seen as a stranger to his son's tragedy. And the same holds for Daniel Paul's brother, Daniel Gustav, who committed suicide in his thirties. As Daniel notes in his *Memoirs*, "There is something rotten in the state of Denmark." In their contributions on the Schreber case, both Freud and Lacan reinforce the message that the law stalks the figure of the disturbances in the judge's desire for an unavailable truth.

The return to the figure of paternity appositely places the case of Schreber in the context of the first law, that of the *oikonomia*, of the family, which in Agamben's work is transformed by the Christian church from an apolitical administration of the household into a mystical and divine practice that is intended to save humanity.[26] It is in the Christian regime of the emotions, the laws inculcated in the *oikos*, modelled on the rules of monastic life, that the order of identity and the classification of gender and sex has its ultimate cause in the West. It is the management of the emotions, the administration of normal behaviours, that make life unliveable through the exclusion of polymorphous jouissance and the denigration, if no longer the prohibition of a self-fashioning body and life. The *oikonomia* pedals a normalizing disciplinary administration of subjects, of bodies and knowledge, of identity and sex, and in doing so limits the modalities of jouissance and bifurcates choice. The biblical restriction of existence to two sexes and the *oikonomic* limitation of gender to normatively prescribed behaviours are the ultimate objects of Judge Schreber's rage, his bellowing, her laughter, and simultaneously the starting point, the fluid and undifferentiated, dislocated, out-of-joint, transitional modes of affective anomie that mark Schreber's journey. When we can say that in the mirror we see not a man or a woman but a multitude of potentials and alternations, only then will Schreber's other law have been inscribed, as another use of bodies that breaks with the cage of a deadening legalism, opening up the future of a beauty the judge sought to make a reality.

NOTES

1 Daniel Paul Schreber, *Memoirs of My Nervous Illness* (Cambridge, MA: Harvard University Press, 1988).

2 In this regard see Patricia Gherovici, *Transgender Psychoanalysis: A Lacanian Perspective on Sexual Difference* (New York: Routledge, 2017); and also her earlier *Please Select Your Gender: From the Invention of Hysteria to the Democratizing of Transgenderism* (New York: Routledge, 2010). For visceral accounts of transition – pharmaco-political and surgical – see Paul Preciado, *Testo Junkie: Sex, Drugs and Biopolitics in the Pharmacopornographic Era* (New York: CUNY, 2016); and Juliet Jacques, *Trans: A Memoir* (London: Verso, 2015). For a radical development of the theory of bodily mutability, and opposition to the binary system of sex, see Paul Preciado, *Counter-Sexual Manifesto* (New York: Columbia University Press, 2018). The cross-dressing, eloquently prolific, and commendably undecided McKenzie Wark is the most recent to challenge the Freudian dismissal of the judge and to invoke the enormity of Schreber's disordering of the universe: https://twitter.com/mckenziewark/status/1270504326516092928.

3 We note here that the ahistorical view that treats psychosis as a consequence of desiring to be feminine is increasingly subject to critique. The real question to be posed is what rigidity or normative categories stop the psychoanalyst from hearing the transitional character of Schreber's discourse and the desire to choose as expressions of resistance and as a tortured manifestation of free will in an epoch of conventional as well as juridical censure.

4 Jonathan Kemp, "Queer(ing) Masculinity: Daniel Paul Schreber & the Madness of the Penetrated Male Body," https://www.academia.edu/3667973/_Queer_ing_Masculinity_Daniel_Paul_Schreber_and_the_Madness_of_the_Penetrated_Male_Body_?email_work_card=thumbnail.

5 On openness to paradox as a defining feature of queer theory, see Noa Ben-Asher, "Law of Sex, Changed," in *Oxford Handbook of Law and Humanities*, ed. Simon Stern, Maksymilian Del Mar, and Bernadette Meyler, 601–18 (Oxford: Oxford University Press, 2019).

6 The refusal of definition is explored playfully in autoethnographic terms in McKenzie Wark, *Reverse Cowgirls* (New York: Semiotexte, 2020). See also her comments in an interview on transitional identity: "The unknowable core of the self is no obstacle to producing selves that do indeed know, in an active and open sense, and who use writing as a way of making themselves," https://bombmagazine.org/articles/mckenzie-wark/.

7 See particularly Gherovici, *Please Select Your Gender*; Noa Ben-Asher, "Conferring Dignity: The Metamorphosis of the Legal Homosexual," *Harvard Journal of Law & Gender* 37 (2014): 243–84; Judith Butler, *Undoing Gender* (New York: Routledge, 2004).

8 On the hetero-patriarchal assumptions in family law and the need to secure the role of "masculine" fathers in the development of "masculine" boys, see, for example, Clifford J. Rosky, "To be Male: Homophobia, Sexism, and the Production of 'masculine' boys," in *Exploring Masculinities: Feminist Legal Theory Reflections*, ed. Martha Albertson Fineman and Michael Thomson, 285–310 (Farnham, UK: Ashgate, 2013); with respect to Schreber, see also Brian Taylor, "Like a Marble Guest: The Nervous Illness of Daniel Paul Schreber," in his *Responding to Men in Crisis: Masculinities, Distress and the Postmodern Political Landscape*, 120–30 (Abingdon, UK: Routledge, 2006).

9 Eric L. Santner, *My Own Private Germany* (Princeton, NJ: Princeton University Press, 1996), xii.

10 Sigmund Freud, "Psychoanalytic Notes on an Autobiographical Account of a Case of Paranoia (Dementia Paranoides)," in *The Standard Edition of the Complete Psychological Works of Sigmund Freud*, ed. James Strachey, 12:12–80 (London: Hogarth, 1958); Jacques Lacan, *The Seminar of Jacques Lacan Book III: The Psychoses* (New York: Norton, 1993).

11 On the pathologies of sadism and masochism in the medico-psychiatric discourse and their genealogical origins in the nineteenth century, in Krafft-Ebing, Sigmund Freud, Havelock Ellis, and the *Diagnostic and Statistical Manual of Mental Disorders* (*DSM*), see Ummni Khan, *Vicarious Kinks: S/M in the Socio-Legal Imaginary* (Toronto: University of Toronto Press, 2014).

12 On the matterphorical, see Daniela Gandorfer, *Matterphorics: On the Laws of Theory* (Durham, NC: Duke University Press, forthcoming), 110, where she argues that doing theory matterphorically means that theory "cannot be confused with a set of rules or a rigid methodology that can be applied to different contexts, but rather encounters complex entanglements and

seeks to understand the material-discursive practices that brought both matter and what matters into being, or destroyed and excluded it from doing so." The body and the violences attracted to it and repelled from it are intrinsic to the theorization of Schreber's law, as Gandorfer spells out in this volume.

13 For an excellent and salutary empirical study of gender representation and norms of masculinity in law firms, see Richard Collier, "Read What the Law Firms Say: Gender and the Representation of Career Success in the Contemporary Legal Profession," chap. 4, in *Men, Law and Gender*, 95–127 (Abingdon, UK: Routledge, 2010).

14 Michel Foucault, *History of Madness* (London: Routledge, 2009), xxviii.

15 See, for instance, Sam Weber's "Introduction to the 1988 Edition," in Daniel Paul Schreber, *Memoirs of My Nervous Illness*, trans. and ed. Ida Macalpine and Richard A. Hunter, 1–28 (Cambridge, MA: Harvard University Press, 1988), as well as additional materials in Hans Israels, *Schreber: Father and Son* (Madison, CT: International Universities Press, 1989).

16 See Elias Canetti, *Crowds and Power* (New York: Farrar, Straus and Giroux, 1984).

17 Schreber, *Memoirs*, 515. See also Peter Goodrich, *Schreber's Law: Jurisprudence and Judgment in Transition* (Edinburgh: Edinburgh University Press, 2018), 99.

18 Goodrich, *Schreber's Law*, 141; Gilles Deleuze and Félix Guattari, *Kafka: Towards a Minor Literature*, trans. Dana Polan, Theory and History of Literature 30 (Minneapolis: University of Minnesota Press, 1986).

19 On the broader political developments of the time, including proto-fascist elements that Schreber's *Memoirs* exposed and in some way subverted, see Eric L. Santner, *My Own Private Germany* (Princeton, NJ: Princeton University Press, 1996); Gilles Deleuze and Félix Guattari, *Capitalism and Schizophrenia*, vol. 1, *Anti-Oedipus*, trans. Robert Hurley, Mark Seem, and Helen R. Lane (London: Continuum, 2004).

20 Shoshona Felman, "Women and Madness," *Diacritics* 54, no. 4 (1975): 2–16.

21 See Judith Butler, *Gender Trouble: Feminism and the Subversion of Identity* (New York: Routledge, 2007); see also Noa Ben-Asher, "Conferring Dignity: The Metamorphosis of the Legal Homosexual," *Harvard Journal of Law & Gender* 37 (2014): 243–84; Joseph J. Fischel, *Sex and Harm in the Age of Consent* (Minneapolis: University of Minnesota Press, 2016).

22 See, for instance, Patricia Gherovici, "Depathologizing Trans: From Symptom to Sinthome," *Transgender Studies Quarterly* 4 (2017): 534–55.

23 See Les Moran, "Judicial Pictures as Legal Life-Writing Data and a Research Method," *Journal of Law and Society* 42 (2015): 74–101; Goodrich, *Schreber's Law*, 140.

24 On the history of this juristic theatrics, see the eloquent and expansive Julie Stone Peters, *Law as Performance: Legal Theatricality, Spectatorship, and the Making of Law in Ancient, Medieval, and Early Modern Europe* (Oxford: Oxford University Press, 2022); on the legal and theatrical scene of the person, see also Katrin Trüstedt, *Stellvertretung. Zur Szene der Person* (Konstanz: Konstanz University Press, 2021), esp. chap. III.2 on a case from Schiller's Pitaval involving a gender transition.

25 On the historical usage of "law books" to describe asylum registers, see Laure Murat, *The Man Who Thought He was Napoleon: Towards a Political History of Madness* (Chicago: Chicago University Press, 2014).

26 Giorgio Agamben, *The Kingdom and the Glory: For a Theological Genealogy of Economy and Government* (Palo Alto, CA: Stanford University Press, 2011); and for inventive commentary and revision of the thesis, see Marinos Diamantides and Anton Schütz, *Political Theology: Demystifying the Universal* (Edinburgh: Edinburgh University Press, 2017).

1 Schreber's Cases: Escaping from Rational Law

WERNER GEPHART

Daniel Paul Schreber's case remains fascinating and endlessly debatable, the current publication being fine proof. I had the privilege of listening, some fifteen years ago, to Zvi Lothane's explanation of soul murder and his defence of Schreber, but I had access to it only as a case in the colourful history of madness and psychoanalysis. Unfortunately, I cannot claim to have found a completely new theory or to have conducted the urgently needed archival examination of his dissertation and professional work. Much has been said, as in the final chapter of this volume, by Davide Tarizzo, about the possible role and symbolic foreclosure triggered by his father,[1] whose name is very much linked for Germans to the restorative physical power and corporeal regimes of the *Schrebergärten*. The "dressage" of the child[2] undoubtedly impresses upon our understanding the expansive meaning of the term "habitus," as invented by Pierre Bourdieu, and referencing the embodied values of society.[3]

While the name of the father, the Lacanian Law putatively foreclosed in psychosis, has received lengthy and erudite exposition, and indictment, as in Mark Sanders's account of the unmooring of language leading also to the disruption of gender perceptions, the judge's juristic background has always seemed to be neglected. The symbolic law of the psychoanalyst always appeared to trump positive legal institutional practices. This is in many respects understandable. I believe in the magic of the law's deontic power to create our notions about society – I call it the birth of sociology from the spirit of the law – and will argue that it is precisely the ontographic power of legality that Schreber sought to conjure and understand, thereby endeavouring to fuse the symbolic and positive manifestations of the law that binds, the norms that hurt.[4] But I am also deeply convinced that the German poet-jurists' ambiguous relationship to the law – from Johann Wolfgang von Goethe to Peter Handke – has to be seen as an expression of the legal culture in which they lived. Friedrich Hölderlin, to our great regret, did not have a legal background or comparable respite, but Goethe, who criticized law as the eternal disease,[5] or Theodor Storm, who inscribed impressive words about the deep suffering caused by the law, were able to escape from law's cruel rationality into poetry and literature. Allow me to quote this remarkable and largely unknown passage from a letter Storm wrote to his wife in 1859: "How strange to my innermost being the profession [of a judge] is, into which I have fallen due to the circumstances in the absence of any other decisive aptitude. But is felt only when it has been distant to me for some time. *I have a formal physical sense of dread of it.*"[6]

The toll of legalism led not infrequently, and does so even now, to disquiet and breakdown. The iron mask of objectivity and the deadening heteronormativity of reason forced wild interior escape attempts, mad letters being one form of revenge and potential cure for that dread that descends upon the conforming legalist. Let me name another case that has been widely discussed but never resolved: the case of Max Weber. The jurist, a brilliant doctor of laws by way of a dissertation about the *Handelsgesellschaften im Mittelalter*,[7] and habilitated scholar in Roman agrarian history free of all legal argumentation,[8] as it is said, fell into a deep depression because he was overloaded with work. But nowhere is it reflected that during his writing *The Protestant Ethic and the Spirit of Capitalism* his attempts at further religious studies – from Japan to China, India to Islamic cultures – and his systematic investigation into the rational character of music may have been an expression of fleeing the "iron cage" of law.[9] Returning to religious imaginations, as judge Schreber did, was not an option for Weber, as he remained exposed to the enchanted garden of modernity. But women were a way out of the traps of rationalization. He began intimate relationships with the piano player Mina Tobler, and with Else Jaffé, the sister of Frieda von Richthofen, the spouse of D.H. Lawrence.[10] The subjacent, if not oppressed, legal authority of the father with whom he had a famous tiff, resurfaces in his monumental yet unfinished novel – known under the title *Economy and Society*.[11] Here it is so profoundly apparent that his sociological notions are directly derived from the law, having "instilled" in them a new meaning, as he said in his methodological reflections. His understanding of systematically rationalized law presents an optimal starting point for a comparative reading of Weber and a contemporary jurist, namely Schreber, who seems to "enjoy" the law and legal argumentation, especially when reading the *Denkwürdigkeiten eines Nervenkranken*, with Peter Goodrich as a legal text,[12] whereas in Weber ambiguity became evident.

"Bound to Relatively Boring Jurisprudence": Some Ambivalences towards Jurisprudence in Weber's Path from Jurisprudence to the Sociological Study of Law

From studying law, to writing a dissertation on law, to taking the assessor's exam, and finally submitting his habilitation to the faculty of law, Weber followed a nearly linear legal career trajectory.[13] This belies his conflicted attitude towards jurisprudence. With his father, Max Weber Sr., being a lawyer, jurisprudence was a more likely fit than a career in the unfledged area of classical economics or the financially unrewarding field of philosophy, let alone sociology, which at that point existed in name only, and merely as the bugbear of French positivist sciences.

In his youthful letters, it becomes apparent which parts of the law attracted Weber.[14] He does not hold criminal law in high esteem, considering it of inferior intellectual value. In order to characterize the time wasted on the dance floor – it is well known that Weber preferred the library to the dance floor – he states, "In that time, one can go through the entire general part of the imperial penal code and at least finish up with the dangerous crimes in the special part."[15]

It is thus unsurprising that little can be found on crime and punishment in Weber's writings on "cultural science" or "sociology." His negative view of *criminal law* doctrine remains unchanged. It would be a real shame, he remarks to its protagonist Georg Jellinek in 1909, to include criminal law, "this [downright] bland stuff," in an academic project.[16] Nevertheless, the rather superficial treatment of criminal law left far-reaching traces, inter alia, in the formulation of a concept of action oriented by criminal law doctrine, with reference to Gustav Radbruch, as well as in the consideration of hypothetical causal developments for the justification of sociological-historical attributive judgment.

Weber, rather, represents the *civil lawyer*, whose schooling in *gemeinrechtlich* (*ius commune*/common law) doctrine offered the contours of the formal rational law he later favoured: "belief in systems" (*Systemglaube*), "gaplessness," "complete subsumability" of reality under legally formed facts, etc.[17] This ideal type of formal rational law is so far removed from the "real" law discovered by the *Freirechtsschule* (school of Free Law) that the facts of law do not even seem to enter into view. But despite his interest in civil law, Weber is not a die-hard dogmatist. Instead, he appears from the outset to have had a legal-historical orientation, an approach that is reflected in his take on Roman law. While a student, Weber complains in a letter to his mother that, although the depiction of "institutions" by the famous teacher of Roman law Ernst Immanuel Bekker may be pleasing, the course on Roman legal history is worthy of criticism: "Roman legal history, on the other hand, which he reads together with the other course, is less pleasing to me, who still has Puchta in mind…, because it is not history, but first and foremost a depiction of the fully formed Roman civil and criminal procedure with few legal comparative intermezzos."[18]

Weber thus exhibits a penchant for the historical consideration of law. To better understand this orientation, one should recall – as Weber alludes to with his reference to Puchta – that *gemeinrechtlich* practice was conceived as legal history, whereas the historically distant Roman law was developed as a model for the formation of dogmatic systems. If one then considers Weber's further studies – besides the legal-historical influence of courses by Theodor Mommsen, Weber also attended Kuno Fischer's lectures on logic – it is hardly surprising that tension should arise towards a course of study aimed at legal practice. From the beginning, Weber aims beyond this practice-based approach to law, which exposed him to familiar problems when facing exams. In another letter to his mother on 17 February 1886, Weber admits that he should have taken a review course to prepare for his exam. Just the previous year, he had reported on a fellow student from the Allemannia fraternity: "He is sweating here in a review course with an assessor – I don't think I could participate in this as well right now."[19] Ultimately, however, cand. jur. Max Weber Jr. is less confident: "I believe to have occupied myself with a great number of things which are of no concern here, and which I could have very well put off until after the exam."[20] It is only before the exam that Max Weber regrets the "great number of things" he could have postponed: "Now I will just have to try it like that, even though any professor will admit that people who let themselves be 'crammed,' without previously doing anything themselves, are far better candidates for an exam than the most studious bright lights among the student body."[21] Weber now at least has a private tutor, Professor Frensdorff, even if he tests him only in German legal history.[22]

It is important for Weber's further development that he turns down an offer from Ferdinand Frensdorff to write his dissertation on German law. His stated reasons once again emphasize his relationship to legal history: seriously pursuing the "mass of political material" in Prussian state law, in addition to educational Roman law, viz. pandect law, cannot simply be reconciled with a "legal education" that is still to be gained.[23] Weber would instead opt to write his dissertation on the history of commercial partnerships in the Middle Ages, under the supervision of Levin Goldschmidt.[24] Despite this clear academic interest, Weber is initially drawn to practising law. In a further letter to Frensdorff, he describes his obvious joy in private practice: "At least one notices during the current work before civil chambers what had long since ceased to be the case: that one does not belong to the degenerate species of legal clerks, but is a lawyer open to multiple uses, drilled in a legal office instead of a mere writer's desk."[25] This assessment continues not to apply to matters of criminal law, which he simply finds "boring" and from which he was "never able to derive meaningful academic interest."[26]

On the basis of a letter to Hermann Baumgartner, it is known that Weber applied for a position as an in-house lawyer. On his failure, he reports with much regret, "I have a great yearning for practical work, and this yearning could perhaps have been satisfied and thus done away with here."[27]

Weber nevertheless pursues an academic career, even though his habilitation encounters problems, because Goldschmidt regards the legal domain of commercial law, which Weber dealt with from a legal-historical viewpoint in his doctoral thesis, overrepresented at the faculty of law in Berlin.[28] The habilitation ultimately deals with *Römische Agrargeschichte in ihrer Bedeutung für das Staats- und Privatrecht* (Roman agrarian history: Its importance for public and private law).[29] As a lecturer, Weber is then obligated to conduct the review courses he himself had rejected as "unscientific,"[30] following which the pedagogical calling he had seen in himself seemed to steadily wane. His application for a chair in classical economics in Freiburg may also have been due to his increasing distance from jurisprudence as a discipline, particularly as Weber confesses in another letter to Baumgarten: "For my part, I have become about a third classical economist over time."[31] His unease with law becomes clear when he expresses his hope of receiving an appointment in Freiburg to his mother: "I would be sorry if I remained bound to relatively boring jurisprudence."[32] It is not as a classical economist, whose legal background should have kept the problem of the relationship of law and economics particularly close to heart, but as a critic of R. Stammler's "'Überwindung' der materialistischen Geschichtsauffassung"[33] ("overcoming" of the materialist view of history) that the substantive interest in law steps into the spotlight from the background of a methodological criticism of a supposed Kantian. It does so to such a degree that the orientation of Weber's contribution to Schönberg's handbook, the later *Grundriß der Sozialökonomik* (*GdS*), is motivationally and substantively fed from the confrontation with Stammler – up to a telling turning point.[34]

The Suppressed Role of Emotions and Legal-Rational Law

Weber draws a sharp distinction between the emotional qualities of prerational law and the rational qualities of modern law. His implicit debate opponent is the romantic school of law, the views of which inform more recent advocates of an emotive theory of law. The meaning of this "sense of fairness and justice" to the finding of law in contemporary methodological theory, however, is debated. Max Rumpf, for instance, attempts to scientifically grasp this legal sentiment.[35] Gustav Rümelin goes so far as to derive a "logic" of a sense of law from a moral urge for order.[36] Rejecting sentiment as a source of law is also a statement against the program pursued by the Freirechtsschule. Such a source is suspicious to Weber, who was perhaps particularly ambivalent towards the emotive realm, not just for its lack of reason, but also its destabilizing effects. On the importance of legal sentiment, he states, "Yet observation has shown how extraordinarily delicately 'legal sentiment' functions so long as it is not guided by the fixed pragma of an external or internal set of interests."[37] The form of legal sentiment or an emotive grounding of law is even less suitable as the basis of collective identity. Weber therefore clearly denounces any theories teaching about a spirit of the people or the law (*Volks-* or *Rechtsgeistlehre*), as well as anyone who supports them: "However, the particularities of 'national' legal developments, this much we know, cannot be derived from differences in how 'emotive' sources function. Highly emotional, 'feeling' is particularly unsuited to stably support assertive norms and is one of the sources of irrational findings of justice."[38] In this vein, Weber denies a relationship between emotional cultures and legal cultures. Weber's line of attack is therefore twofold and central to the understanding of his *Rechtssoziologie.* The differences between "national legal cultures" cannot be derived from diffuse emotive and traditionally entrenched deep layers of an emotive culture, but are understandable and explainable only from other constellations. Hence, even though Weber does claim that certain aspects of the world can be "rationalized," "emotions" are exempted. In Weber's understanding of legal rationality, there is thus neither space for legal sentiment (*Rechtsgefühl*) nor a feeling of justice (*Gerechtigkeitsgefühl*) as a corrective of gross injustice. Rationalization of law rather implies "overcoming" legal sentiment. This statement by Weber must be taken in the way it was formulated in his time without insight into the possibilities of a state of systemic injustice, such as the Nazi "unculture" of law, whose "injustice" often existed in mobilizing collective feelings of exclusion.[39]

In the Traps of a Jurist in His Class Situation during the German Empire

In agreement with several other studies,[40] Schreber's *Denkwürdigkeiten*[41] must here, too, be viewed as an important source for the understanding the judge's case. His narrative about his second crisis is linked to his work as president of Dresden's Court of Appeals in 1893. Let us take a closer look at this situation: Minister Rudolf Schurig, we are told, had personally communicated his nomination to this high position in the hierarchical structure of the realm of normativity. On the same page, Schreber tells of his central dream, in the immediate context of his nomination: "It was the idea that it must actually be quite lovely to be a woman and succumb to copulation."[42] We know from Freud's interpretation that this phrase can be read as a latent confession to homosexual tendencies.[43] Perhaps it is not too farfetched to decipher it as an image of a female existence that does not have to bear on her shoulders the professional expectations of a judicial corpus and the ambience of being part of a certain status, namely the *Juristenstand,* a commonly shared "honour." Schreber's extreme commitment to obligation, but also to perfection and being without fault, is clearly laid out in his following avowals. Allow me to quote at length, because this background is unfortunately, even in juristically oriented studies like Ruben Marc Hackler's,[44] hidden in a footnote:

> On October 1, 1893, I took office as the president of the Senate of the Higher Regional Court of Dresden. The workload that awaited me was, as already mentioned, tremendously large. In addition, there was the desire, which on my account was fed by ambition, but nevertheless needed in the interest of the office, to gain the necessary respect among my colleagues and other sacred circles (lawyers, etc.) through the indisputable efficiency of my services. This task was all the more difficult and also placed even greater demand on the pace of personal communication, as the members of the five-judge faculty that I had to lead were almost all far older than I (up to twenty years) and, on top of that, in a certain respect more familiar with the workings of the court that I had newly joined.[45]

Ambition, respect in the circles involved, and tactful behaviour in personal relations are the sociological keywords in this narrative: ambition as an expression of a superego tautly trained by his father, whatever may be thought now about this perhaps not so dark pedagogy as had previously been thought.

Respect by significant others, that is the social circle Schreber and Weber were thrown in, which simultaneously demanded discretion towards elder colleagues, who had not been nominated though a principle of *ancienneté* that would have led to an election as president in their favour. Instead, Schreber had to cope with this discrepancy of age, lack of competence, and hierarchical superiority, which demanded tact, that is empathically projecting himself into the other's soul in order to avoid harm to the other's self.[46]

All these objective shadows over his brilliant professional success culminated in the fact that the mechanisms of societal integration into this new "society" did not work: "There was almost no opportunity for social distractions, which would have certainly done me good, with our non-acquaintances in Dresden – as I gather from the fact that I slept considerably better after the one time we were invited to an evening party."[47] Sociability (*Geselligkeit*) was lacking, and there was no access to the joys of his class, namely a soirée (*Abendgesellschaft*) by invitation that celebrates the type of aimless communication that our social soul needs. Lack of social integration, if not isolation, combined with his overcommitment to external norms that are radicalized by his habitus as *Homo juridicus*,[48] left no place for *Homo ludens*,[49] *Homo aestheticus*,[50] or the "zoon politikon"[51] to whom a political role in the Reichstag had been refused. No wonder that playing the piano brought him some relief, though a resistance is symbolically expressed by a strange story about him bursting piano strings.[52] Although these are, of course, the dialectics of bourgeois society, it should be remembered that he himself sketched this structural picture of his position in society. It is composed of a lack of social integration, high ambitions, and an overcommitment to the normative order, lacking a real *Weltordnung* (world order) as we know from his writings.[53] In 1897, Émile Durkheim published *Suicide*.[54] His distinction between anomic and egoistic as well as fatalistic and altruistic suicide condenses in Schreber's figure. Though, correctly speaking, Durkheim's pursuits were not addressed to individual behaviour but rather suicide rates as the explanandum of sociological explanations, the prototype of the anomic suicide being the sufferings of the Young Werther (Goethe) and the unlimited drive for love in Don Juan (Molière). Let us not forget: he tried several times to commit suicide, and it is not entirely plausible that an analysis of this has not been done.[55]

Before trying to follow his path from suicidal tendencies to phantasmagorical wishes to really transforming into a woman, the missing link, namely his relation towards law, justice, and jurisprudence in his lifetime, must be analysed in a much more precise way.

Elements of Schreber's Image of the Law

A reading of Schreber's dissertation would be useful (if it exists at all and he actually had to produce a written text to pass, a customary part of today's doctoral procedure). The search for it was unfortunately not successful. Different articles published by Schreber, luckily identified by Lothane,[56] did not hold what they might have promised for my special purpose either. This is why a reading of judgments that fall into the period around his second outbreak of mental illness seems to be a promising methodology to adopt. Is there any reason to think that the brilliant jurist was so greatly affected by those cases that he fled from the discipline, which paradoxically, did help him out of the asylum: the jurisprudence of late nineteenth-century Germany?

From the judgments that were accessible in the Dresden files,[57] a decision from 11 November 1893, stands out from all which were signed by Dr. Schreber in the Third Civil Senate of the Royal Higher Regional Court of Dresden (k.S.O.C.G.). The case concerned an appeal from a decision of the Zwickau Regional Court's determination of the incapacity of a former miner, Karl Louis Wagner, and an order of wardship by virtue of his disabling mental illness. Wagner found himself in the same precarious situation as the undersigned Judge Schreber was soon to find himself, namely that legal incapacity also affects the ability to stand trial. In this case, the guardian had refused to agree to the annulment of the incapacitation order, and so resisted the appointment of an advocate for Wagner, for which reason the appeal was lodged, i.e. the former miner Wagner had requested that the court assign him a lawyer to file the suit. The case was, of course, dismissed by the chairman of the court. The appeal was also rejected by Schreber, as can be seen from the renewal of the order, signed by Schreber himself, stating that it was "rejected because of the hopelessness of the intended prosecution."[58] The appeal is then also directed against this decision.

The appeal, however, could have been successful only if the reason for his incapacity had meanwhile ceased to exist, "i.e. his state of mind should have returned to normal."[59] At this point, however, the power of the medical definitions intervenes, insofar as expert opinions from district physician Dr. Barth, as well as written submissions "quite undoubtedly" concur that such a normalization had not occurred. The request to call in a lawyer to represent the incapacitated person's interests, therefore, was also rejected by the pre-trial court "with full rights."[60] The appeal against this decision was similarly unsuccessful. Thus the proleptic irony that the order of the Third Civil Senate of the Royal Higher Regional Court of Dresden on 11 November 1893, affirming the incapacity of the plaintiff and denying him legal representation, was signed by Dr. Schreber!

This date seems to be of importance when Schreber starts his second stay at the Nerven-Klinik Leipzig on 21 November, only ten days later. Medical records from the very first day had already reported that he was "very out of tune. He has now been happily made crazy, suffered brain softening, inaccessible."[61] When Schreber made the decision ten days earlier on the incapacity of the former miner Wagner, he had already experienced a hospital stay, from 8 December 1884 to 1 June 1885; it had to be clear to him that his own condition had deteriorated again. Unfortunately, both expert opinions from Dr. Barth and statements made by the incapacitated person remain unavailable, and thus it is only possible to speculate on the plausibility of the medical assessments and the justifications for the appellate court's determination. It should have been clear to Judge Schreber, however, from his own experience how precarious such a situation had to be in a total institution of surveillance and disfranchisement, where the risk of losing even his civil rights was vividly before his eyes! Yet the cold tenor of this judgment can hardly be surpassed, the decision is that of the a priori futility of a lawsuit, which made the assignment of a lawyer, according to § 620 para. 1 of the Civilprozessordnung (C.P.O.), superfluous![62]

We know that with legal effort and bold argumentation of two truths Dr. Schreber was able to ingeniously resist his own legal incapacity through the intelligent use of jurisprudence. In this case, however, legal formalism does not in any way allow him to have any understanding for someone who is in the same situation, as his own illness will very soon lead him into experiencing and recording in lengthy and vivid detail! This also seems to be a "memorable" feature of the Schreber case. It will not be possible to claim that this decision is the cause of his own relapse into illness, but he does show the dangers of a juridical formalism in which empathy and compassion, a sense of material justice, have no place. In this sense, other judgments of Dr. Schreber's also appear meaningful. They mainly concern questions of bankruptcy law and security rights in credit transactions, in which – to put it simply – the protection of creditors seems to ignore everything else and especially refuses any legal hearing for the economic misery of the debtors.

There is, however, one exception: in a decision from 11 November 1893, an appeal by seven creditors against enforcement proceedings was partially upheld. The constellation provides a socio-historically fascinating picture of Saxon society, for the creditors are butchers, merchants, reindeer keepers, fertilizer producers, and members of an agricultural credit association. The creditor, Karl von Burchardi, however, is an owner of a manor (*Rittergutsbesitzer*) who seized potatoes, pigs, fish from the garden pond, and apples on the trees, because of insolvency. In addition to interesting considerations regarding the protection of agricultural holdings against seizure, which are based on the motifs of the C.P.O. that came into force in 1879, there are also other interesting examples; the law is by no means on the side of political domination, in particular when, in a decision from 14 November, a complaint by the aforementioned Karl von Burchardi for failure to comply with a time limit established in 537 C.P.O. is declared inadmissible. We similarly see judge Dr. Schreber shining on questions of jurisdiction between the Court of Appeals and voluntary jurisdictions (order of 7 October 1893), for example, in an order on questions of lawyer's fees for the reimbursement of several appeals lodged, which is admissible only in the case of collusion (order of 28 October 1893), determinations of the value of the disputed status of an action for rescission in the context of bankruptcy proceedings (3 November 1893), and so on.[63]

In this respect, a fairly consistent picture emerges: even beyond the well-known rhetorical-legal art of Dr. Schreber – as will be shown in the following paragraph – which is handed down in the "memorabilia," a sharp and argumentatively adept lawyer appears in the decisions for which he is responsible. In those decisions, he has to deal with the subtlest of questions concerning the C.P.O, which defines limits on this kind of procedural rationality, as it is incarnated in civil procedural laws, and which then come into play again when the strange case of Wagner's incapacity is addressed and seems strangely to anticipate Schreber's own destiny.

With the Help of the Hatred Law: The Paradoxical Role of Law in Schreber's Case

As Hackler has rightly pointed out, Schreber used his juristic competence strategically in order to demonstrate that somebody who was capable of such refined and detailed juristic argumentation could not be deprived of his right to rights in everyday matters, a description of *Geschäftsfähigkeit* (legal competence).[64] The appellate court in his own case and the judgment from 14 July 1902 correctly reiterates Schreber's argumentation: "Anyone who knows how to carefully administrate in self-written procedural documents and expertise such a difficult and complicated legal matter, such as the one presented here, and perform this tactfully and discreetly if the opinions of others are considered, should also be trusted of being capable to reasonably handle the rather much simpler and less important affairs of civic life."[65] This was already accepted first in his decision and is repeated in a second instance, which reiterates that "in its incapacitation decision in favour of the plaintiff, the administrative court itself assumes that he still is capable of presiding over the judges' college, ruling on the most complicated of trials, and submitting the most difficult of legal opinions with resounding legal reasoning."[66]

The judgment of the Royal Higher Regional Court of Dresden even goes beyond this recognition of juristic competence when fairly stating in its *Entscheidungsgründe* (reasoned judgment), "The way in which the struggle against the incapacity imposed on him and its planned implementation was personally taken up, the sharpness of logical and legal operations developed in the process, the prudence of his actions, and, last but not least, the moderate attitude in his opposition towards the expert and prosecutor: all of this delivers irrefutable proof that the plaintiff does not require any custodial protection in this area, that he is rather able to independently and entirely safeguard his interests when handling his procedural affairs better than any other person could."[67] This passage is very important for my argument because not only have his doctrinal deliberations, as logically coherent arguments, been underlined, but also his extra-juristic capacities to deal with members of his own profession ("the moderate attitude in his opposition towards the expert and prosecutor") who – let us not forget – to his displeasure, did not include him in their social circle. He is held to be competent, to be capable of exhibiting the necessary tact and strategic competence to be an excellent jurist beyond the letter and the law in the books. Communicative competence ("the prudence of his actions"), so obviously lacking in the heart of that isolated soul, is taken as an argument for determining him to be legally competent (*Geschäftsfähigkeit*).

The Power of the Differentiation of Spheres

The argumentative miracle of Schreber's plea for regaining his basic civil rights as a civis was not understood by the court. Goodrich, however, has pointed to the fact that "madness and judgement, lunacy and legal practice can co-exist, without the one impacting on the other."[68] And, in fact, this is the very sense of the canonical invention of the office (*Amt*), that the state of mind of the biological person who assumes an office has no impact on the sacred effect of his official actions (differentiation between "personal grace" and "institutional grace" (*Anstaltsgnade*). This differentiation is the basis of modern institutions and the modern state. Schreber is aware of its religious implications, though he does not quote canon law but rather Luther's theory of the two realms, the *Zweireichelehre*: "'I could say that my kingdom is not of this world as far as Jesus Christ is concerned."[69] Schreber quotes the passage that is the basis for Luther's conception of a dual validity of the *Weltordnung*, a sacred sphere and a profane sphere that have to be held in difference and distance. *Sphärenfrevel* (sphere offence), as I argue elsewhere, is the gravest crime in a modern and thus differentiated society,[70] and Schreber uses it with brilliance. He is obliged to argue that the probability that his apparent madness, or at least his outward seemingly less rational behaviour, as, for example, his wearing of jewellery, or his feminine attire and colourful ribbons, worn in front of the mirror, is extremely low, and in any event is certainly less harmful than the ladies' décolletages responsible for producing colds![71] Whether this comical element is voluntary or further proof of Schreber's capacity to ironically distance himself from his foolish behaviour and thereby gain the sympathy of his former fellow judges remains unknown – a nice indicator of how harmless, to our eyes, his crazy behaviour has become.

What in an extremist position might be and had been regarded as a kind of schizophrenia proves to be nothing other than the expression of the very trait of modernity: the differentiation of roles and spheres. Reading Schreber does not only reveal a theory of law, as Goodrich has argued,[72] or disenchantment in the genealogy of the clinic as an institution of surveillance, but also demonstrates that he is a child and a propagator of the principle of differentiation – an idea that has been described as the motor of modernity in Georg Simmel's *Über soziale Differenzierung*[73] and in Durkheim's *Division du travail social*,[74] the very year of Schreber's second illness.

Conclusion

In the end, I cannot claim to have found a really new solution to the Schreber case. If one places Daniel Paul Schreber in the ranks of those who have escaped formal law and its iron cage, some of the peculiarities of his fate are put into perspective. We learn indirectly how dangerous an over-rationalized law can be. We witness the harm occasioned by a juridism that gives space to emotions only as the source of criminal motives for action, for killing out of greed, vindictiveness, mad passion, instead of trusting in the mobile and emotive force of a sense of justice, which has been so painfully lacking in the German history of injustice.

In the end, we understand Daniel Paul Schreber, the unhappy lawyer, the repressed and tortured transitional better if we relate his confusion, which seems not simply harmless but positively insightful to us today, to his legal socialization. It was only the clarity of the legal mind that brought him out of his immaturity, that forced the vivid confrontation and lucid account of experience that the *Memoirs* relate and that the Court of Appeals confirmed even back then, in shadows of the closing of the nineteenth century. We live with these ambivalences and fissures of the law even today, when we are on the one hand annoyed by the contingency of formal corona etiquette and on the other hand indulge in a belief in regulation that is even supposed to have medico-epidemiological effects. Perhaps these paradoxes can no longer be resolved in legal theory or medical history, but only in a third sphere, aesthetically, imaginally, virtually, as in the film, currently planned as the next entry in my study of the art of the jurist, colours of law.

NOTES

My thanks go first and foremost to Peter Goodrich for his patience and encouragement, to my old friend Henry Lothane for his benevolent support, and last but not least to my former assistant, Aline Azevedo, who was extremely helpful during my research and decision-making at the Dresden State Archives. I would also like to express my gratitude to Felix Rissel for his extremely careful transcription of the documents and to Jure Leko for his help in putting everything together.

1 Zvi Lothane, *Seelenmord und Psychiatrie. Zur Rehabilitierung Schrebers* (Gießen: Psychosozial-Verlag, 2004), 211. For the conflict between father and son, see Tarizzo, "The Delusional Metaphor," in this volume.

2 Émile Durkheim, *Fonctions sociales et institutions. Textes III* (Paris: Les Éditions de Minuit, 1975), 361.

3 Pierre Bourdieu, *Pascalian Meditations* (Stanford: Stanford University Press, 2000). On the heritage of Durkheim in Bourdieu's work, see esp. Daniel Witte, *Auf den Spuren der Klassiker. Pierre Bourdieus Feldtheorie und die Gründerväter der Soziologie* (Konstanz: UVK, 2014); Daniel Witte, "Der Staat und die gelehrigen Körper. Zur politischen Transformation von Subjektivierungsweisen bei Michel Foucault, Norbert Elias und Pierre Bourdieu," in *Foucault und das Politische. Transdisziplinäre Impulse für die politische Theorie der Gegenwart*, ed. Oliver Marchart and Renate Martinsen, 211–33 (Wiesbaden: Springer VS, 2019).

4 Werner Gephart, *Gesellschaftstheorie und Recht. Das Recht im soziologischen Diskurs der Moderne* (Frankfurt am Main: Suhrkamp, 1993).

5 Johan Wolfgang von Goethe, *Faust: Part One* (New York: Dover, 1994), 58. In this context, see also Werner Gephart, *Goethe als Gesellschaftsforscher. Und andere Essays zum Verhältnis von Literatur und Soziologie* (Münster: LIT Verlag, 2008).

6 Theodor Storm, *Ein rechtes Herz. Sein Leben in Briefen dargestellt von Bruno Loets* (Wiesbaden: Dieterich'sche Verlagsbuchhandlung, 1951), 207 (my translation, emphasis added).

7 Max Weber, *Zur Geschichte der Handelsgesellschaften im Mittelalter 1889–1894. Max Weber-Gesamtausgabe Band I/1* (hereinafter *MWG I/1*), ed. Gerhard Dilcher and Susanne Lepsius (Tübingen: Mohr Siebeck Verlag, 2008).

8 Max Weber, *Die römische Agrargeschichte in ihrer Bedeutung für das Staats- und Privatrecht 1891. Max Weber-Gesamtausgabe Band I/2* (hereinafter *MWG I/2*), ed. Jürgen Deininger (Tübingen: Mohr Siebeck Verlag, 1986).

9 For the "iron cage" metaphor, see Weber, *MWG I/2*. See also in Peter Goodrich's most elegant and elucidating *Schreber's Law: Jurisprudence and Judgment in Transition* (Edinburgh: Edinburgh University Press, 2018). He is using the same metaphor of Weber in order to characterize Schreber's need to "slip out of the iron cage of legal science" (10). For an overview of Weber's religious studies in regard to law, see Werner Gephart, *Law, Culture, and Society: Max Weber's Comparative Cultural Sociology of Law* (Frankfurt am Main: Klostermann, 2015). For the relationship between music and law, see Werner Gephart and Jure Leko, "Introduction," in *Law and the Arts: Elective Affinities and Relationships of Tension*, ed. Werner Gephart and Jure Leko (Frankfurt am Main: Klostermann, 2017), 12.

10 The erotic motif in Weber's life is fully played out by Martin Green, *The von Richthofen Sisters: The Triumphant and the Tragic Modes of Love* (London: Weidenfeld & Nicolson, 1974). Joachim Radkau places it at the centre of his interpretation of Weber, losing sometimes in this kind of fixation the genius "work" of Weber: *Max Weber: Die Leidenschaft des Denkens* (Munich: Carl Hanser Verlag, 2005). Rainer M. Lepsius puts it less into keyhole perspective by meticulously telling Weber's relationship to the world of women on the basis of the latter edition's sources: *Max Weber und seine Kreise: Essays* (Tübingen: Mohr Siebeck Verlag, 2016), 210–51. But the real question for the historian of the social and cultural sciences remains open: What does the "discovery" of masochistic traits in his relationship to the beautiful Else Jaffé mean for the understanding of his famous doctrine of domination (*Herrschaft*). This, in turn, deals with obedience (*Gehorsam*), motifs of obedience (*Fügsamkeitsmotive*), command structures (*Befehlsverhältnisse*), and the discovery of the masochistic, commonly shared understandings of submission (*Herrschaftseinverständnis*), badly translated as "consensus." This question has not yet been answered.

11 Edited in six volumes in the historical and critical edition of Weber's work: *Wirtschaft und Gesellschaft. Die Wirtschaft und die gesellschaftlichen Ordnungen und Mächte Nachlaß* (*MWG I/22*, 1–6).

12 See esp. Goodrich, *Schreber's Law*, 61–86.

13 Important notes can be found in Jürgen Deininger, "Einleitung," in Weber, *MWG I/2*, 4–13. See also Gerhard Dilcher, "Einleitung," in Weber, *MWG I/1* (here 8–14). See further, Realino Marra, *Dalla comunità al diritto moderno: la formazione giuridica di Max Weber 1882–1889* (Turin: Giappichelli, 1992).

14 On the knowledge of Weber as a legal clerk, see Max Weber to Ferdinand Frensdorff, 22 January 1887, *Briefe 1887–1894, Max Weber-Gesamtausgabe*

Band II/2 (hereinafter *MWG II/2)*, ed. Rita Aldenhoff-Hübinger, with Thomas Gerhards and Sybille Oßwald-Bargende (Tübingen: Mohr Siebeck Verlag, 2016), 214–16.

15 Weber to his mother, 24 January 1888, *MWG II/2*, 289 (own translation).

16 Weber to Georg Jellinek, 16 July 1909, *Briefe 1909–1910. Max Weber-Gesamtausgabe Band II/6* (hereinafter *MWG II/6*), ed. M. Rainer Lepsius and Wolfgang J. Mommsen, with Birgit Rudhard and Manfred Schön (Tübingen: Mohr Siebeck Verlag, 1994), 189 (own translation).

17 See the listing of characteristics of formal rational law by Weber, "Die Entwicklungsbedingungen des Rechts," in Weber, *Wirtschaft und Gesellschaft. Recht. Max Weber-Gesamtausgabe Band II/22,3* (hereinafter *MWG II/22,3)*, ed. Werner Gephart and Siegfried Hermes (Tübingen: Mohr Siebeck Verlag, 2010), 305.

18 Weber to his mother, 2 May 1882, *MWG II/1*, 41 (own translation).

19 Weber to his father, 2 November 1885, *MWG II/1*, 185 (own translation).

20 Weber to his mother, 17 February 1886, *MWG II/1*, 202 (own translation).

21 Weber to his mother, 17 February 1886.

22 See Weber to his mother, 24 January 1886: *MWG II/1*, 200; on the lasting closeness to his father's university friend, see Weber to his mother, 13 April 1909, *MWG II/6*, 101.

23 Weber to Ferdinand Frensdorff, 22 January 1887, *MWG II/2*, 216.

24 Weber, "Entwickelung des Solidarhaftprinzips," partial print of Weber, *MWG I/1*; see also in the editorial report, Weber, "Entwickelung des Solidarhaftprinzips," 127.

25 Weber to Ferdinand Frensdorff, 16 July 1887, *MWG II/2*, 247 (own translation).

26 Weber to Ferdinand Frensdorff, 22 January 1887, *MWG II/2*, 215 (own translation).

27 Weber to Hermann Baumgarten, 3 January 1891, *MWG II/2*, 326 (own translation).

28 Weber to Hermann Baumgarten, 3 January 1891.

29 *MWG I/2*.

30 See the list of courses given by Weber in the summer semester of 1892 through summer semester 1894, which shows him offering a tutorial on commercial law five times: *Allgemeine ("theoretische") Nationalökonomie. Vorlesungen 1894–1898. Max Weber-Gesamtausgabe Band III/1* (*MWG III/1*), ed. Wolfgang J. Mommsen, with Cristof Judenau, Heino H. Nau, Klaus Scharfen, and Marcus Tiefel (Tübingen: Mohr Siebeck Verlag, 2009), 5.

31 Weber to Hermann Baumgarten, January 1891, *MWG II/2*, 327 (own translation).

32 Weber to his mother, 26 July 1893: *MWG II/2*, 372 (own translation).

33 Weber, "R. Stammlers 'Überwindung' der materialistischen Geschichtsauffassung," in Max Weber, *Gesammelte Aufsätze zur Wissenschaftslehre* (Tübingen: Mohr Siebeck Verlag, 1985), 291–359.
34 Gephart, *Law, Culture, and Society*, 13.
35 Max Rumpf, *Gesetz und Richter. Versuch einer Methodik der Rechtsanwendung* (Berlin: Otto Liebmann, 1906).
36 Gustav Rümelin, *Über das Rechtsgefühl*, in Kanzlerreden (Kanzler der Universität Tübingen 1970–1889) (Tübingen: Mohr Siebeck Verlag, 1907).
37 *MWG I/22,3*, 444 (own translation).
38 *MWG I/22,3*, 444.
39 Werner Gephart and Siegfried Hermes, "Einleitung," in *MWG II/22,3*, 7.
40 Esp. Goodrich, *Schreber's Law*; also Ruben Marc Hackler, "Die Allianz von Recht und Medizin um 1903: eine Fallstudie zu Daniel Paul Schrebers Selbstbehauptungsstrategien im Rechtsstreit um seine Geschäftstüchtigkeit," in *BIOS – Zeitschrift für Biographieforschung, Oral History und Lebensverlaufsanalysen* 23, no. 1 (2010): 114–26.
41 Daniel Paul Schreber, *Denkwürdigkeiten eines Nervenkranken* (Berlin: Kulturverlag Kadmos, 2003).
42 Schreber, *Denkwürdigkeiten*, 27.
43 Sigmund Freud, *Werke aus den Jahren 1909–1913. Gesammelte Werke Bd. VIII* (Frankfurt am Main: Fischer Verlag, 1969), 239–316.
44 Hackler, "Die Allianz von Recht und Medizin," n16.
45 Schreber, *Denkwürdigkeiten*, 27.
46 For an analysis of this complex structure of mutual expectations, see esp. Georg Simmel: *Soziologie. Untersuchungen über die Formen der Vergesellschaftung 1908. Georg Simmel-Gesamtausgabe Band 11* (hereinafter *GSG 11*), ed. Otthein Rammstedt (Frankfurt am Main: Suhrkamp, 1992), 13–62.
47 Schreber, *Denkwürdigkeiten*, 27.
48 I take this concept from Alain Supiot, *Homo juridicus. La fonction anthropologique du droit* (Paris: Seuil, 2005).
49 Johan Huizinga, *Homo Ludens: Vom Ursprung der Kultur im Spiel* (Reinbek bei Hamburg: Rowohlt, 2017).
50 Ellen Dissanayake, *Homo Aestheticus: Where Art Comes From and Why* (Washington, DC: Washington University Press, 1995).
51 Aristoteles, *Politik* (Stuttgart: Reclam, 1989).
52 Schreber, *Denkwürdigkeiten*, 119–28.
53 Schreber, *Denkwürdigkeiten*, 34–46.
54 See Émile Durkheim, *Le Suicide: Étude de sociologie* (Paris: Félix Alcan, 1897); interpreting the logic of the suicide typology as related to the normative ordering of society, see Werner Gephart, *Strafe und Verbrechen. Die Theorie Emile Durkheims* (Opladen: Leske und Budrich, 1990), 76–101.

55 Lothane, *Seelenmord und Psychiatrie*, 583–7
56 Fußnote nicht gefunden... vielleicht Zvi Lothane, *Seelenmord und Psychiatrie.*
57 Sächsisches Hauptstaatsarchiv Dresden 11025, Oberlandesgericht Dresden (1893), Nr. 973.
58 Beschluß des dritten Civilsenats des k.S.O.C.Gs. vom 11. November 1893 zu III. C. 198/93 (own translation).
59 Beschluß des dritten Civilsenats des k.S.O.C.Gs. (own translation).
60 Beschluß des dritten Civilsenats des k.S.O.C.Gs. (own translation).
61 Cited by Zvi Lothane, *Seelenmord und Psychiatrie*, 584 (own translation).
62 Beschluß des dritten Civilsenats des k.S.O.C.Gs. vom 11. November 1893 zu III. C. 198/93 (Ruling of the k.S.O.C.G's Third Civil Senate from 11 November 1893 on III. C. 198/93).
63 Beschluß des dritten Civilsenats des k.S.O.C.Gs.
64 Hackler, "Die Allianz von Recht und Medizin."
65 Urtheil des Königlichen Oberlandesgerichts Dresden vom 14. Juli 1902, in Schreber, *Denkwürdigkeiten*, 325 (own translation).
66 Urtheil des Königlichen Oberlandesgerichts, 324 (own translation).
67 Urtheil des Königlichen Oberlandesgerichts, 337 (own translation).
68 Peter Goodrich, "The Judge's Two Bodies: The Case of Daniel Paul Schreber," *Law Critique* 26 (2015): 119.
69 Schreber, *Denkwürdigkeiten*, 301 (own translation).
70 Werner Gephart, "Einleitung: Grundelemente einer Theorie sozialer Sphären," in *Sphärendynamik I. Zur Analyse postsäkularer Gesellschaften*, ed. Georg Pfleiderer and Alexander Heit, 13–58 (Baden-Baden, 2011).
71 "Gerichtsärztliches Gutachten," in Schreber, *Denkwürdigkeiten*, 275–80.
72 Goodrich, *Schreber's Law.*
73 Georg Simmel, *Über sociale Differenzierung. Sociologische und psychologische Untersuchungen* (Leipzig: Duncker & Humblot, 1890).
74 Émile Durkheim, *De la division du travail social* (Paris: Félix Alcan, 1893).

2 Primal Scene

MARK SANDERS

As noted in the introduction to this volume, one of the principal claims made by Jacques Lacan in his seminar on the psychoses (1955–6) is that, in Schreber, as with psychosis generally, we observe a *Verwerfung* (rejection) by the subject of a "primordial signifier" or a "fundamental signifier."[1] Because this signifier organizes signification more generally – it is a condition of possibility for signification – its resulting lack or absence has profound consequences for the subject's relation to language. And because signification is linked to what Lacan calls the "Symbolic" and "Law," to which the subject accedes by the Oedipus complex, and *Verwerfung* of the primordial signifier is also thought to be a *Verwerfung* of the idea of castration, this lack or absence not only leads to the psychotic unmooring of language and thought from a common frame of reference – what has always been a sign of madness – but also an unmooring of sex/gender. The "imaginary disturbance"[2] that Lacan identifies when the Law and the Symbolic (Other with a capital *O*) are short-circuited is that, literally – although Lacan does not refer to the relevant passages – Schreber looks in the mirror and sees not a man but a woman.[3]

In this seminar, Lacan is on the move, constructing a theory, altering terms, keeping the construction loose. For this reason, I prefer it to the summary included in *Écrits*,[4] and, naturally, to the schematic summaries of the master sometimes presented, with an air of self-evidence, by professed Lacanians. Summaries by others, such as Eric Santner and Jodi Dean, in the course of their analyses, respectively, of Schreber and of paranoid American conspiracy theories are, however, highly instructive.[5] But they, like the disciples, quietly close the book on how, Lacan being under way, is moving with, as well as away from, certain other ideas, deftly displacing a theoretical system that comes down from Freud and his elaborators. This is, of course, the import of Lacan's "return to Freud."

Lacan himself is almost silent about certain displacements he makes. A first clue, in this seminar that is mainly about Schreber, is Lacan's reliance on Freud's case history of the Wolf Man.[6] Lacan refers – in ways that have been challenged because of their liberty with Freud's text,[7] – to the Wolf Man's memory of a boyhood hallucination of having severed his finger with a pocket-knife:

> The scene is as follows. While playing with his knife he cut his finger, which was left hanging on by only a small piece of skin.... Then he sat on a bench, beside his nurse, ... and he didn't dare mention it to her. How significant is that suspension of all possible speech! – and precisely with the person he used to recount everything to, and especially things of that order! There is an abyss here, a temporal submersion, a rupture in experience, following which it turns out that he has nothing at all wrong with him, it's all over, let's drop the subject. The relation that Freud establishes between this phenomenon and this very special *knowing nothing of the thing, even in the sense of the repressed* expressed in this text translates as this – what is refused in the symbolic order re-emerges in the real.[8]

The word "refuse" (*refuser*) is Lacan's translation of the German verb *verwerfen*,[9] which becomes nominalized as *Verwerfung*. What is refused in the symbolic, according to Lacan's interpretation, is the threat of castration: "It can happen that a subject refuses access to his symbolic world to something that he has nevertheless experienced, which in this case is nothing other than the threat of castration."[10] In other words, when not given access to words, the experience returns as an image. One scene takes the place of another. Discussing the scene of the severed finger, Lacan refers explicitly only once to the central focus of Freud's case – the primal scene – although it was what Freud was discussing immediately before he refers to the memory of the hallucination of the severed finger, and it is where Freud nominalizes the term *Verwerfung*. The primal scene, Freud explains, is subject to a "deferred comprehension ... and an explanation of the part played by women in the sexual act" (*nachträgliches Verständnis ... und Aufklärung über die Rolle der Frau beim Geschlechtsakt*).[11] The consequences of this *Nachträglichkeit* are, in short, that, at the genital stage, the remembered event, in which the boy identifies with the mother in the scene of sexual intercourse because it will gain him his father's love, is understood as entailing her, and therefore his own, castration. This leads to the *Verwerfung* of the idea of castration.[12]

In an 1896 letter to Fliess setting out his neuropsychology, Freud posits a *Wahrnehmungszeichen*, an "indication of perception."[13] Interpreting the word *Zeichen* as "sign," Lacan calls this an "initial putting into signs," a "primordial signifier." Lacan draws on the terminology in Freud's letter to argue that the primal scene, even before the subject has language, and before the advent of the genital stage, is "already signifying," that it is a "signifier [that] is ... primitively given."[14] Missing, however, for the Wolf Man, is a bringing of that scene into his "history" – which, when he speaks as an adult analysand, has long since brought him into genital maturity. Just as, in his recollection of his boyhood hallucination, he does not tell his nurse about his severed finger, the Wolf Man does not own the primal scene by putting it into words that would make it subject to the law of the "symbolic." The scene is a signifier, but it "remains nothing" until it is spoken by the subject. As Lacan has said, "all access to the register of the symbolic function, the fact that any assumption of castration by an *I* has become impossible for him."[15]

> In *The Wolf Man* the primitive impression of the famous primordial scene has remained over the years, serving no purpose, though already signifying, before having its word to say in the subject's history. The signifier is thus primitively given, but it remains nothing as long as the subject doesn't cause it to enter into his history, which becomes important between the ages of one and a half and four and a half. Sexual desire is effectively what man uses to historicize himself, insofar as it's at this level that the law is introduced for the first time.[16]

In *The Psychoses*, Lacan appears to be displacing the primal scene – which, in contrast to standard usage, he calls the "primordial scene" (*scène primordiale*) – with the "primordial signifier" (*signifiant primordial*). In the history of psychoanalysis and its theorization of psychosis, this is consequential, implying a moving to the side of the assumptions elaborated out of Freud by Melanie Klein, Ida MacAlpine, and others, which align the psychoses with regression to primitive instinctual/libidinal fixation points.[17] The solution to the Wolf Man case, by far the most intricate of Freud's case histories, is to understand, by analysis of the primal scene, how these points of fixation are recoded – or not – by subsequent libidinal positions. As Freud sums up, referring to the Wolf Man, "He rejected castration, and held to his theory of intercourse by the anus."[18] In the normal course of development, the Oedipus complex would bring those fixation points under the law of the father and distribute gender/sex accordingly.

The primal scene is thus an almost silent presence as Lacan sets out his ideas about the primordial signifier. Giving it a voice, amplifying it, projecting it, will make more clear what is at stake – beyond psychoanalysis – for law as organizing principle or *archē* of origins and first causes.[19] There are points of convergence, of course – the one looking, the one who was or will have been looking, still at the level of what Lacan calls the "imaginary," still supposedly *infans*, asks, Who am I? Where do I come from? – whereas the psychotic cannot answer that, because language functions for him in the peculiar way that it does, and not just because he is stuck in a particular phase of development.

I propose the following argument: The "scene" works as a silent presence in law, or at least in the theory of "law." There is, in what we term "law," an irreducible trace of a "scene." This scene might not be identifiable as a primal scene in the narrow sense, and a trace or "mark" is not self-identical in any case,[20] but be something along the lines of what Derrida calls a "scene of writing" – a term that he uses when he discusses the unstated conditions for certain theorizations by Freud and Lacan.[21] In a word, the theorist looks for causes, but, in the end, she is left with scenes and images – which are as insistent and immovable in their silence as the words that, given to us by the system of language, clamour to be heard. It is what is called psychosis that – especially with Lacan's distinctions, which indicate a misfiring of language – demonstrates a divergence of word and image that is typically smoothed over or ignored. What are the points of convergence and divergence, then? I shall be reading two passages from Schreber, but first let us read a passage from Lacan.

1

The key words, the signifying words of Schreber's delusion, *soul murder, nerve-contact, voluptuousness, blessedness,* and a thousand other terms, revolve around a fundamental signifier, which is never mentioned and whose presence is in command, is determinant. He says it himself. I shall give you an indication and, to reassure you by showing you that we are in our own domain, I shall tell you that in Schreber's entire work his father is cited only once.[22]

I do not wish to comment in detail on a certain imprecision, even contradiction, in Lacan's formulations, but they need to be noted: "never mentioned" but "cited once." To be cited, surely, is also to be mentioned – and, as Lacan seems to suggest, to be *cited* is an important way of being mentioned – as it indicates reference to an author and authority (here the main *auctor*). Another important point is that, although the signifier is not *mentioned*, it is present in some sense – and that "presence is in command" – in other words, it is not exactly "absent," as Lacan has said a few paragraphs earlier. I am not going to try to iron out these inconsistencies – I refer to the remarks on "misunderstanding" and "not quite understand[ing]" that Lacan addresses to those attending his seminar.[23] Lacan's pedagogical strategy may be another reason why the theoretical formulations presented in the seminar are, as it were, on the move.

With that in mind, let us move ahead, and address the next paragraph:

> [H]is father is cited only once. This is on the subject of his most well-known, if not his most important, work, which is called *Manual of Bedroom Gymnastics*. It's a book that I did everything to obtain, full of little diagrams. The only time Schreber mentions his father by name is when he goes and looks in this book to see whether what the voices tell him about the typical position of men and women when they make love really is true. You will admit that it is an amusing idea to go in search of this in a *Manual of Bedroom Gymnastics*. Everyone knows that love is an ideal sport, but all the same.[24]

Shortly after making this reference, Lacan ends his seminar for 13 June 1956. He does not return to the *Manual of Bedroom Gymnastics*. Let us, however, explore it a little further. Lacan terms Daniel Gottlob Schreber's book the *Manuel de gymnastique de chambre*, which the translator renders as *Manual of Bedroom Gymnastics*. "Manual" has been made part of the title, perhaps by the transcriber or note-taker (the volume does not explain the provenance of the text, edited by J.-A. Miller). The French translation of the title of Moritz Schreber's *Ärztliche Zimmergymnastik*, which was widely used, and published in English as *Medical Indoor Gymnastics*, obviously leads the reader toward the bedroom, when it could have been any room, probably[25] – except for the *son*, as Lacan cannily implies. What Lacan wishes to tell his seminar about is "a signifier that is primordial but excluded for the subject. I named this signifier ... *Thou art the one who is*, or will be, *a father*. As a signifier it can in no way be received, insofar as the signifier represents an indeterminate support around which there is grouped and condensed a number, not even of meanings, but of series of meanings, which come and converge by means of and starting from the existence of this signifier. Before the Name-of-the-Father there was no father, there were all sorts of other things."[26] But what he incidentally also asks his audience to bear witness to is the/a primal scene.

The relevant passage from *Memoirs of My Nervous Illness* comes after Schreber tells us how "[a] very prominent part was played in the 'soul-conception' by ideas about the relation between the two sexes and their respective mode of occupation, their tastes, etc. For instance beds, hand-mirrors and rakes were considered feminine, basket-chairs and spades masculine; of games, chess as masculine, draughts as feminine, etc."[27] It is as if he is receiving sexual difference in the form of law. Schreber continues: "Souls knew very well that a man lies on his side in bed, a woman on her back (as the 'succumbing part,' considered from the point of view of sexual intercourse). I myself, who in earlier life never gave it a thought, have only learned this from the souls. From what I read in for instance my father's MEDICAL INDOOR GYMNASTICS (23rd Edition, p. 102), physicians themselves do not seem to be informed about it."[28] Lacan's interpretation seems to be that, if the man and the woman are making love, the "man" is Schreber's father – and the son is the "woman." The same verb (*unterliegen*) is used as in the much-discussed passage in chapter 4, when Schreber wakes up with the "idea that it really must be rather pleasant to be a woman succumbing to intercourse."[29] Lacan is canny – since the passage is ostensibly about one's position in "bed" – but the reason for one's position in bed given – but only for the woman – is her position during sexual intercourse. Latent content is deftly translated into manifest content.

When Lacan reads that "physicians themselves do not seem to be informed about it," which is Schreber's point, Lacan asks, Why on earth would Schreber be looking for this information in a book of therapeutic exercises? Lacan does not elaborate on his inklings. It would be interesting, however, for us to do so. What can we infer about what Schreber was expecting to find? And about why he was expecting to find it *there*? As Schreber tells us, the book does not distinguish between sleeping positions for men and women, but it does distinguish between the two sleeping positions that he identifies. And those positions are highly invested for Schreber. Two passages in *Ärztliche Zimmergymnastik* do refer to one's position in bed. They both contrast lying on one's side with lying on one's back. Lying one one's back is preferable because it allows easier breathing, and exerts less pressure on the liver and spleen.[30]

An exception is made, however, in cases of "morbid, enfeebling frequency of nocturnal emissions."[31] In those cases, in addition to a series of exercises, cold sitz baths, cold-water enemas, and washing of the genitals and perineum with cold water in the morning, the book prescribes "at night … instead of the back position, making a habit of the alternating side position."[32] This appears to be the passage that Schreber cites (I have a later edition, the thirty-third, but the page number is the same as that given in the *Memoirs*). Although, of course, a prescription for over-frequent nocturnal emissions by definition applies to males, there is, as Schreber notes, nothing in either of these passages to associate lying on one's side with being male, or lying on one's back with being female. But why might he have expected to find such a distinction in his father's book?

The train of association that one needs to reconstruct in order to begin to account for his looking up this passage includes Schreber's "idea that it really must be rather pleasant to be a woman succumbing to intercourse," something that was *sonderbar*, as well as his "quite unusual number of pollutions (perhaps half a dozen)," both being elements of the prodrome to his second illness as described in chapter 4 of the *Memoirs*.[33] The twenty-third edition of *Ärztliche Zimmergymnastik* was published in 1889, and he may have consulted it in order to account for and to remedy his excessive nocturnal emissions, which date to early 1894. But by early 1895, from when the recollections appear to date, the book is playing a more complex role. It was as if Schreber was expecting to find instruction from his father on what he needed to do if he were to be a woman, with sexual intercourse being the template for this instruction. With being a woman, as under-lying, associated with nocturnal emissions in the *Memoirs*, it is possible for Schreber to read the linking of lying on one's back to such emissions in *Ärztliche Zimmergymnastik* as promising an account, and perhaps a prescription, for femininity. And there is also the anal eroticism, be it only infantile, inevitably associated with the prescribed enemas. It is possible to read it as promising a look at the primal scene – although it would be an odd coupling, or non-coupling, with the man lying on his side and the woman on her back.

Thus, although the ostensible object of this passage is to show the superiority of the knowledge he has derived from the "rays" to that of physicians, including his father, the display reveals that his father is actually the one whose word is sought – and *found*, if one takes the word of the "voices" to be related to Schreber's reading of his father's book. If it is a citation, the citation of the father is, in a word, psychotic (and may be compared to Schreber's inaccurate citations of Byron, which Freud sees as a clue to incest).[34] The father is "in command," not because of what he actually wrote, but rather for what he did not. Thus, in bringing to the fore the role of the "primordial signifier" and "Name-of-the-Father," Lacan also entertains (or allows us to entertain) the role of the primal scene. It is significant, given Freud's account of the primal scene, that when the name of the father appears in *Memoirs of My Nervous Illness*, it does so in a discussion of sleeping position of the two sexes, which is then associated with position in sexual intercourse (for the woman). Recall that, in Freud, fear of castration, which is *verworfen*, stems from a deferred comprehension of the role of the woman in sexual intercourse.[35] Because the son is putting himself in the place of the woman, one could, of course, also call his citation a seduction of the father.

There is the law, but it is a psychotic version of it, without common terms or a common text, in which (the father says/prescribes that) the position in which a man or a woman sleeps is thus, because that is the position that women (and men?) adopt in sexual intercourse. Knowledge stems from a primal scene that, as a *scene*, is irreducible. The *Memoirs* actually only refer to the position of the woman, and, except, by a complex train of association, the *Zimmergymnastik* tells Schreber nothing about the respective positions of the sexes, either in sleep or during sex. In this respect, his father's manual fails to provide a workable version of the primal scene, one that would align with the Law and assign Schreber his gender – which is what he requires/demands from the/his father. But this should not prevent us from suspecting that, more generally, bound up with any invocation of the law is the need to look – to observe a *scene*. Such a scene or *Vorstellung* may, of course, be subject to subsequent negation of conscious thought, as in chapter 4 of the *Memoirs*, in which, although Schreber, "whether still half asleep or already awake I cannot remember ... had a feeling ... the idea [*Vorstellung*] that it really must be rather pleasant to be a woman succumbing to intercourse," which "thinking about it later when fully awake [*beim späteren Nachdenken in vollständig wachem Zustande*], struck me as highly peculiar.... I may say I would have rejected it with indignation if fully awake [*bei vollem Bewußtsein mit solcher Entrüstung zurückgewiesen haben*]."[36] The lack of alignment of scene and Law, evident both in Schreber's initial rejection of the female position, and in his citation of his father's book in order to affirm that position, suggests that a scene is irreducible, not only for gender, but, more generally, for law, if the latter involves a locating of origin, purpose, and so forth. One could say, with Lacan, that the signifier is "primordial," but then one would have to say the same of the scene – as Lacan, in fact, does, when he refers to the impression of the primal scene on the infant as a *Wahrnehmungszeichen*,[37] although he proceeds, in the seminar sessions that follow, as if it were self-evident that this unconscious trace were somehow functionally equivalent to what he terms the "Name-of-the-Father." With Schreber's help, I am questioning this apparent self-evidence.

2

This brings me to a second passage in Schreber, which seems to have within it a reference to the primal scene – although a link to the father, and to the question of the father, is not made right away.

> Because of its very characteristic meaning I must devote a few more remarks to the above-mentioned question [asked by the voices] "Why do you then not shit?," however indelicate the subject may be. Like everything else in my body, the need to empty myself is also called forth by miracles; this is done by forcing the faeces in the bowel forwards (sometimes also backwards) and when owing to previous evacuation there is insufficient material present, the small remnants in the bowel are smeared on my backside. This miracle, initiated by the upper God, is repeated every day at least several dozen times. It is connected with the idea which is quite incomprehensible for human beings and can only be explained by God's complete lack of knowledge of the living human being as an organism, that "sh..." is to a certain extent the final act; that is to say when the miracles produce the urge to sh... the goal of destroying my reason is reached, and so the possibility afforded for a final withdrawal of the rays. Trying to trace the origin of this idea one must assume some misunderstanding of the symbolic meaning of the act of defecation, namely that he who entered into a special relationship to divine rays as I have is to a certain extent entitled to sh... on all the world.
>
> At the same time, however, the whole perfidy of the policy conducted towards me is clear. Whenever the need to defecate is produced by miracle, some other person in my environment is sent to the lavatory – by exciting the nerves of the person concerned – in order to prevent me from emptying myself; this I have observed so frequently (thousands of times) and so regularly that one can exclude any thought of it being coincidence. The question "Why do you then not sh... ?" is followed by the capital answer "Because I am somehow stupid." The pen almost resists writing down the fantastic nonsense that God in His blindness and lack of knowledge of human nature in fact goes so far that He assumes a human being could exist who – something every animal is capable of doing – cannot sh... for sheer stupidity. When I do empty myself – usually in a bucket because I almost always find the lavatory occupied – this act is always combined with a very strong development of soul-voluptuousness. Liberation from the pressure of faeces present in the guts creates an intense feeling of well-being, particularly for the nerves of voluptuousness; the same happens when I pass water. For that reason all rays have always and without exception been united during evacuation and passing water; and for this very reason, namely to avoid a union of all rays, one attempts (usually unsuccessfully) to miracle away the urge.[38]

Giving examples of what he calls "compulsive thinking," Schreber tells us, "The infringement of the freedom of human thinking or more correctly thinking nothing, which constitutes the essence of compulsive thinking, became more unbearable in the course of years with the slowing down of the talk of the voices."[39] "To say 'But naturally' is spoken B.b.b.u.u.u.t.t.t.n.n.n.a.a.a.t.t.t.u.u.u.r.r.r.a.a.a.l.l.l.y.y.y, or 'Why do you not then shit?' W.w.w.h.h.h.y.y.y d.d.d.o.o.o.......... ; and each requires perhaps thirty to sixty seconds to be completed."[40] In the German, the word *scheißen* is only spelt out when the typography illustrates its "slowed down" form; on other occasions, only the first three letters of the word appear, followed by ellipses: "sch..." or "Sch...." Schreber distinguishes his usage from that of the voices, employing the euphemism *ausleeren* (to evacuate). I shall comment later on the elision. After describing some of the ways in which he counteracts the compulsion to think (*Denkzwang*), Schreber elaborates: "Because of its very characteristic meaning I must devote a few more remarks to the abovementioned question 'Why do you then not shit?,' however indelicate the subject may be."[41]

The meaning attached to the words of the question – or the "idea" – is interwoven with the act of evacuation and its vicissitudes, which, if not in fact given a meaning, is given an explanation: "Like everything else in my body, the need to empty myself is also called forth by miracles; this is done by forcing the faeces in the bowel forwards (sometimes also backwards) and when owing to previous evacuation there is insufficient material present, the small remnants in the bowel are smeared on my backside. This miracle, initiated by the upper God, is repeated every day at least several dozen times."[42] Two things here are worthy of note. First, the hyperbole: "several dozen times" daily, just as something else has been observed "thousands of times." What does this suggest? A repetition, and the significance of the act residing in its repetition. Second, applying a Freudian framework, we notice how an anal eroticism is associated with the repetition: "forcing the faeces in the bowel forwards (sometimes also backwards)," and, a little later, "th[e act of evacuation] is always combined with a very strong development of soul-voluptuousness. Liberation from the pressure of faeces present in the guts creates an intense feeling of well-being, particularly for the nerves of voluptuousness." This also applies to "passing water" (*pissen*).[43] We know, from the *Three Essays on the Theory of Sexuality*, that the pleasurable alternation of forward and backward movement of the feces involves a differentiation of activity and passivity, which, in turn, is the condition of possibility for a differentiation between masculinity and femininity.[44]

Freud, however, is careful to describe infantile anal eroticism in terms that do not depend on this subsequent sexual differentiation. In

Freud's analysis of the primal scene in the case of the Wolf Man, this is of immense importance: Freud introduces an analytic "construction" to the effect that the infant Wolf Man produced a stool, a pleasurable occurrence, when he observed his mother and father coupling.[45]

This brings us to the lineaments of the primal scene to be found in this passage. A key detail in Schreber's description of the miracle is that "whenever the need to defecate is produced by miracle, some other person in my environment is sent to the lavatory – by exciting the nerves of the person concerned – in order to prevent me from emptying myself." This cannot be a "coincidence." The structure of the primal scene is close to the surface. Their nerves being excited, somebody else is receiving sexual pleasure (passively), what Schreber calls "soul-voluptuousness." And this person is preventing Schreber from receiving the same thing. The coupling to which he is urged is already taking place, but with that "other person": "I almost always find the lavatory occupied."

In Freud, the observation of the primal scene is linked to a questioning: Who am I? Where did I come from? It is bound up, for obvious reasons, with the sexual theories of children, and to the *Wißtrieb*. Melanie Klein would elaborate.[46] It is thus no great surprise that, in this passage, we see how an episode repeating the primal scene is associated with questioning the meaning of the words used in the question "Why do you not shit?" The compulsion to think produces from Schreber the answer: "Because I am somehow stupid." But he is not content with that answer and has been conducting further analysis. The "miracle" of evacuation, the forward and backward movement of the feces, is connected to an "idea," to a "symbolic meaning." The rays have the wrong idea, namely "that 'sh…' is to a certain extent the final act; that is to say when the miracles produce the urge to sh… the goal of destroying my reason is reached, and so the possibility afforded for a final withdrawal of the rays." But this is a "misunderstanding of the symbolic meaning of the act of defecation, namely that he who entered into a special relationship to divine rays … is to a certain extent entitled to sh… on all the world." Schreber asserts his supremacy, but when one reads "misunderstanding," one can, as elsewhere in Schreber's book, reverse the term and guess that this is, in fact, the better understanding and closer to the symbolic meaning. The appeal to the *Volksmund* in order to assert supremacy is all very well, and there is something manic about shitting on all the world. But the idea that shitting could be the last act, or simply "what is last (*das letzte*)" – the translators insert "act" – is quite interesting.

Two comments: First, if we follow Freud, the phase of anal eroticism is a *liminal* one. Involving activity and passivity, it is the condition of possibility for subsequent binary sexual differentiation.[47] It is, in some sense, the beginning of life as human life. It is, in these terms, the condition of possibility for accession to the Law, for the system of language, and so forth. This account is comparable to the fable in Klein of free-floating, oscillating good and bad part-objects, and how they coalesce into features of a single object and thus become applicable, like language generally, to any other object.[48] It is thus not hard to imagine how, if defecation is an act of initiation, it can also be a last act, in the sense of a dissolution, a *lysis*. On the other hand, if we continue to reverse Schreber's terms, the last can be first, and Schreber is repeating his beginning. Except that he cannot, because the lavatory is occupied.

Second, if, provisionally, we emulate Schreber in his philological and etymological researches, we can see how the word *scheißen* connotes a separation. I open the online etymological dictionary, which notes that *scheißen* comes from the Proto-Indo-European *skei – "to cut, split, divide, separate" (see schizo-). Thus *scheiden* and *scheißen* in German, and *skei* and *skyt* in Afrikaans. Opening a new chapter of his *Memoirs*, in which he continues the pattern of questioning, Schreber writes of "a kind of recompense for the wrong done me."[49] "I must … mention the mentally stimulating effect compulsive thinking has had on me. Throwing into my nerves unconnected conjunctions expressing causal or other relations ('Why only,' 'Why because,' 'Why because I,' 'Let it be then,' 'At least,' etc.) forced me to ponder many things usually passed over by human beings.… I am forced or at least stimulated in immeasurably greater degree than other human beings to contemplate the reason or purpose behind them."[50] Reason or purpose: *"Grund oder Zweck"* in the German. "Stimulated by compulsive thinking," Schreber relates, "I occupied myself a great deal with etymological questions which I must say had interested me in earlier days of health. Finally a very ordinary event to illustrate the above: I meet a person I know by the name of Schneider. Seeing him the thought automatically arises 'This man's name is Schneider' or 'This is Mr. Schneider.' With it 'But why' or 'Why because' also resounds in my nerves.… My nerves perhaps answer first: Well, the man's name is Schneider because his father was also called Schneider. But this trivial answer does not really pacify my nerves."[51] Thus begins a new "chain of thought," about name-giving "among different peoples at different times."

A "very ordinary event," a "trivial answer." We know Schreber well enough now to guess: well, not exactly ordinary, not all that trivial. And, having read what Lacan has said about *Verwerfung* of the "Name-of-the-Father," we do not have to believe that an appearance, in this book, where Schreber *père* is cited only once, of "his father" is simply by chance. So what if Mr. Schneider were Mr. Schreber, or at least his doppelgänger? And "his father" is Mr. Schreber's? I leave aside for the time being the multiplication of the "sch-" and "schr-" and "schn-" sounds. His name is Schreber because his father was also called Schreber. In this form, it is an answer that does not pacify Schreber's nerves. Why? He does not explain. But the fact that he then appeals to the naming systems of other peoples could be a clue to what is going on. He is missing something systematic. We do not have to be Lacanians to see that the reason that the tautological answer that "the man's name is Schneider because his father was also called Schneider" does not pacify Schreber's nerves is that the correct answer is: the man's name is Schneider because Schneider *was his father*.[52] This is the law of the father. No contingency of father and son, males with the same name, but a *necessity* of the patronym and the right to it. And this law/structure, as theorists from Freud to Derrida, including Lacan, have pointed out, is not one that can be derived from nature – from what Schreber calls *Grund und Zweck*.

In this case, the "symbolic meaning," alluded to a few pages earlier,[53] is a red herring. No "etymological" investigation will produce this answer – and, arguably, no version of the primal scene. We can certainly follow Lacan and see this instance of Schreber missing the correct answer as related to the *Verwerfung* of the name of the father as "primordial signifier," and, with it, the resultant loss of capacity to think consequentially. But if we did, we would also have to say that this *Verwerfung* has nothing dramatic about it (as Freud describes repression in his notes on Schreber),[54] just a certain pervasive vagueness about paternity and filiation – and thus, I would add, in a more Freudian vein, about origin, a vagueness that the primal scene, repeated symbolically, does and does not dispel, over and over. This applies as much to Schreber, whose fecal miracles happen thousands of times, as to the Wolf Man, whose boyhood dream, which Freud interprets as a memory of the primal scene, is recurrent. The image or scene is an irreducible trace, which will not necessarily be resolved into words. If the origin, as Derrida says, describing the trace, is constituted retrospectively by the non-origin,[55] as with Freud's *Nachträglichkeit*, there is no guarantee that this constitution will take place, or will always take place.

It is thus no accident that Schreber turns to "picturing" and toward his feminization. The "ability to 'picture' … has truly often been a consolation and comfort in the unending monotony of my dreary life, in the mental tortures I suffered from the nonsensical twaddle of voices."[56] Language, for Schreber, does not cohere into what Lacan calls the Symbolic or the Law, whereas his mirror, allowing a short circuit that bypasses language and the structures of kinship, makes identification possible and produces the "consolation and comfort" of the image. The topic of "picturing" (*Zeichnen*, or drawing) enjoys a careful set of definitions, drawn from Schreber's "Little Studies" XLIX of 29 October 1898. "To picture (in the sense of the soul-language)," Schreber explains, "is the conscious use of the human imagination for the purpose of producing pictures (predominantly pictures of recollections) in one's head, which can then be looked at by rays."[57] After giving some brief examples, Schreber devotes several sentences to the "picturing" involved:

> I can also "picture" myself in a different place, for instance while playing the piano I see myself at the same time standing in front of a mirror in the adjoining room in female attire; when I am lying in bed at night I can give myself and the rays the impression that my body has female breasts and a female sexual organ; I mentioned its great importance and the reason for it in Chapter XIII. The picturing of female buttocks on my body – *honi soit qui mal y pense* – has become such a habit that I do it almost automatically whenever I bend down.[58]

Looking and seeing are crucial to Schreber. Anybody can directly see certain things about Schreber's body, but then there is the mediation of the mirror in order to produce the "illusion" or "impression" of femaleness: "I venture to assert flatly that anybody who sees me standing in front of a mirror with the upper part of my body naked would get the undoubted *impression of a female trunk* – especially when the illusion is strengthened by some feminine adornments."[59] The scene, as described, is ambiguous. Assuming that the spectator is standing behind Schreber (and not behind the mirror), she or he could be observing Schreber's back, or the image in the mirror. The latter makes more sense, for Schreber wants the observer to see him as he says he sees himself – in the mirror, as corresponding to the image in the mirror, as identical to the image in the mirror. It resolves the impossibility registered at the level of the Symbolic. By appealing to the presence of the other – "anybody" – who affirms, or who at least has the *unzweifelhaften Eindruck*, registering one amid two (*zwei-*) – the big Other also speaks, and it authorizes. In this instance, as in hardly any other instance in the *Memoirs*, it speaks and authorizes because "somebody" has been presented, by means of a technics of the mirror, with a scene or image that leaves one – mistakenly – with no doubt. For Schreber, then, the Law speaks and authorizes, and it does not – just as when he opens Moritz Schreber's *Zimmergymnastik*, and the father's name is both authorizing and *verworfen*.

It would remain, of course, in this scenario, for the observer to identify himself or herself in the process, since he or she would probably also be able to see his or her own image in the mirror. Who is the observer, though? The "serious specialist"? Schreber's wife? The "rays," for whom Schreber's "picturing," more generally, takes place? And what would the observer see? These questions are not answerable. The present investigation may, however, conclude by observing that, by displacing the primal scene, in order to argue for the *Verwerfung* of the "primordial signifier," Lacan not only elides the repetition of Schreber's struggle to signify but also the irreducibility of the image in law.[60]

NOTES

1 Jacques Lacan, *The Seminar of Jacques Lacan; Book III: The Psychoses 1955–1956,* trans. Russell Grigg (New York: Norton, 1993), 171. Page numbers for *The Psychoses,* which are given in the margin of Grigg's translation, refer to the original French edition. It should be noted that the terms used by Lacan change in the course of the seminar, as does what signifier it is that is *verworfen* – inter alia, the idea of castration, the feminine, the male, the Name-of-the-Father. Lacan, *Psychoses,* 21, 99–100, 286, 344.
2 Lacan, *Psychoses,* 54.
3 Drawing on the notion of "the push-towards-Woman," developed by Lacan in the early 1970s, Patricia Gherovici views Schreber's feminization in more fundamental terms: "Schreber will not become a woman (or change his gender) but he will become Woman: here is a founding exception that can function as a sort of name-of-the-father." Patricia Gherovici, Schreber's *Grande Bellezza,*" in this volume. It will be clear from what follows that my reading of passages relating to the primal scene, in Schreber and in Lacan's 1955–6 seminar, would not lead me to such an interpretation.
4 Jacques Lacan, "On a Question Prior to Any Possible Treatment of Psychosis," *Écrits: The First Complete Edition in English,* trans. Bruce Fink (New York: Norton, 2007), 445–88.
5 Eric Santner, *My Own Private Germany: Daniel Paul Schreber's Secret History of Modernity* (Princeton, NJ: Princeton University Press, 1997); Jodi Dean, *Democracy and Other Neoliberal Fantasies: Communicative Capitalism and Left Politics* (Durham, NC: Duke University Press, 2009), 145–75.
6 Sigmund Freud, "From the History of an Infantile Neurosis," in *Standard Edition of the Complete Psychological Works of Sigmund Freud,* ed. and trans. James Strachey et al. (London: Hogarth, 1953–), 17:7–123.
7 See Elisabeth Roudinesco, *Jacques Lacan: Outline of a Life, History of a System of Thought,* trans. Barbara Bray (New York: Columbia University Press, 1997), 282–3. The translator's footnote quotes the relevant sentences from the English and the German, but, unfortunately, omits the phrase "daß er sie verwarf, so ist die nächste Bedeutung," which in the English is

translated as "that he rejected it [i.e. castration], the first meaning of the phrase is." Lacan, *Psychoses*, 21n10.

8 Lacan, *Psychoses*, 22.

9 Lacan variously translates *verwerfen* as "refuse," "reject," and "exclude," before settling, in the final session of the seminar, on "foreclose." Lacan, *Psychoses*, 21, 56, 171, 344, 361. For further commentary, see Roudinesco, *Jacques Lacan*, 283. In a highly suggestive analysis, Davide Tarizzo translates *Verwerfung* as "anathema," or "malediction," arguing, "This means that the delusional metaphor was not there to compensate for the original foreclosure of the paternal metaphor, as Lacan maintains. Rather, it was there to sanction its malediction. In many respects, the anathema 'God is a whore' testifies to the fact that the paternal metaphor had never been completely absent from Daniel's subjectivity." Davide Tarizzo, "The Delusional Metaphor: On Schreber's Anathema," in this volume.

10 Lacan, *Psychoses*, 21.

11 Freud, "From the History of an Infantile Neurosis," 77–8.

12 Freud, "From the History of an Infantile Neurosis," 77–84.

13 Freud, "Letter 52 from Extracts from the Fliess Papers," in *Standard Edition*, 1:234.

14 Lacan *Psychoses*, 177. For Freud, this *Wahrnehmungszeichen* "is quite incapable of consciousness, and arranged according to associations by simultaneity." Freud, "Letter 52," 234.

15 Lacan, *Psychoses*, 21.

16 Lacan, *Psychoses*, 177.

17 See, for instance, Melanie Klein, "Notes on Some Schizoid Mechanisms," in *Envy and Gratitude, and Other Works, 1946–1963* (1975; London: Virago, 1988), 1–24; Ida MacAlpine and Richard A. Hunter, "Translators' Analysis of the Case," in Daniel Paul Schreber, *Memoirs of My Nervous Illness*, trans. MacAlpine and Hunter (Cambridge, MA: Harvard University Press, 1988), 369–416.

18 Freud, "From the History of an Infantile Neurosis," 84.

19 Writing elsewhere about Schreber, I explore the nexus of law, mourning, and guilt. Mark Sanders, "Psychoanalysis, Mourning, and the Law: Schreber's Paranoia as Crisis of Judging," in *Law and Mourning*, ed. Austin Sarat and Martha Merrill Umphrey, 117–147 (Amherst, MA: University of Massachusetts Press, 2017).

20 Jacques Derrida, "Signature Event Context," in *Margins of Philosophy*, trans. Alan Bass, 315–18 (Chicago: University of Chicago Press, 1982).

21 See Jacques Derrida, "Freud and the Scene of Writing," in *Writing and Difference*, trans. Alan Bass, 196–231 (Chicago: University of Chicago Press, 1978); Derrida, "To Speculate – On 'Freud,'" and "Le facteur de la vérité," in *The Post Card: From Socrates to Freud and Beyond*, trans. Alan Bass, 257–496 (Chicago: University of Chicago Press, 1987).

22 Lacan, *Psychoses*, 320
23 "It is with a deliberate, if not entirely deliberated, intention that I pursue this discourse in such a way as to offer you the opportunity to not quite understand. This margin enables you yourselves to say that you think you follow me, that is, that you remain in a problematic position, which always leaves the door open to a progressive rectification." Lacan, *Psychoses*, 184.
24 Lacan, *Psychoses*, 320.
25 The book actually addresses this; Daniel Gottlob Moritz Schreber, *Ärztliche Zimmergymnastik; oder System der ohne Gerät und Beistand überall ausführbaren heilgymnastischen Freiübungen als Mittel der Gesundheit und Lebenstüchtigkeit für beide Geschlechter und jedes Alter*, 33rd ed., revised and expanded by Rudolf Graefe (Leipzig: Friedrich Fleischer, 1913), 33.
26 Lacan, *Psychoses*, 344.
27 Schreber, *Memoirs*, 165–6. When making reference to this book, I use the page numbers from the original German edition, provided by MacAlpine and Hunter in the margins of their translation.
28 Schreber, *Memoirs of My Nervous Illness*, 166.
29 Schreber, *Memoirs of My Nervous Illness*, 36.
30 Daniel Gottlob Moritz Schreber, *Ärztliche Zimmergymnastik*, 98.
31 Daniel Gottlob Moritz Schreber, *Ärztliche Zimmergymnastik*, 101.
32 Daniel Gottlob Moritz Schreber, *Ärztliche Zimmergymnastik*, 102.
33 Schreber, *Memoirs*, 36, 44.
34 Sigmund Freud, "Psycho-Analytic Notes on an Autobiographical Account of a Case of Paranoia (Dementia Paranoides)," in *Standard Edition*, 12:44.
35 Freud, "From the History of an Infantile Neurosis," 77–8.
36 Schreber, *Memoirs*, 36.
37 Lacan, *Psychoses*, 177.
38 Schreber, *Memoirs*, 225–7.
39 Schreber, *Memoirs*, 223.
40 Schreber, *Memoirs*, 223.
41 Schreber, *Memoirs*, 225.
42 Schreber, *Memoirs*, 225–6.
43 Schreber, *Memoirs*, 227.
44 Sigmund Freud, *Three Essays on the Theory of Sexuality*, in *Standard Edition*, 7:198–9. See also Freud, "From the History of an Infantile Neurosis," 84.
45 Freud, "From the History of an Infantile Neurosis," 80–1.
46 See, for instance, Melanie Klein, "Early Stages of the Oedipus Conflict," in *Love, Guilt and Reparation, and Other Works 1921–1945* (London: Hogarth, 1975), 188–91.
47 Freud, *Three Essays on the Theory of Sexuality*, 198–9.
48 See, for example, Melanie Klein, "A Contribution to the Psychogenesis of Manic-Depressive States," in *Love, Guilt and Reparation*, 264.
49 Schreber, *Memoirs*, 228.

50 Schreber, *Memoirs*, 228–9
51 Schreber, *Memoirs*, 230–1.
52 Samuel Weber argues in another direction, speculating that the deeper reason that the "trivial answer" does not put Schreber at ease is that the word "Schneider" (tailor), which may denote the profession of Mr. Schneider's forebear, is, through a mass of cognates of the verb *schneiden* (to cut) in the *Memoirs*, also associated with castration. Samuel M. Weber, "Introduction to the 1988 Edition," trans. Benjamin Gregg, in Schreber, *Memoirs*, xlvi–il.
53 Schreber, *Memoirs*, 226.
54 Freud, "Psycho-Analytic Notes," 71.
55 Jacques Derrida, *Of Grammatology*, trans. Gayatri Chakravorty Spivak (Baltimore, MD: Johns Hopkins University Press, 1976), 61.
56 Schreber, *Memoirs*, 233–4.
57 Schreber, *Memoirs*, 232. The definitions are elaborated in a footnote appended to this sentence.
58 Schreber, *Memoirs*, 233.
59 Schreber, *Memoirs*, 280.
60 For a systematic overturning of the teleology of image-becoming-word, see Peter Goodrich, *Schreber's Law: Jurisprudence and Judgment in Transition* (Edinburgh: Edinburgh University Press, 2018).

3 The Office of Pleasure: On Schreber's Minor Jurisprudence

RAJGOPAL SAIKUMAR

A Minor Jurisprudence

Daniel Paul Schreber's *Memoirs of My Nervous Illness* is an exemplary text. Schreber's life, in all its *jouissance*, his dramatic testimonials of love, passion, and betrayals, his kinky sexual experimentation, embodies a minor jurisprudence. Her transgressions gesture at an opening. Her disobedience leads to a trial, an exemplary case that holds the potential to found new law and nurture new precedents. Schreber's trial is exemplary in the sense in which Angela Condello and Luke Mason suggest exemplarity functions in relation to the law: "When the law generates a landmark case, breaking with the past or dealing with a novel situation, this incorporates into the law social narratives and normativities from outside the law in a general way, but does so through a single case, a single story, with its own singular meanings and narratives."[1] Re-founding the law and bringing newness into the world: this is Schreber's gift, albeit one that needs to be rediscovered. This chapter, like others in this volume, is an attempt to decode this minor jurisprudence and return to (and reapply) this exemplary precedent for the future.

Minor jurisprudence describes any species of legal knowledge that has escaped the "phantom of a sovereign and unitary law."[2] Christopher Tomlins draws out two modes of engagement with minor jurisprudence:[3] One, broadly associated with Peter Goodrich, is a plural, subversive, and subaltern jurisprudence arising from the "rebels, critics, marginals, aliens, women and outsiders."[4] In this register, minor jurisprudence is a challenge to the law of the masters: disruptive, antagonistic, and historically anti-foundational. The other register, associated with Panu Minkkinen, is capable of initiating new foundational perspectives. It is in this latter register that I read Schreber.

Whereas Schreber initially conceived of their "emasculation" as a conspiratorial persecution, over time they embraced their sexuality and started to see it as a moral duty to God. Examining this shift, my intuition is that Schreber invokes some notion of being divinely "chosen" to occupy what we might call the "office of pleasure" that justifies his trans* eroticization as being sane, moral, legitimate, obligatory, and legal.[5] In claiming to be vested with this office, Schreber justifies her transgressions on the grounds of a "higher law," a sort of natural justice. But if she claims that God's interference in humanity is against the Order of the World, then her natural law is paradoxically grounded in the "unnatural" moment of interference.

A Dis-ease of Positive Law

Schreber's *Memoirs* were published in 1903. In 1893, following his investiture as *Senatspräsident* or presiding judge of the Superior Court of Dresden, Schreber had a mental breakdown, and a psychotic illness plagues the rest of his life. As Eric Santner argues, one might read this as an "investiture crisis."[6] In January 1900, the German Civil Code came into effect. This marked the culmination of a long process of secularization of law that began in the late seventeenth century. This secularization challenged law's traditional sources of authority, rendering its demands for deference and obligation suspect, and thus necessitating thinking anew the question of what makes a legal order legitimate.[7] The solution to this lack was twofold: First, the coronation of a peculiar "legal rationality," with its purportedly scientific character, and a formal, professionalized, bureaucratic organization. It is this legal rationality that evolves into the "positive law" that Peter Goodrich diagnoses as the cause of Schreber's illness.[8] And second, a popular acceptance of law in the name of another peculiar fiction called the "citizen" and the People, generated by a discourse of nationalism.

Werner Gephart's chapter elaborates on the disease of the subject of positive law via Max Weber's characterization of modernity's iron-caged, disenchanted, bureaucratized, and rationalist legitimization of law that Schreber rebelled against. Daniela Gandorfer examines the sickness from positive law in the *Memoirs* stylistic symptoms that reveal the judge's inability to think, weigh, and judge the mechanical repetition of rules, the robotification of decision-making, the fragmentation and algorithimization of language, the effacement of "becoming," the weakening hold of creativity and ethical comportment. And Katrin Trüstedt shows how positivist jurisprudence conflates justice and proceduralism: "*Just* is whatever is produced by the right means:

by rational procedures." She suggests that the *Memoirs* are an elaborate endeavour to report his experiences in the language of this procedural-rationality, ultimately transforming his psychic experiences into a legal case that in turn is capable of transforming the law itself.

This chapter takes seriously Schreber's illness (from positive law) and traces his gradual, reparative, self-healing. Schreber never wholly recovered from his psychosis all his life, but by self-healing I mean here the attempt to convert his singular experience into an exemplary case capable of transforming the law. The memoir, deployed as evidence in his own legal trial, is of reparative value. What makes possible this self-healing in and through Schreber's memoir? How did he translate rebellious transgressions, first experienced as paranoid suffering and then as responsible pleasure, into the language of law, evidence, argument, and judgment? Reading it with Freud's *Totem and Taboo* and *Moses and Monotheism*, I show how Schreber believed that God's divine intervention and grace demanded his trans* eroticization as a service to God, and it was therefore his duty to disobey the positivist legal command. In other words, God had appointed him to a new office, and his appointment was at the pleasure of God and to pleasure God.

This formulation of an office whose role is to glorify God resonates with as well as disrupts Agamben's archaeology of duty.[9] In gesturing to Ernst Kantorowicz, Goodrich's "The Judge's Two Bodies" suggests a political theology that takes the *persona-ficta* of royal power seriously.[10] The bureaucratic rationality of modern law is mediated by a vast and complex network of officers, employees, typists, scribes, scriveners, Gogol's clerks, Bartlebys, and Kafka's doormen that signifies not a straightforward disenchanted secularization but a redistribution of sovereignty whose new bearer is a bio-politically produced entity called the People. As Eric Santner puts it in *The Royal Remains*, the early-modern period initiates "the passage of royal sovereignty into the body and life of the people, the 'horizontal' or democratic dissemination of the dynamics of the King's Two Bodies in the domain of popular sovereignty."[11] This redistribution of that "fleshly excess" of sovereignty generates novel pressures and excitations on every individual bearer of sovereign power. In modernity, therefore, the "citizen" comes to occupy the sacred *office*, the erstwhile seat of the sovereign. Santner's narrative is not a secularization of disenchantment but the displacement of an enchanted royal materiality into everyday life, as the elusive materiality of modern biopolitical life. Schreber describes a similar model of dissemination of royal remains figuratively in the "divine rays" that radiate from God, who comes in contact with the world, against the order of nature, communicating with humans through a complex network of "nerves." Schreber seems to think that this transfusion of power between sovereign and the human, body-to-body through nervous systems, caused his madness. His bellowing, his multiple orgasms, his imagined anatomical changes, the inability to "weigh himself," are symptoms of this sublime and "fleshly excess" as it becomes infused in him when appointed to the office of the judge. But the crucial point here is that the sublime and mystical body of the sovereign that becomes displaced in modernity, as Victoria Kahn suggests, is essentially an elaborate and spectacular legal fiction.[12] The body of the king was not identical with his office. The Crown is a *persona ficta* separable from the king.[13] It is this separability that opens up the space, via proliferating fictions, for re-imagining politics. This is what Schreber does by hallucinating an investiture of the "office of pleasure." He invents a spectacular *persona ficta,* as a cross-dressing, trans* sexual, desiring, caring, becoming a nurturing mother.

A Freudian Detour

Sigmund Freud traces the genesis of law and religion to the absence of the primal father. In his *Totem and Taboo* it is only after the sons have killed the primal father out of hatred and envy that they begin to identify with him, and the repressed affection makes itself felt.[14] So the murder creates a loss of the father that is experienced as remorse and guilt, which then leads to the law against murder. After killing the father, Freud surmises, the brothers quarrel for succession but soon realize the futility of that violence. This realization leads to a union among the sons, a patriarchal social contract to institute stable social organizations accompanied by the renunciation of instinctual gratification and incest prohibitions – in short, the beginnings of morality and law.[15] Freud is interested in the ambiguous relation between fathers and sons, but equally important are the excluded women over whom the men fight, and that is what Schreber points towards. The sons envy the father because the father controlled the women. After killing the father, the sons form of a "fraternity" and pass rules of kinship to regulate the role of women in the community. By becoming-woman, Schreber transgresses this "sexual contract" of the brotherhood, thus disrupting the terms of the original social contract.[16]

Totem and Taboo, however, needs to be read with *Moses and Monotheism.* The thematic and genetic proximity of these two texts have been discussed elsewhere, therefore one can safely assume that Freud saw a deep continuity between these works even though separated by over two decades.[17] As per Freud's fable, to save the religion of Aton from extinction, Moses, a fervently monotheist Egyptian priest, headed an oppressed Semitic tribe from their bondage in Egypt to create a new nation of Israel for them. Moses (like the primeval father in *Totem and Taboo*) was strong, powerful, and strict, and he preached a spiritualized and imageless form of monotheism. But when the former slaves could not bear the severe demands of the new faith, they murdered Moses and repressed the memory of the murder. The Israelites went on to forge an alliance with other Semitic tribes of the region, fusing the god of Moses with those other polytheistic religions. However, over centuries, the submerged tradition of the true faith and its founder resurfaced and gathered sufficient force to reassert itself. This is the stage of the "return of the repressed." The memory of the murder of Moses comes back, and they return to that earlier monotheism. Freud argues that the return to monotheism reminds the Jews that they are the "chosen people," therefore they are invested with a psychic power of confidence, creativity, and coherence. In Eric Santner's political theology, influenced by Kantorowicz, it is the People who come to be the "chosen one," vested with rights and powers. But, unlike Freud's Israelites, the effect of this investiture is not always "self-confidence," but rather the fleshly vibrant anxiety that comes from having to occupy that office to which they have been specially and involuntarily called.

Office of Pleasure

Schreber's *Memoirs* are written in a hybrid style that mixes poetic and fantastically rich descriptions of bizarre visual and auditory hallucinations, along with a concept-laden, abstract, evidence-driven, methodologically rigorous and theoretically lucid prose. In his fabulation of the strange and the familiar, the old and the new, there is a prefiguring of the dialectic between the rule and the facts, the precedent and the singularity of the present. And through this encounter newness enters the world.

Schreber suffered his first mental breakdown in 1884, at age forty-two. He was admitted to a psychiatric clinic and discharged in six months. His condition got worse when he was appointed to the position of *Senatspräsident* of the Superior Court of Dresden in June 1893. He experienced the stresses and pressures of the job in severe physical exhaustion. He tried to escape the profession of judging by turning to politics, but he couldn't enter politics for want of democratic approval.[18] During this period, Schreber also showed signs of what Mark Sanders calls his "crisis of judging."[19] He found himself unable to evaluate his actions and unable to judge, or to even "weigh himself" by balancing the choices he faced. He saw himself in the mirror metamorphosing into a woman. Constantly hearing voices in his head, echoing and compulsively repeating the same phrases, Schreber suffered from sleeplessness. This eventually led to his mental collapse after a particular night, during which he had a "quite unusual number of pollutions." Freud saw "nocturnal emissions" as a sign of weakness and lack of self-control.[20]

After this nocturnal event, Schreber's paranoia intensified. He started seeing signs of communication with supernatural powers. He interpreted his hallucinations as revelations concerning the nature of God. God, who was made up of "nerves," had established "nerve contact" with him.[21] He called these nerves "divine rays." This "nerve contact," being against the "order of the world," led to the destruction of the world. He was now the last man alive while all other human beings were not real people but miraculously created "fleeting-improvised-men." This context of the destruction of the world, an apocalyptic crisis in social order, is the condition in which Schreber's written reflections begin.

Freud's interpretation of Schreber focuses on its homosexual content. He postulates that Schreber suffered from "an outburst of homosexual libido," sublimating his attraction to figures like Professor Flechsig into conspiracy theories. Freud suggests that his struggles with the libidinal impulse produce these symptoms.[22] Freud notes how Schreber's "delusions" of becoming a woman begin around the time he was appointed to the senior office of the *Senatspräsident* in Dresden.

In what follows, I want to focus on one specific and decisive shift that happens in his psyche. In the initial periods of his psychosis, Schreber regarded his emasculation as an act of persecution. He experienced being sexually abused by God, possibly in conspiracy with his psychiatrist Dr. Flechsig: "It was in consequence very natural for me to see my real enemy only in Professor Flechsig or his soul and to regard as my natural ally God's omnipotence.… It occurred to me only much later, in fact only while writing this essay did it become quite clear to me, that God Himself must have known of the plan, if indeed He was not the instigator, to commit soul murder on me, and to hand over my body in the manner of a female harlot."[23] In this stage of his illness Schreber was deeply ashamed of his "unmanning." He felt vulnerable, as if a victim of sexual abuse being persecuted by powers of the greatest might that have complete control over him. Michael Warner frames the connection between shame and sex pithily: "Perhaps because sex is an occasion for losing control, for merging one's consciousness with the lower orders of animal desire and sensation, for raw confrontation of power and demand, it fills people with aversion and shame."[24]

How did Schreber overcome this shame that arises from the confrontation of power and desire? Over time his shame was replaced by the pleasure he found in the "unmanning." He became less hesitant and developed pride about his trans* experimentations. As his psychiatrist from Sonnenstein noted in his medical report to the court: "In the clean shaving of his face, in his pleasure in feminine toilet articles, in small feminine occupations, in the tendency to underdress more or less and to look at himself in the mirror, to decorate himself with gay ribbons and bows, etc., in a feminine way, the pathological direction of his fantasy is manifested continually."[25]

This regaining of a selfhood, which I understand as his embracing the dynamism of "becoming-trans*," was possible when he took up his delusional "office of pleasure," where the cultivation of his femininity was coded as an obligation: "I have to imagine myself as man and woman in one person having intercourse with myself, or somehow have to achieve with myself a certain sexual excitement, etc. – which perhaps under other circumstances might be considered immoral.... This behaviour has been forced on me through God having placed Himself into a relationship with me which is contrary to the Order of the World." So, when asked what justified his voluptuous transgressions, he responded, *"Dieu le veut"* (God wishes it).

This reparation perhaps was a result of his realization (via hallucinations) that God was not persecuting him but had "chosen" him for his higher design of giving birth to a new world. Schreber saw his emasculation as a submission to God's calling, and that he had a duty to cultivate his voluptuousness in response to the demand and to recreate humanity. Freud suggests that this shift in delusion was "a magnificent victory" because now Schreber was able to make his voluptuousness God-fearing and "God Himself never tired of demanding it from him."[26] As Schreber put it, "I have frequently referred in this book to the close relationship which exists between voluptuousness and everlasting Blessedness. Voluptuousness can be considered as part of everlasting Blessedness and is in a sense inherent in man and other living beings."[27] He suffused his sexuality with spirituality, invested it with authority, and made it a legitimate expression rather than something to be ashamed of.

When reflecting upon his persecution complex, Schreber suggested that "the crisis that broke upon the realms of God was caused by somebody having *committed soul murder;* at first Flechsig was named as the instigator of soul murder but of recent times in an attempt to reverse the facts, I myself have been 'represented' as the one who had committed soul murder."[28] The allusion to the soul murder makes the connection with *Totem and Taboo* obvious. Schreber felt guilty for this soul murder. This recollection of soul murder was an important stage in overcoming the latency period necessary for the return of the repressed. It is similar to what Freud suggests is special to the Mosaic religion: the self-confidence and independent will as the psychic effect of being "chosen" by God. Taking a different route, Santner also gives us a genealogy of the "People" as the chosen inheritors of sovereignty in modernity. But unlike Freud, Santner does not believe that being chosen leads to optimism and self-confidence. Rather, it leads to an anxiety from the fleshly excesses, whose symptoms include, amongst other things, commodity fetishism, our 24/7 workaholic culture, becoming busybodies, aversion to idleness, and ultimately, the ills of neoliberalism.[29] What Schreber's psychosis prevents, however, is a resistance to passive acquiescence of the displaced sovereignty that Santner traces. Instead, Schreber transformed the sublimity of the royal via his kinky and exciting transsexual experiments. In doing so, Schreber moved beyond *Totem and Taboo*'s father-and-son heteronormative patriarchy, to envision other natalities from the standpoint of the mother, whom Freud ignores.

Freud's "return of the repressed" as a "return of the patriarch/ authoritarian father" and idea of being the "chosen one" to renew a world in disorder can be a discomfortingly conservative heroic narrative as well. Yet the move Schreber made was to orient himself to the past so that the past enabled his insatiable desires for the future. She remade her sense of self by being undone by the forces of desire. The rhetoric of obligation to God comes across in the real world as a naughty, rebellious, disobedient, and intransigent comportment. The visions of being the "chosen one" here is not of being the "chosen son" but a more playful excess, of being chosen to become-other, to become trans*, all pluralities-in-one. Schreber ultimately carved for herself this heterotopic space of autonomy as the pleasurable mode of inhabiting the law.

Eric Santner's political theology is bleak in how it traces the redistribution of sovereignty/God/Father into the bio-politically constituted flesh of the People who collectively form the nation state, which has been the agent of unspeakable violence since the nineteenth century. When Schreber took up the office of the judge in the name of the "People," he experienced the fleshly anxieties as crisis of symbolic investiture that led to his mental breakdown. But he turned it around by resignifying the distribution of the king's sublime body via fictions of trans* multiplicities and multitudes rather than the singular national principle of the "People." In his re-signification of the People as a trans* multitude, we can infer a trans* nationalism that critiques the monad of the nation state, the jurisdictional condition for modern law.

On the basis of medical reports of his mental illness, the District Court of Dresden placed him under tutelage of the state. In challenging this juridical order treating him like a minor, he put his minor jurisprudence to trial before the Appeals Court and ultimately won back their autonomy. The judgment unequivocally noted that the "Court is in no doubt that the appellant is insane."[30] But the question before it was whether Schreber was able to manage their own affairs or not (a question of *Oikonomia,* as Goodrich puts it in the Introduction). It was a matter of whether Schreber was able to carry on his daily business correctly and fulfil his duties as a social being. In a secular vein, the court categorized "ordinary civil life" and "religious life" as distinct, and since he was able to manage the former, his religious beliefs were less relevant. Schreber himself would find this departmentalization of the secular and divine untenable. But in ultimately legitimizing his experiments and being freed from tutelage, Schreber's case became an exemplar. And exemplarity is itself a source of new norms.

NOTES

1 Angela Condello and Luke Mason, "*Make It New!* The Redeeming Modernism of Law and the Collapsing of Its Polarities," *Polemos* 13, no. 1 (2019): 161.

2 Peter Goodrich, *Law in the Courts of Love: Literature and Other Minor Jurisprudences* (New York: Routledge, 2013).

3 Christopher Tomlins, "Foreword, 'Law As…' III – Glossolalia: Towards a Minor Historical Jurisprudence," *University of California Irvine Law Review* 5 (2015): 239–61.

4 Tomlins, "Foreword," 241–2.

5 For my use of the term "trans*," see Jack Halberstam, *Trans: A Quick and Quirky Account of Gender Variability* (Oakland, CA: University of California Press, 2018).

6 Eric Santner, *My Own Private Germany: Daniel Paul Schreber's Secret History of Modernity* (Princeton, NJ: Princeton University Press, 1996).

7 For a version of this argument on the loss of foundations of legal authority, especially in the German context, see Roger Berkowitz, *The Gift of Science: Leibniz and the Modern Legal System* (Cambridge: MA: Harvard University Press, 2005).

8 Peter Goodrich, *Schreber's Law: Jurisprudence and Judgment in Transition* (Edinburgh: Edinburgh University Press, 2018).

9 Giorgio Agamben, *Opus Dei: An Archaeology of Duty,* trans. Adam Kotsko (Palo Alto, CA: Stanford University Press, 2013). Also see Agamben,

The Kingdom and the Glory, trans. Lorenzo Chiesa and Matteo Mandarini (Palo Alto, CA: Stanford University Press, 2011).

10 Peter Goodrich, "The Judge's Two Bodies: The Case of Daniel Paul Schreber," *Law & Critique* 26, no. 2 (2015): 117–33.

11 Eric Santer, *Royal Remains: The People's Two Bodies and the Endgames of Sovereignty* (Chicago: University of Chicago Press, 2011), 44.

12 Victoria Kahn, "Political Theology and Fiction in *The King's Two Bodies*," *Representations* 106, no. 1 (2009): 77–101.

13 On the literary-historical usage of *persona ficta*, see Stephen Greenblatt, *Renaissance Self-Fashioning: From More to Shakespeare* (Chicago: University of Chicago Press, 1980): 166–7.

14 Sigmund Freud, *Totem and Taboo*, trans. James Strachey (New York: Norton, 1950).

15 Also see Sigmund Freud, *Moses and Monotheism*, trans. Katherine Jones (New York: Vintage, 1959), 104.

16 On the term "sexual contract," see Carole Pateman, *The Sexual Contract* (Palo Alto, CA: Stanford University Press, 1988).

17 See Richard J. Bernstein, *Freud and the Legacy of Moses* (New York: Cambridge University Press, 1998).

18 Goodrich, "Judge's Two Bodies," 118–19.

19 Mark Sanders, "Psychoanalysis, Mourning and the Law: Schreber's Paranoia as Crisis of Judging," in *Law and Mourning*, ed. Austin Sarat and Martha Merrill Umphrey, (Amherst: University of Massachusetts, 2017), 117–47.

20 Sigmund Freud, *Three Essays on the Theory of Sexuality*, trans. James Strachey (New York: Basic Books, 2000).

21 Schreber's conception of "nerves" has a mechanistic or physicalistic connotation that hints at a world that works by scientific laws rather than any transcendent God's arbitrary wishes. Schreber considers himself to be a "doubter," and as per his physicalist view of the world, God's rightful place could have been only as the prime mover, and once this function has been performed, his presence was no longer required. This view of "deism," dominant in the eighteenth century, conceived God as one who did not intervene in the universe.

22 Sigmund Freud, "Case History of Schreber," in *The Standard Edition of the Complete Psychological Works of Sigmund Freud*, trans. James Strachey (New York: Vintage, 2001), 12:43.

23 Daniel Paul Schreber, *Memoirs of My Nervous Illness*, trans. Ida Macalpine and Richard A. Hunter (New York: New York Review of Books, 2000), 66.

24 Michael Warner, *The Trouble with Normal: Sex, Politics and the Ethics of Queer Life* (Cambridge, MA: Harvard University Press, 1999), 3.

25 Daniel Paul Schreber, "Appendix A," in *Memoirs*, 335.

26 Freud, "Case History of Schreber," 56.
27 Schreber, *Memoirs,* 249.
28 Schreber, *Memoirs,* 34.
29 Eric Santner, *The Weight of All Flesh: On the Subject-Matter of Political Economy* (New York: Oxford University Press, 2015).
30 Schreber, *Memoirs,* 422.

4 Schreber's Double Process: Legal and Literary Transformations in the *Memoirs of My Nervous Illness*

KATRIN TRÜSTEDT

In *Denkwürdigkeiten eines Nervenkranken* (Memoirs of My Nervous Illness) judge Schreber writes about his "transformation into a woman"[1] as a "reversal of that developmental process"[2] that had once constituted him as male.[3] "In the first months of pregnancy the rudiments of both sexes are laid down and the characteristics of the sex which is not developed remain as rudimentary organs at a lower stage of development, like the nipples of the male."[4] Schreber's transformation into a woman thus highlights the fundamental reversibility of processes that had constituted him as the subject he is but remain open-ended and latent potentialities. At the same time, this process of becoming woman at the centre of the *Memoirs* meets a second-order process of *writing* about it, turning these experiences into a legal and scientific case. On the first level – the level of *what is being described* – there are the numerous steps involved in the transformation of the previously sober and manly judge into a woman. The techniques in performing this transformation and the steps of this metamorphosis that Schreber painfully transcribes are attributed to the agency of others (ultimately God). On the level of the *description* of this transformation – the textual level – it is itself transformed into a legal and scientific case that Schreber uses to win the legal battle about his internment, proving his legal competency – his delusions notwithstanding. In what follows, I suggest to read judge Schreber's *Memoirs* from the perspective of the transformational techniques and practices, processes and procedures that are at work in the different layers of the text – legal procedures, but also scientific and of course textual ones that, instead of expressing some definitive message or diagnosis, constitute a performative and dynamic constellation.

Many ingenious readings of his *Memoirs*[5] have been informed by the idea that, for Schreber, entering the world of his delusions meant leaving behind the role and the concerns of the judge, lifting the restrictions of his office, and finding access to a wealth of repressed psychic and social conflicts. As the following reading focusing on the double process at work in the *Memoirs* suggests, however, Schreber did not turn away from the law in his delusions, but rather deepened his sense and expanded his view for the procedural character of the law. His transformation into a woman reflects back on the law as a subjectivizing procedure and brings out its potentials and aporias, its productivity and costs. It does not leave law behind; instead it develops a different perspective on it that can open up its procedures to a different use. So is his reintroduction of his delusions as evidence in a legal case that resulted in the court rescinding an earlier ruling that Schreber be subject to tutelage – that is, guardianship by the courts.

In this sense, Schreber's *Memoirs* use legal procedures to expand our sense of their possible use, unearthing their latent, hidden potentials ("like the nipples of the male"). The *Memoirs* cannot be read just as a reservoir of rich delusional images allegorizing underlying psychic or social conflicts – they are also an oblique contribution to a theory of the law,[6] to the theory of law *as procedure*. Schreber's account highlights a tension that is present in the procedural character of the law, yet covered up in its modern positivistic understanding. To conceive of law as procedure means to base the legitimacy of its results on the openness of the outcome of proceedings and its responsiveness to the singularity and heterogeneity of the material entering the proceedings. On the other hand, the legal process imposes a selective legal form that reduces this very singularity and aims at a repeatability and a finality of its results that effectively remove the procedural openness. The reality of the modern law thus consists in the reduction of its own procedural complexity that Schreber, in his own way, retrieves.[7] Read against this background, Schreber's *Memoirs* reveal the dynamism and potential reversibility of all procedures so excessively that they go beyond the limited and rationalizable confines of the law, opening them up to new usage. The different "use of bodies" at the heart of Schreber's transformation – the violent but pleasurable transformation into a woman that Schreber aligns with his legal case – opens up a new perspective on the law's grasp of the body. And while starting out from and thus apparently reinforcing binary oppositions – male and female, law and poetry, rationality and madness – the dynamic and latent processes that are at the heart of this text ultimately undermine such binary logic that has limited our conception of the law.

I will proceed in four steps: I will first introduce general features of procedures (*Verfahren*) by turning to Luhmann's theory of legal procedure (1). In the main part, I will then unfold the two main layers of proceedings in the *Memoirs* that make up this case: the transformation into a woman as he describes it (2), and his *writing* of the transformation by which he turns it into a legal and scientific case (3). In the concluding section I will indicate in what sense Schreber exceeded Luhmann's procedural theory and points to another use of procedures (4).

1. Towards a General Theory of Procedure

The intellectual culture of Schreber's time can be characterized, among other things, by the fundamental and constitutive and yet often overlooked role it attributed to *procedures*. This role concerns the normative realm of the law just as much as the alethic realm of scientific truth and the aesthetic realm of beauty.[8] A positivist conception of the law conceived of it as generated by legal procedure;[9] the experimental paradigm of the sciences, extended to the life sciences in the nineteenth century, thought of scientific truth as the product of experimental procedures.[10] And the aesthetic conception of art as "technique" conceived of the beautiful as the product of aestheticization.[11] While the ancient European tradition was articulated teleologically and oriented by evident *ends* (the good, the true, the beautiful) that could lead to and justify the appropriate means, the modern tradition understood itself technically: *just* (in legal decisions) or *true* (in the natural sciences) or *beautiful* (in the arts) is whatever is produced by the right means – the right kinds of procedures.

In the realm of law, this procedural orientation is connected to a legal positivism that refrains from basing the normative order on hierarchies of values or goals or authorities based on natural law.[12] Rather, justice is understood as the technical product of the right type of procedural arrangement and engagement, and authoritative decisions do not issue from a self-evident truth, sovereign power, or manifestation of a higher will.[13] A ritualized invocation of "supernatural decisions" instead yielded to codified procedures that begin with "open possibilities" and only thereby result in binding decisions.[14]

In modernity, the systematicity, repeatability, and rationality of scientific procedures were likewise conceived of as legitimizing and supporting the results they produced. Just like legal and political procedures, they tend to deflect from the uncontrollability and contingency, the openness and improvisation, that accompany the turn towards open-ended experiments and processes that are in constant flux themselves. The so-called age of the life sciences, which is characterized by an "experimentalization of life" has extended the corresponding new perspective on knowledge and the procedures of its production.[15] Following the shift from a classificatory approach of a natural history towards a biological science that grasps life as a dynamic force, the new sciences of life in the nineteenth century were trying to capture and understand the dynamic of life by experimental procedural settings: living entities were put in controlled environments and subjected to reproducible procedures to learn about the procedures already inherent in the objects (or rather, subjects) of these experiments.[16]

The turn of the last century conceived of not only law and science, but even art as the product of generative "techniques" or "procedures." Rather than a final product of artistic creation or a monument to last unchanged through the ages, literature – and art more generally – appears as a dynamic process, reflecting and potentially questioning matters from life and art, and thereby also other procedures like those of the law and of life sciences in its own open and experimental second-order procedure.

Niklas Luhmann's analysis of the fundamental significance of the procedural self-conception for modern legal and social systems in his *Legitimation durch Verfahren* (Legitimation through procedures) is especially illuminating in its stakes and challenges. As Luhmann's title already conveys, the central aspiration of procedures is to provide legitimation, without having to rely on self-evident grounds or a superior authority. Simply by following the right kinds of procedures, we can hope to generate binding results. Even though Luhmann is convinced about the social effectiveness of procedural mechanisms, he questions the narratives that depict procedure as restraining sovereignty effects and as guaranteeing rational outcomes. Instead of praising the normative idea that procedural arrangements are the true sources of justice, he gives a critical and rather polemical account of the social functions and mechanics, the ambiguous results and costs of this paradigm. He does not subscribe to the narrative that "procedural safeguards" function mainly "as restraints on executive and judicial power in insuring personal security."[17] Instead, he claims that the social function of legally ordered procedure is the legitimization of power, the social authorization of legal systems and of decisions. By becoming involved in a procedure that seems open at its beginning and by being granted participation, people become so enmeshed in the concatenation of proceedings that they will eventually, even if grudgingly, accept the outcome. A procedural conception of the law thus is a powerful tool to create binding effects for contingent decisions whose rationality is not self-evident. According to this modern and positivistic setting, decisions are thus not the manifestation of a truth evident from the beginning, but the outcome of a procedure that everyone had (implicitly or explicitly) agreed to accept by becoming an active participant.[18]

This is how they generate legitimacy in legal proceedings, but also in political decision-making, as Luhmann demonstrates with regard to voting procedures in democratic regimes. Similarly, scientific truth appears not as self-evident or as issued by the higher power of an infinite intellect, but as the outcome of scientific procedures that vindicate the result. In all of these cases – just decisions, legitimate policy, and scientific truth – if the procedure is understood to be trustworthy – fair, open, rational, etc. – the adequacy of the procedure validates its own result and suggests that the outcome is to be accepted. Luhmann writes, "In contrast to the course of ritual, which is without alternative, it is characteristic of procedures that the uncertainty over their outcome and its consequences and the openness of alternative behaviors are included and dealt with in the context of action and its motivational structures. Not the predefined concrete form, gesture, the correct word drive a procedure, but the selective decisions of those involved. These decisions eliminate alternatives, reduce complexity, absorb uncertainty, or transform the undefined complexity of all possibilities into a definable, graspable problematic."[19]

Luhmann's quote points to an inherent tension within such procedures that he uncovers but does not focus on: On the one hand, the procedures are to be reliable and reproducible in order to generate the consistency of binding results. On the other hand, they need to be open to the specific material of the case, and open to the diverse contributions of the participants. This is a genuine tension, since both the reproducibility and the openness are necessary to produce the legitimizing effect: The parties of the procedure can be moved to participate only because the decision still seems open and the procedure promises to be responsive to their contributions. Yet if the procedure fails to narrow down in the course of its process and to produce consistent and binding results, it will appear to be random. This tension is reflected also in the peculiar character of the outcome that is, on the one hand, legitimized as a performatively produced fact that should supposedly bind us, but that is on the other hand, as such a procedural product, always open to being questioned by new procedures. As a result of its dependence on the generative and genuinely open procedure, the result does not rest on its own and cannot be shielded from the question whether it is to be regarded as definitive or open to revision.

The openness of the procedure that is the very basis of the legitimacy of its results – any outcome of a process that is seen as "rigged," be it a trial, a democratic election, or a scientific experiment, would not be accepted – at the same time undermines its definitive and final character and thereby also questions its ability to fulfil its presumed social function, which is to reduce complexity and conflict. Although the shift towards procedures acknowledges complexity and ultimately recognizes the impossibility of any ultimate, final decision, the social implementation tends to cover up this side, in favour of securing their binding function.

It is part of Schreber's legacy to bring out this inherent tension. And he sharpens our sense for the acute and incisive formative effects that any procedure exerts on what is to enter in it. To provide a preliminary analytic grid of these incisive effects, let me point to five general features of procedures in legal but also in scientific contexts that are relevant here:

1. *Selection*: Procedures filter what becomes part of the procedural arrangement and what does not. Thereby procedures are, obviously and for structural reasons, not neutral, as is usually the claim. The decision about what is admitted and not admitted into evidence is what Derrida has called "pre-judice."[20] This selectiveness also means that any procedure implies entitlement to disregard and to ignore any evidence outside the procedure, as Luhmann points out.
2. *Isolation*: Procedures isolate the material they have selected, take it out of its original context, and put it into a different one, namely the new context of the procedural arrangement.
3. *Transformation*: Procedures shape, reframe, or reconstitute the material so that it can enter the procedure and be processed by its techniques. Whatever might have happened or occurred has to be rephrased and translated in order to become part of the legal procedure. This transformative nature of any procedure concerns not only the material of the procedure, but also the participatory roles within the procedure: whoever wants to enter the legal sphere has to take on a specific and distinct role (judge, attorney, clerk, defendant, etc.), even if that is, as in the case of witnesses, the role of "oneself" – those are the hardest roles to play, according to Luhmann. There are expectations about how those involved ought to behave and about role consistency limiting the possibilities of action within the procedure.
4. *Generalization and particularization*: A fourth feature is the tension between the *general rule* and *particular case*, to be unfolded in but not eliminated by the procedure.[21] This also applies to truth procedures, as one can see in the function of the example in philosophical judgment (Kant), the paradigm in scientific research (Kuhn),

and model organisms in scientific research (Latour): the singular "case" refers to something more general, and yet this relation of representation has to remain "somewhat hazy" if the example, paradigm, or model is to have a productive, generative, and genuine function beyond mere illustration of a general rule.[22]

5. *Positing its own other*: I would like to point out a fifth feature that Luhmann's account uncovers, even though it does not sufficiently develop it: procedures are self-instituting and self-delimiting and thereby *reconstitute their own other*. By positing the law as a procedural legal realm with selective entry conditions and required transformations, the law also posits its own other, the realm of non-law. Insofar as the law goes along with the claim to normatively regulate and do justice to the realm of non-law – to whatever occurs in the world and enters the legal realm – the law is confronted with an especially challenging task: to respond to what is other than itself and to do justice in its own procedures to what is not yet informed by the just/unjust difference.

In light of all these features, we can appreciate the challenging character, the incisive formative effects, and the inherent tension of procedures that can work to subvert or suspend their legitimizing function. What seems striking in Schreber's *Memoirs of My Nervous Illness* is the inherently dynamic character and the multiplicity of layers of proceedings interacting in this complex case story, by means of which he retrieves the complexities that positivistic law makes itself blind to in the service of producing and asserting its results. In his elaboration of these complexities, Schreber uses terms like procedure (*Verfahren*[23]), process (*Prozeß, Vorgang*[24]), performance (*Vollzug*[25]) extensively throughout. In the following, I will now sketch the two main levels of procedure in Schreber's *Memoirs*: the transformation into a woman as he describes it, and his *writing* of the transformation by which he turns it into a legal and scientific case.

2. Becoming a Woman

At the heart of Schreber's *Memoirs* is a process of becoming woman that Schreber is undergoing, according to his own report. It is both a physical and a mental process of considerable complexity. If we speak about the processes as "visions," those visions, Schreber insists, had "method" to them.[26] After resisting his transformation during the first sequence of procedures directed at him, Schreber then starts to participate in them and does his part by engaging in producing corresponding imaginations, by dressing up, exposing himself to the sun, etc. The whole transformation is an elaborate endeavour with different steps, sequences, operations, and agents involved. It is described as not having been finalized and as partly having been taken back. So it seems that this procedure is open-ended, moving back and forth, still ongoing, opened up to an uncertain future.

First, there are general procedures (in line with feature 3 of procedures: *transformation*), which are in accordance with the universal "Order of the World," as Schreber describes them.[27] On the other hand, there are all the proceedings that are, according to Schreber's own account, exceptional, causing considerable disarray in the order of things and all kinds of attempted corrective measures. "The process of unmanning itself" is, as Schreber claims, in fact part of the general procedures "innate in the Order of the World," according to which a "human being ('a seer of spirits')" must "under certain circumstances be 'unmanned' (transformed into a woman) once he has entered into indissoluble contact with divine nerves (rays)."[28] Also in accordance with the Order of the World, even if rare in the course of events, is the process of becoming woman in order to give birth to a new human race: "unmanning with the purpose of creating new human beings" occurs "in consonance with the Order of the World."[29] Physically the unmanning generally involves "the (external) male genitals (scrotum and penis) being retracted into the body and the internal sexual organs being at the same time transformed into the corresponding female sexual organs.... [T]he skeleton (pelvis, etc.) had also to be changed."[30] For that transformation, Schreber was selected and isolated from his family and normal living conditions, making him the selected and isolated object of the procedure (thus undergoing the procedural selectiveness and isolation mentioned under features 1 and 2): he was "completely cut off from the outside world, without any contact with my family."[31] It is also part of the general rule, relevant to every instance of unmanning, that "everything feminine attracts God's nerves. Hence as often as one wishes to withdraw from me, one attempts to make the female characteristics which are evident on my body recede by miracle; the effect is that the structures which I call 'nerves of voluptuousness' are pushed a little under the surface."[32] Here we can see the tendency of the procedure to go back and forth (attraction and withdrawal) and operate with degrees of latency ("under the surface").

What makes Schreber's case particular and exceptional, and brings it into tension with the general order of things (feature 4: generalization and particularization), seems to be, at first glance, a minor procedural deviance, a slight change in the quality, degree, and duration of contact with the divine rays: "In my case, however, since my nervous illness took the above-mentioned critical turn, my nerves have been set in motion from without incessantly and without any respite."[33] While it is in accordance with a general rule that through "nerve-contact a *temporary* connection was effected between divine rays and the nerves of that person," that connection was calculated to "last only a short time.... To succumb permanently to the power of attraction of such nerves would endanger God Himself; therefore one had to attempt to get away again when the purpose was achieved."[34] To "get away" required its own countermeasures, so-called interferences: "One only had to produce little noises by miracle (the so-called 'interferences') ..., and this short period of diverted attention sufficed the rays *in the case of nerves not as highly excited as mine*, to give up the nerve-contact and enable them to withdraw from the person."[35] And yet, in Schreber's case, the attraction of female Schreber is not temporary, but too strong for the withdrawal, as "the nerves concerned have ... taken on the character of *female nerves of voluptuousness* and apart from this have given my body a more or less *feminine stamp*.... God, who used to be an immense distance away, had been forced to draw nearer the earth.... [T]he change thus wrought is *contrary to the Order of the World*[;] it is connected with certain *disadvantages even for God Himself*."[36] Considering the hypothesis that Schreber is here engaged in an oblique reflection of what it means to become the object of a procedure, it seems that he highlights how its direct effect is a fundamental and violent transformation that it forces upon the subject entering into it. Entering into a procedure involves a change in being. What makes this consequence especially grave, even maddening in Schreber's case, is the fact that as a result of his special case, this transformation is not temporary anymore (dependent on a fleeting circumstance or on a certain required product – the new race to be produced). Schreber is caught up in a procedure that becomes unending, finds an object in him that the procedure itself cannot let go anymore. Schreber thus highlights the violent transformative grasp of the procedure and the inherent threat of a procedure without end.[37]

A further element that Schreber focuses on is the multiplicity of agents and operators that become involved and turn him into a site of conflict. To become the subject of a procedure thus does not simply mean to be possibly irreversibly transformed, it means to become the site of a war of forces intersecting in oneself. The agents involved include operators of its own counter-processes, not only in the form of contact with rays and interferences to disrupt this contact, but also the process of unmanning itself. "The rays of the lower God (Ariman) have the power of producing the miracle of unmanning; the rays of the upper God (Ormuzd) have the power of restoring manliness when necessary."[38] Different agents seem to be responsible for opposite directions of the process. There is not one source of authority authoring this overall process; even God is split into two contrasting agents. "The posterior realms of God were (and still are) subject to a peculiar division, a lower God (Ariman) and upper God (Ormuzd) being distinguished."[39] Ultimately such a variety of agents involved seems to have undermined, made impure, and sabotaged the integrity of the process itself. That it "was even reversed again, was due only to the fact that, apart from the pure rays of God, other rays were present led by 'tested' (impure) souls…, Flechsig's rays and others, which prevented the completion of the process of transformation in its purity and in accordance with the Order of the World."[40] This is how the infamous Professor Flechsig, Schreber's first doctor and director of his first asylum, factors into the process, manipulating the nerve contact: "Professor Flechsig in some way knew how to put divine rays to his own use."[41] Accordingly, new measures had to be taken, involving yet new agents again. "The Eternal Jew was maintained and provided with the necessary means of life by the 'fleeting-improvised-men' … that is to say souls were for this purpose transitorily put into human shape."[42] It is, however, important to note that it is not only Flechsig's influence that makes Schreber's case run partly contrary to the Order of the World, but his own nervous condition, as well as God's incapacity to understand the human material the process is dealing with, as we will see further on. "Later, apart from Professor Flechsig's nerves, direct divine rays also entered into contact with my nerves. This influence has in the course of years assumed forms more and more contrary to the Order of the World … and I might say become increasingly grotesque."[43]

The particular case of Schreber, it seems, interrupts, challenges, and subverts the general mode of operation. In some way, every case contains a challenge for the general rules to be applied to it. That is the irreducible tension between case and rule, inherent in the very idea of procedure. Yet Schreber's exceptional case is, on his own account, not just in a productive tension with the general procedures but in fact suspends[44] and ultimately threatens the order itself: "Through my case fundamental changes have come about in these conditions [i.e., conditions in consonance with the Order of the World.]"[45] The unintended consequences interrupt the course of the proceedings and prompt new procedures that must be found along the way (in the course of the very process, on the fly, as it were), challenging the Order of the World and the set of techniques that was supposed to reproduce it. Schreber sometimes expresses this by referring to his special case as interrupting the "plan": "The power of attraction of my nerves was however so strong that this plan could not be carried out."[46] The "plan" often had to be changed during the proceedings. For instance, instead of taking the measure of subjecting Schreber to compulsive thinking, as planned, "one was soon driven to take refuge in a system of falsifying my thoughts."[47]

In an experimental style, all kinds of measures are tried to see whether they move the proceeding in the right direction, often achieving the contrary effect. "One continually tried to stop the attraction, in other words to break free again from my nerves.... All other conceivable methods were therefore tried in the course of time, but with regard to the efforts to unman me it was soon found that the gradual filling of my body with nerves of voluptuousness (female nerves) had exactly the reverse effect, because the resulting so-called 'soul-voluptuousness' in my body rather increased the power of attraction."[48]

The cascade of procedures introduced to interrupt the entanglement, which was supposed to be temporary, only reinforces and expands it. Introducing these further procedures, which are meant to realign the outcome of the procedure with the expected and typical result, reintroduces the general openness that constitutes all procedures to an excessive degree. Introducing these further procedures thus neither helps to close or interrupt and exit the process, nor brings it to a definitive result. Rather it creates a "system of vacillation [System des Lavierens],"[49] a system of procedures that indefinitely holds everyone involved, constantly going back and forth, and moving in all kinds of directions without final resolution. The undermining of the general rule thus actually becomes the rule. Because of other rays and a "*fundamental misunderstanding*," such a "system of vacillation" began, in which "attempts to cure my nervous illness alternated with efforts to annihilate me as a human being who, because of his ever-increasing nervousness, had become a danger to God Himself. From this developed a policy of half measures ('half-heartedness' is the expression which I heard repeatedly)."[50] The term of a "system of vacillation" appears paradoxical, but it highlights the crux of procedures: they constitute an open *agencement* that takes on a dynamic of its own, ultimately threatening the systematicity of the system and the reproducibility of its outcomes it is supposed to ensure. Schreber's procedure takes on a dynamic of its own in which it blossoms exuberantly: it "become[s] increasingly grotesque" as he writes. With humour he describes the tendency of procedures to become self-instigating: "*L'appétit vient en mangeant*: it is therefore quite probable that after the first, more soul murders were committed on the souls of other people."[51] On the other side of that openness is the repetitiveness of procedures. As Schreber notes, the procedures that are locked in the system of vacillation tend to become mechanical, a fact highlighted especially by the repetitive mechanization of speech: "It is true the souls had at that time still their own thoughts … whereas for a long time now the talk of the voices has consisted only of a terrible monotonous repetition of ever-recurring phrases (learnt by rote)."[52] While agents in the form of "souls" would contribute "their own thoughts" to the process, which adds to its general openness, the necessary repetitiveness of procedures leads to the opposite effect. In turn that affects the subject taken up and transformed by the procedure: Schreber himself: "I was tired of all miracles."[53]

Different agents, like the various "souls," are not only involved in executing the procedure, of which Schreber is the sole material or object; they become part of the material itself ("I was in contact for some time with the nerves of Professor Paul Theodor Flechsig and of Daniel Fürchtegott Flechsig … and had parts of their souls in my body."[54]) The border between instrument and object thus becomes increasingly blurry and hard to draw. Correspondingly, the object Schreber – at first resistant to the procedure – will become an active agent or instrument of the proceedings, initiating measures himself to steer proceedings in a particular direction "to assist God in His fight against the 'tested souls,'"[55] or cultivating becoming a woman, when he "wholeheartedly inscribed the cultivation of femininity on my banner."[56] In this way, Schreber highlights how the roles in procedures are influenced and co-defined by one another. In a legal trial, for instance, judge, plaintiff, defendant, state's attorney, jury, witness, referee, etc. give each other shape and influence each other's behaviour in a dynamic way that is not fully accessible to someone external to the proceedings.

The tension between the general Order of the World and the particular case of Schreber, and the dynamic interaction between the agents involved in the procedure lead not only to deviant trajectories, but also to misuse and infringement, most prominently by Director Flechsig. God could have eliminated him for that misuse, but instead let it slide. "Perhaps one did not think it necessary to proceed immediately with the most drastic measures against the presumed soul murderer, while his trespass consisted at first only of abuse of contact with divine nerves, and the eventuality of soul murder seemed remote."[57] The Order of the World did not sanction the transgression against its rules, but rather allowed it to continue. There seem to be "proceedings" and "measures" to deal with transgressions, but it is a question of consideration whether or not to use them. Schreber often uses "one" (man) instead of an identified subject of the procedure ("Perhaps *one* did not think it necessary to proceed"), thereby emphasizing that there is no single authority (God), and that the procedure is impersonal and decentred.

Resistance to the process is not limited to the material, but rather also concerns the instruments involved. "For God's nerves also it is unpleasant and against their will to enter into my body."[58] The resistance of God's nerves points to the paradoxical role of God himself as being both the external orchestrator outside of the procedure and a party within it, working both within the bounds and against the rule of the Order of the World: "The Order of the World reveals its very grandeur and magnificence by denying even God Himself in so irregular a case as mine the means of achieving a purpose contrary to the Order of the World. All attempts at committing soul murder, at unmanning me for purposes contrary to the Order of the World … have failed. From this apparently so unequal battle … I emerge … victorious, because the Order of the World is on my side."[59] The singularity of Schreber's case forces the general order into conflict with itself. According to his diagnosis, God was at odds with himself, and Schreber employed God's own true powers and attributes against him in his self-defence: "God, whose power by rays is essentially constructive in its nature, and creative, came into conflict with Himself when he attempted the irregular policy against me … God Himself was on my side in His fight against me, that is to say I was able to bring His attributes and powers into battle as an effective weapon in my self-defense."[60] Interestingly, this mirrors the way Schreber thinks of himself in the legal battle that this narrative eventually becomes a part of in which he defends himself against being denied legal competency. Schreber did come out of his other "unequal battle" victoriously, working both with and against the law.

The resistance to the process performed by the material, by the instruments, and ultimately by the highest authority of the proceedings itself (God), indicates that the elements involved are in an important sense foreign to the process itself. This foreignness is already highlighted by the "event" in 1893, which started the process of turning Schreber into woman: "It was the idea that it really must be rather pleasant to be a woman succumbing to intercourse. This idea was so foreign to my whole nature that I may say I would have rejected it with indignation if fully awake; from what I have experienced since I cannot exclude the possibility that some external influences were at work to implant this idea in me."[61] The conditionality of resistance ("I *would have* rejected it with indignation if fully awake") points to an ambivalence in this resistance. It seems not to be due to the given manly "nature" of Schreber. Rather, the pleasure of the transformation as well as the resistance to it seem to be part of the process itself. It is undecidable where the line between given material and manipulated outcome would have to be drawn. Rather, the material itself is in part constituted by the process as its own other.

The transformation into a woman produces – according to the self-limiting character of procedures – its own other as the material that is to be transformed: "In my earlier life ... I had been a person of calm nature, without passion, clear-thinking and sober, whose individual gift lay much more in the direction of cool intellectual criticism than in the creative activity of an unbounded imagination. I was by no means what one might call a poet."[62] Only in the past tense – "I *had been* a person of calm nature," "I *was* by no means what one might call a poet" – do we learn of Schreber's "nature," now already caught up in its transformation. This "other" of the procedure, the material existing prior to it that is only retroactively evoked as such, is put into a binary contrast: the opposition between calm nature, clear-thinking, and sober, cool intellectual criticism on the one hand, and passion, creative activity of an unbounded imagination, and poetic capacity, on the other.

To "wholeheartedly inscribe ... the cultivation of femininity on my banner"[63] on Schreber's own account means to forego her manliness and by extension to leave behind the law associated with it: "The pursuit of my previous profession, which I loved wholeheartedly, every other aim of manly ambition, and every other use of my intellectual powers in the service of mankind."[64] One side is associated with manliness and law, as well as the natural sciences ("I had occupied myself too much with the natural sciences"[65]), the other with poetry and femininity, with "soul-voluptuousness,"[66] "sensuous pleasure,"[67] and "female sexual enjoyment,"[68] but also with madness,[69] dreams, "feminine feelings" in contrast to "being retained on the side of men."[70] There are many descriptions in this vein, referring to the "wild play with miracles in my dreams," "the whole garden" that was "luxuriantly in bloom,"[71] "French-speaking ladies,"[72] "Moonshine-Blessedness," which "was to represent the female state of Blessedness."[73] To "float in voluptuousness," an "indescribable feeling of well-being corresponding to feminine feelings of voluptuousness"[74] pervading "my whole body," is associated not only with letting "my imagination play on sexual matters," but also with "reading a particularly moving part of a poem, playing a piece of music on the piano which particularly pleases me aesthetically."[75] What becomes clear in the course of Schreber's account, the opposition in fact traverses him in such a way that the two sides are inseparable. The two opposed sides can thus occur simultaneously in one and the same "whole person": "At times I enjoy the highest voluptuousness up to my neck, while my head is in a bad way."[76] This *coincidentia oppositorum* can even produce "amusing effects" and "a touch of the comic,"[77] as Schreber attests. As we will see in the next section on the method with which Schreber transforms the experience of his nervous illness so that s/he can give a calm, clear-thinking, sober account of it that convinces the court of hir legal competency, Schreber effectively insists on hir doubleness, the wholehearted commitment to femininity notwithstanding.

There are two further levels accompanying the primary procedure of Schreber's transformation. The transformative process of "unmanning" is immanently coupled with two further levels of procedure: accounting and examination. The transformation Schreber undergoes is in this sense connected of an accounting process, producing a large apparatus of files on the subject of this transformation, and a process of examination and interrogation, testing him in order to identify possible means of finalizing the transformation.

In the accounting, there are, first and foremost, the famous "writing-down systems," *Aufschreibesysteme* in the original German, recording his every thought. Friedrich Kittler's famous study *Aufschreibesysteme 1800/1900* from 1984 adopts Schreber's term as a generic concept referring to the "technologies and institutions that allow a given culture to select, store and produce relevant data."[78] The writing-down system that Schreber describes is a massive surveillance system: a quasi-technical apparatus of anonymous writing agents that produce a huge number of files on Schreber. "Books or other notes are kept in which for years have been written-down all my thoughts, all my phrases, all my necessaries, all the articles in my possession or around me, all persons with whom I come into contact, etc."[79] While at first glance it appears to be neutral – simply recording what is already there – the writing-down system reveals itself to be anything but neutral, as most recording procedures and media eventually do. Rather, it seems to severely affect, even terrorize the thoughts it is supposedly only there to objectively record: during the continuous recording neither repetitions of thoughts nor thoughtless blanks are accepted, and both lead to active interventions: "When any of my earlier thoughts recurred ..., the approaching rays were sent down with the phrase 'We have already got this.'"[80] Pauses in thinking, on the other hand, need to be filled no matter what. On Schreber's account, in fact previous writing-down material is used to do so, producing the very repetitions he is supposed to avoid. "The writing-down-material, mainly my previous thoughts ... serves to fill in these pauses (that is to say to give the rays something to talk about even during these pauses)."[81] Schreber informs us that he intended to add a collection of certain phrases, laid down in these *Aufschreibesysteme*, as an appendix to the book, recording in turn, the system recording him: "I will perhaps append an anthology of these phrases to the present essay."[82] If the pauses in thinking were not filled, it was assumed that his thoughts had been exhausted. "The writing-down also serves as another peculiar trick which again is based on a total misunderstanding of human thinking. It was believed that my store of thoughts could be exhausted by being written-down."[83] Schreber insists on the inexhaustibility of this individuality by this recording mechanism. It is a mere temporary fix in view of the unattainable nature of the human: the writing-down system thus "belongs even for me to the realm of the unfathomable because the objective it pursues must be recognized by all who know human nature as something in itself unattainable. It is obviously a *stop-gap measure* and it is difficult to decide whether it arises from a wrong (that is contrary to the Order of the World) intent or from faulty reasoning."[84]

Who exactly performs these acts of accounting, Schreber cannot be sure: "I cannot say with certainty who does the writing down.... I presume that the writing-down is done by creatures given human shape on distant celestial bodies after the manner of the fleeting-improvised-men, but lacking all intelligence; their hands are led automatically, as it were, by passing rays for the purpose of making them write-down, so that later rays can again look at what has been written."[85] The technical process of recording, however, at points merges into a poetic or creative endeavour, highlighting again the active interference of a supposedly objective measure: "The divine rays read my thoughts correctly, without falsifying them, as has been done without exception since; they even gave them verbal expression in a rhythm corresponding to the natural movement of human nerves."[86] While the writing down is claimed to be "correct" and "without falsifying," the writing is being given in a particular "verbal expression" and a particular "rhythm," thus blurring the line between an "objective" and neutral recording on the one hand, and a creative translation on the other. In line with the binary oppositions informing his unmanning, this poetic rhythm is then opposed to his former existence as *Senatspräsident*. "For this reason the phrases learnt by rote used in the writing-down-material ... chose and still choose preferably words in *discord* with this natural cadence, as for instance my own title 'Senatspräsident.'"[87] Schreber's legal existence is – as part of the process – being reconstituted in opposition to what the transformation is to produce.

Other devices affecting the records apart from the writing-down systems include the "listening-in-thought[s]";[88] the "creation of a false feeling" (the mood-falsifying miracle);[89] the "thinking-it-over-thought"[90] that "leads a person to turn his will power in the opposite direction ..., but which on further consideration automatically causes doubts";[91] the "tying-to-celestial-bodies"[92] (linked with the speaking birds); the "not-thinking-of-anything-thought[s]";[93] the "musical-not-thinking-of-anything-thought[s]"[94] as they were called in the "soul-language." The "human thought-of-recollection" was used to "indicate man's automatic need to imprint on his mind 'soul-conception.'"[95] Then there is the measure of compulsive thinking, including the "system of not-finishing-a-sentence," which "my nerves have to supplement to make up the sense."[96] The example "Lacking now is only the leading idea, that is – we, the rays, have no thoughts,"[97] performs in a self-reflective way the technical nature of such a "system." The "intellectual deliberation"[98] had the same effect. A very prominent part in the "soul-conception" was played by "ideas about the relation between the two sexes and their respective mode of occupation, their tastes, etc. Souls knew very well that a man lies on his side in bed, a woman on her back (as the 'succumbing part,' considered from the point of view of sexual intercourse)."[99] It becomes unclear to whom we should attribute the binary opposition of the sexes that informs Schreber's discourse throughout – to Schreber himself or to these instruments (in the ambivalent "soul-conception").

A third level of procedures apart from the transformative procedures turning him into a woman and the accounting procedures recording his thoughts is the level of constant "examinations." They are prompted by the complex issues with the recording systems and the false premises they are based upon. God is so unexperienced with humans and incapable of appropriately "judging" them[100] that any pause in thinking – from the perspective of the premise of the procedure – takes on the meaning that Schreber's thoughts might have been exhausted. "Every time my thinking activity ceases God instantly regards my mental powers as extinct.... And so the withdrawal action is started, and to achieve it an 'interference' produced." [101] An absence of thoughts to be recorded here becomes itself meaningful and in fact generates massive action in turn. Among these measures is the "so-called bellowing-miracle ... produced by the lower God.... It seems to serve a double purpose, namely to create by 'representing' the impression of a person bellowing because he is demented; and also to drown by bellowing the inner voices which the upper God started so that he could withdraw to a greater distance."[102] Not only are the effects of the procedure attributed to the object that is supposedly only recorded; the two main agents of the procedure work in opposite directions, making it ultimately impossible to make out Schreber's actual thoughts and absence of thoughts.

In order to "read" the material accordingly, Schreber has to be tested all the time. "The way this examination takes place is very peculiar and hardly understandable for anybody who knows human nature. People around me are made to say certain words ... to find out ... whether I have enough reason left to comprehend these words."[103] The recording of Schreber and the interferences it triggers make the records unreliable and generate the need for examinations that further distort the situation. To "examine" Schreber's supposedly own capacities and thoughts, manipulations are performed that ultimately make it harder and harder to discern what they are supposed to establish.

Schreber explains the "erroneous" premises of the procedures as a result of the distance between the agents administering the procedure and its subject matter. "The lower and the upper God apparently have in common that they are not able to understand the living human being as an organism while they are at a distance."[104] A grave error, however, seems to stem from their inability to clearly distinguish the initial material entering the procedure from the results of the procedure itself: "Both in particular seem to be caught up in the mistaken notion ... that everything which becomes appreciable to them from the nerves of a human being in my position, mostly only in consequence of the falsification of thoughts by the rays, is to be regarded as the manifestation of the human being's own thinking activity."[105]

All these "erroneous ideas" seem only to be given up when "God has come closer."[106] And yet, once God has been drawn closer and into the process, "[it] seems to be impossible for God to draw a lesson for the future from such an experience" and "to change his usual mode of action,"[107] suggesting that whatever happens in a procedure is not easily translatable to an outside. "The more correct insight is only gained by the most forward nerve endings which are however already condemned to dissolve in my body; those parts at a distance which start the withdrawal action do not partake in this impression."[108]

To this confusing network of recording and examining devices, Schreber reacts by engaging and responding with hir own internal mechanisms of representations. With the measure of "picturing," Schreber responds to the recording and examining devices with "reversed miracles," projecting back to these devices images of how s/he is to be registered by them.

> Man retains all recollections in his memory, by virtue of lasting impressions on his nerves, as pictures in his head. Because my inner nervous system is illuminated by rays, these pictures can be voluntarily reproduced.... All this naturally only in my imagination, but in a manner that the rays

> get the impression that these objects and phenomena really exist. I can also "picture" myself in a different place, for instance while playing the piano I see myself at the same time standing in front of a mirror in the adjoining room in female attire; when I am lying in bed at night I can give myself and the rays the impression that my body has female breasts and a female sexual organ.... The picturing of female buttocks on my body ... has become such a habit that I do it almost automatically whenever I bend down. "Picturing" in this sense may therefore be called a reversed miracle. In the same way as rays throw on to my nerves pictures they would like to see especially in dreams, I too can in turn produce pictures for the rays which I want them to see.[109]

Picturing includes imagining "myself as man and woman in one person having intercourse with myself, or somehow have to achieve with myself a certain sexual excitement,"[110] and giving "divine rays the impression of a woman in the height of sexual delight; to achieve this I have to employ all possible means."[111] Such a reversed procedure – in the same way as rays throw pictures on to hir nerves they would like to see, s/he in turn produces pictures for the rays that s/he wants them to see – evokes its very own countermeasure: "Attempts are regularly made by countermiracles to blot out what I have 'pictured.'"[112] Schreber is thus very actively involved in the fabrication of the female image of himself, even if it goes against the direction of the procedure.[113] And s/he hirself in turn also "represents" God, or rather "what appears in my head when the nerves of the upper God come down," also as female, after the painting *Liebesreigen* by Pradilla: "In the left hand upper corner of this picture a woman is seen, descending with arms stretched before her and folded hands."[114] The creative process of "picturing" thus reflects itself. Both Schreber and God on two sides of the process are "pictured" as female, creating not only an image of the outcome of the transformation – Schreber as female – but also an image of the process itself ("what appears in my head when the nerves of the upper God come down") as in some way female.

3. Becoming a Text: The Writing of Schreber Becoming Woman

Mirroring Schreber's transformation into a woman, there is Schreber's *writing* about the transformation, hir very own accounting and examination that already includes internal accounting and examination. Although the *Memoirs* might seem like one coherent text, they are themselves the result of a complex process involving multiple textual and temporal layers, kept legible in the resulting text.[115] Let me reconstruct the material entering this text and the transformative operations of Schreber's complex text.

(1) The basic source material of this text is constituted by immediate observation notes Schreber took as a kind of "simultaneous" writing, mirroring the automatic "writing-down-system," as can be seen in several quotes: "My notetaking consisted at first only of a few unconnected thoughts or words which I put down; later – beginning with the year 1897 – I started to keep regular diaries, in which I entered all my experiences; earlier – but still in 1896 – I was limited to meager entries in a small calendar."[116] Schreber notes about the night of the 14 March 1900, there was "wild play with miracles in my dreams," which he "immediately wrote … down on paper," in order to decide "exactly how far objective facts were at the basis of my earlier similar visions."[117] Making a selection of what from these notes becomes part of the *Memoirs* (see next point), Schreber mentions the writing-down system: "From the content of these notes I will here only quote that … an attendant of the Asylum … was … eating smoked tongue or ham with beans.… The words used for these items of food are closely connected with the writing-down-system."[118] As we can see, Schreber hirself makes a – somewhat displaced – reference to the writing-down system that hir own immediate writing down seems to copy. These notes are characterized by hirself as quite systematic and extensive records and studies of the processes of transformation: "These notes are contained in little diaries which I have kept for years; I enter under consecutive numbers and with dates, thoughts about impressions gained, about possible future developments, etc., in the form of little studies."[119]

(2) In order for the source material to enter the process of writing hir *Memoirs*, it has to pass the characteristic selection and isolation. This is necessary for it to constitute a comprehensible account. As Schreber writes, "My body has continuously been the object of divine miracles. If I wanted to describe all these miracles in detail I could fill a whole book with them alone."[120] While certain parts of the notes become part of hir *Memoirs*, Schreber keeps other notes as supplements to the *Memoirs* ("the notes in these diaries may form a valuable supplement to my 'Memoirs'"[121]), thereby relating the coherence of the *Memoirs* back to a broader material that can supplement but also possibly question the *Memoirs*. By referring the *Memoirs* back to this additional material s/he highlights the fact that they are in a sense incomplete in their

coherence, dependent on gaps for their systematicity. The same goes for previous sketches of hir *Memoirs* that are part of its larger dossier: "I also started to sketch my future 'Memoirs,' which I had already planned. This sketch is contained in a little brown book, entitled 'From my Life'; it has served me as a welcome support of my memory while elaborating the present 'Memoirs.' Anybody interested in this sketch – which was kept in shorthand – would find there many more items which I have not incorporated into my 'Memoirs.'"[122]

(3) In order to establish hir *Memoirs*, Schreber not only produced a large collection of protocol notes and sketches of possible organizations of the material, but also provides these data with context. To do so, s/he had to rely on descriptions from a certain distance. This included, first, the description of hir external living situation, including ground plans of the various places, such as the Nerve Clinic of the university, and ground plan and sketch of Dr. Pierson's asylum (the "Devil's Kitchen"). Second, it involved the account of hir physical and mental processes from a certain remove that would allow hir to integrate time frames and partial perspectives (see also point 6, the narrative reworking). The account of the *Memoirs* thus adopts mostly a retrospective perspective, which allows Schreber to link the "ongoing" nature of certain processes to their further development into a future that is for a writer already a determinable past. The account adopts a reflective stance from which it becomes possible to characterize partial perspectives as various sides of an implicitly split subject.

(4) A further level of contextualization is provided by references to other writings, such as Kraepelin's *Textbook of Psychiatry* (5th edition, Leipzig, 1896), footnotes providing further commentary, the rather large *Postscripts to the "Memoirs,"* and references to further addenda, among them a legal essay entitled "Under What Circumstances Can Mental Patients Be Held in Public Institutions against Their Will?" that Schreber tried to get accepted for publication in a law journal. Such references give the *Memoirs* not only the air of a scientific study, but also highlight the openness of the text, as it frequently points beyond itself. As always, invoking context can provide assurance by referring to evidence and reasoning provided elsewhere, but also opens up the main body of the text to possible challenges awaiting the text in its margins.

(5) A main part of the transformative procedure giving rise to the text is the examination or "scientific evaluation" of Schreber's experiences that s/he engages in in the *Memoirs*. Here, Schreber

> partly corrects hir "visions," explains and evaluates them. Thus, s/he decides what becomes a crucial part of the case and what is thrown out as insignificant or irregular. In this "scientific" process, s/he insists on "proving" that he was (and is) in the process of becoming a woman. The scientific evaluation includes analytic elements: quoting and commenting on the diagnosis of hir doctors, Schreber adds hir own analysis (and already foreshadows the psychiatric and psychoanalytic literature that adopts and overwrites this case).

Visible throughout the whole account is a careful scientific language that often contrasts with the outlandish character of what it describes. Take the famous description of the "event" in 1893, starting the very process of the transformation into a woman: "It was the idea that it really must be rather pleasant to be a woman succumbing to intercourse. This idea was so foreign to my whole nature that I may say I would have rejected it with indignation if fully awake; *from what I have experienced since I cannot exclude the possibility* that some external influences were at work to implant this idea in me."[123] The different time frames at work in a procedure stretched out in time become visible here, as well as the complex set of agents possibly responsible for hir feelings, split by this careful account into the pleasure of Schreber half sleeping, the "real nature" of Schreber that "would have rejected it with indignation if fully awake," the "external influences" that may have been "at work to implant this idea," and the narrating subject who later raises doubts about the experience (*"from what I have experienced since I cannot exclude the possibility that ..."*). Such critical examinations of previous experiences occur throughout the whole account of the *Memoirs* and are presented by Schreber as themself a product of the unusual transformations s/he had undergone: "I had a number of experiences which led me to a critical examination of my ideas about the 'fleeting-improvised-men,' 'play-with-human-beings,' and suchlike, in consequence of which I arrived at a slightly different point of view."[124]

Against the general tendency of self-certainty that is usually ascribed to paranoia (Schreber's commonly accepted diagnosis), the writer of the *Memoirs* openly admits tensions in his account and open questions, without providing a solution. "Obviously what I have said above about the changed behavior of the upper and lower God and about the kind of phrases the latter used, contains a tangle of contradictions which cannot be unraveled."[125] It seems that a "system of vacillation," which Schreber describes as being in place in the policies transforming him into a woman, is also in place in hir examination of this transformation:

"Earlier ... I stated the contrary opinion. This is because these matters, by their very nature, make any absolutely final opinion impossible; hence I *vacillate* even now as new impressions seem to favor first one conception and then the other."[126] With such examinations, Schreber again mirrors the examination by the rays s/he describes. S/he does not cover up but instead highlights the open, ambiguous, and latent character of the processes he is examining.

(6) The transformative procedure of the *Memoir* further involves a *narrative reworking* of the account by means of which Schreber not only reflects and scientifically evaluates what happens to hir, but finds ways of organizing it narratively and thereby aiming at making it into a coherent story. S/he openly attests such narrative interventions, writing, for instance, "In the above description I have anticipated somewhat in time for the sake of coherence; in actual fact the development described belongs in part to a much later period."[127] In order to produce a more compelling or revelatory trajectory, Schreber, the writer, rearranges time frames and sequences, recalling a practice of bricolage.[128] This narrative reworking involves more than a mere rearrangement of elements, but entails a full reconstitution and transformation. The mechanisms and forces are recast as protagonists in a conflict or a struggle, contingent events take on deeper significance as plot turns, the complex web of processes is organized into conflicting trajectories, and so forth. In this sense the whole material is submitted to a "secondary revision" (*sekundäre Bearbeitung*, to use Freud's term).

(7) Even though the *Memoirs* were published as a personal memoir in 1903 that would then constitute one of the main cases of the psychiatric and psychoanalytic literature, it is crucial not to forget that Schreber produced the *Memoirs* in view of a legal proceeding and designed them to corroborate hir arguments for hir own legal competency. The material being taken up in this *Memoir* is thus not simply selected, contextualized, brought into a peculiar distanced perspective, and narratively reworked; it is furthermore re-articulated in terms of a legal account in which Schreber assesses and evaluates the legal implications and ramifications of hir case. Not only are the *Memoirs* full of legal terms and maxims, they have in fact also become part of the legal dossier of the case and articulate themselves as support for hir motion brought before the law.

The exposition in the proceedings before the Country Court in Schreber's appeal against the judgment of the District Court, asking the Court to rescind hir placement under tutelage is a legal document that had a specific function in a legal procedure. The main body of the *Memoirs* refers the reader to the open legal procedure and incorporates the respective exposition as an addendum: "In general I want to refer to my exposition in the proceedings before the Country Court in my appeal against the judgment of the District Court, an excerpt of which I will therefore insert as Addendum C." The specific open mode of articulation characteristic of the *Memoir* is very much informed by the role it was supposed to play in the legal case. As Schreber makes clear in the very beginning of the *Memoirs*, it was supposed to convey the idea that although Schreber clearly had a nervous illness, it did not preclude hir from taking care of hir own affairs and act in hir own person.

> Although I have a nervous illness, I do not suffer in any way from a mental illness which would make me incapable of looking after my own affairs (§ 6, B.-G.-B. for Germany) or which would allow my detention in an institution against my will on the grounds of administrative law. When I therefore learnt some years ago that I had been placed under temporary tutelage as early as 1895, I approached the authorities last autumn (1899) demanding a decision as to whether the temporary tutelage was to be made permanent or whether it could be rescinded. Contrary to my expectations, a formal order for my tutelage was made in March 1900 by the District Court Dresden, based on a medical expert's report from this Asylum and a court hearing of January of that year. Because I considered the grounds for the decision unsubstantiated I brought an action in accordance with procedure against the Prosecuting Authority, to have my placing under tutelage rescinded. The decision of the Court, the Country Court Dresden, is still outstanding, but can be expected in the course of this year.[129]

Avoiding the paranoid tendency for absolute certainty, Schreber again uses careful, legal, and scientific language. S/he asks the participants in the legal proceedings to demonstrate equal care in the study of the *Memoirs* that can, so s/he argues, disprove their false assumptions: a "consideration raised by the Court is to be found in the sentence at the end of the judgment, namely that I suffer from hallucinations.... If one takes the trouble to read carefully those parts of my Memoirs dealing with this matter, this consideration at once proves invalid."[130] Similarly, in their discussion of the medical reports, Schreber dismisses "the tacit assumption that everything I reported in my *Memoirs* ... rests only on pathological imaginings."[131]

Although considering first to "exclude every discussion of my supposed hallucinations and delusions from the points at issue in the case, the purpose of which is the contesting of my tutelage," Schreber ultimately decided to tie the legal case to an "appreciation of my so-called delusions."[132] While being aware that "the attention of the Court would be diverted," Schreber thus couples the one process – the legal trial – to the other, his transformation into a woman. In this way, s/he links the acceptance of hir legal arguments to at least some appreciation of his transformation into a woman, and hir legal and rational capacities to his supposed other – her feminine, poetic, mad existence. Their ability to make rational and legal arguments and to navigate a legal procedure are on display, when, for instance, s/he argues that "the onus of proof lies with my opponent, the Public Prosecutor.... [I]t is strictly speaking the duty of him who requests that a person be placed under tutelage to furnish the Judge with the required factual proofs."[133] Schreber not only makes hir own selective decisions about what is and what is not to be part of the legal process, s/he also evaluates and checks the selective decisions of the other agents involved. Schreber dismisses, for instance, the remark in the judgment that "through unreasonable actions 'the relationship with my wife would be destroyed'"[134] on the grounds that it does not factor into the legal argument at hand, even if outside of the process, it is very much a factor ("although of great importance for the emotional life of the persons concerned, [it] could hardly have a legal bearing on the question of my legal capacity"[135]). In this second transformation, Schreber was in fact surprisingly successful – a litigation by means of which he managed to attain hir release from tutelage. The courts confirmed the order and determined that Schreber was legally competent and that he was "capable of presiding over a panel of judges, of deciding the most intricate cases and delivering most difficult counsel's opinions with striking juristical reasoning."[136] Peter Goodrich pointed out the irony of the fact that the Appeals Court affirms the psychotic's schizophrenic division of the world in which "the lunatic and the lawyer, psychosis and reason, lunacy and law" are clearly separated.[137] From a procedural perspective, one could add that this very division has been created by Schreber's double process itself. The transformation into a woman introduced the opposition between the male, rational judge and the excessive, female madman and provided Schreber with the very division s/he re-entered into the legal proceeding to convince the court that hir legal competency remained intact.

Schreber's way of relating back to the other of the law is double. On the one hand, in hir appeal before the court s/he makes use of the other of law – the "legally incompetent," mad, female Schreber – in order to distance hirself from it. S/he makes reference, for instance, to the previous conviction of the mad Schreber that no other humans exist anymore – which would make the whole trial superfluous. It is evoked by the Schreber appealing in court as a mad delusion of a former Schreber now transformed into the rational subject to be judged legally capable, who can make sane and sober legal arguments and reason what is and is not part of the legal procedure. On the other hand, Schreber introduces the material – the alleged experiences and revelations of the mad and female Schreber – into the case and forces the process to not only transform this other – again into the legally competent, reasonable judge s/he used to be, from the position of hir *Memoirs* – but at the same time to accept this other as part of the process and of the law. Schreber insists on tying hir feminine existence that might be deemed unreasonable by the Court to hir person and suggest that we have to take it as part of hir legally capable persona: "The only thing which could be counted as somewhat unreasonable in the eyes of other persons is, as mentioned by the medical expert, that at times I was seen standing in front of the mirror or elsewhere with some female adornments (ribbons, trumpery necklaces, and suchlike), with the upper half of my body exposed."[138] Referring to hir *Memoirs* once again, Schreber dismisses other judgments except his own: "I cannot heed other people's judgment as to whether or not these measures are appropriate."[139] In this paradoxical way, Schreber introduces the process of transformation into the legal process, both as its own other and as part of it, tying them together in arguing in Court to be both: legally competent *and* the subject undergoing the transformations described in the *Memoirs*, asking the law to accept and recognize both at the same time.

(8) By constituting the *Memoirs* as part of a legal proceeding, Schreber finally transforms the material incorporated in them in such a way that it is opened up to other further procedures. The legal process itself comes with a certain open-endedness. As precedence for other cases of tutelage, it points beyond the specific case, as Schreber makes clear with the essay on the general question "Under what circumstances can mental patients be held in public institutions against their will?" And Schreber calls for further scientific examinations, both as part of and beyond the legal trial. "I might consider demanding a physical examination by the doctors of this Asylum or other doctors, perhaps including if feasible the

> application of Roentgen-Rays in order to ascertain this state of affairs."[140] The two processes linked by Schreber – hir transformation into a woman and the transformation of this transformation into a legal case – both in turn point to anticipated future scientific procedures of a broader nature, including, for instance, philosophical and theological investigations, but possibly also the study of "the legends and poetry of all peoples."[141] Even as part of the trial, such examinations are supposed to stimulate much wider scientific research beyond the particular case. "I plan to submit my Memoirs for examination to specialists from other fields of experience, particularly theologians and philosophers … to prove to the Judges that my 'Memoirs,' however strange much of their content may be, could yet form an appreciable stimulus to wider scientific circles."[142] Such examinations on the one hand should extend the critical examination of his transformation, already begun by Schreber: "I would then have to leave to other people to elaborate scientifically the conclusions I have hinted at and perhaps to correct some details."[143] On the other hand, they should, starting from this particular case, challenge, broaden, und ultimately change the general status of the sciences itself. "In my case one may be dealing with manifestations which lie outside the field of usual scientific experience."[144] Hir case "may possibly lead to new scientific insights in this field,"[145] as Schreber quotes from the note that s/he sent to the directors of the asylum where s/he has been placed under tutelage. Hir calling for wider scientific procedures ultimately also challenges hir legal trial, and particularly the notion of rationality, that plays such a crucial role in making hir case to be legally competent. "Mere rationalism will naturally deny from the start that divine miracles are the cause. But happily rationalism, in Goethe's words, 'What cannot be accounted for, does not count,' is almost nowhere in science the guiding principle."[146]

In this way, Schreber is both calling for further examination of hir particular case and for hir particular case to prompt science to open itself up.

> During the first years of my illness it would in my opinion have been an easy matter by a thorough examination of my body with the help of medical instruments and above all with Roentgen-Rays (not then discovered) to demonstrate the most obvious changes in my body…. This would be much more difficult now. If it were possible to make a photographic

> record of the events in my head, of the lambent movements of the rays coming from the horizon, ... then the observer would definitely lose all doubt about my intercourse with God. But unfortunately human technique has not yet the necessary apparatus for investigating such sensations objectively.[147]

Just like the roentgen rays had not been invented in the beginning of the process, Schreber anticipates further inventions and developments in human technique that would allow for a procedure to investigate these "sensations objectively."[148] The publication of the *Memoirs* is supposed to "offer my person as object of scientific observation for the judgment of experts.... I can only hope that at some future time such peculiarities of my nervous system will be discovered."[149] The three procedures – the textual, the legal, the future scientific – working somewhat independently and yet in connection to one other, point beyond themselves, opening themselves up to and tying themselves to each other.

4. Conclusion

Schreber's double process consists of two transformations: Schreber's transformation into a woman, and the transformation of this transitional experience into the account of the *Memoirs*.[150] The two main sets of procedures at work in the *Memoirs* imply not only multiple steps and sequences, but also multiple roles. In the first process that s/he describes, Schreber is – at least in the first part – the *object* (not the subject) of the transformation into a woman, that is orchestrated by external agents (God, fleeting-improvised men, rays, Dr. Flechsig, speaking birds, etc.), who at times are in conflict with each other and at times become part of hir. In hir *writing* about that transformation, on the other hand, Schreber is the subject, the witness, the accuser, the prosecution, the judge, the analyst, and the scientist. S/he seems to play all the parts hirself[151] and is situated on both sides of the case: the analysed object in the transformation, and the analysing subject in the process of writing about it. The metamorphosis[152] into a woman and that of hir writing about it are, as I tried to show, complementary:

(1) The process of turning into a woman depends on material that is selected, isolated, transformed or manipulated, recorded and examined in multiple steps, by multiple instances. The main site of the process is Schreber hirself, the difference between the material (the body, the nerves, the soul) and the techniques and instruments "processing" the material (the rays, the nerves) is

constantly shifting.[153] More importantly, the "original material" of the transformation, the rational *man* and Judge Schreber that is being transformed into a woman, is established in its distinct and differential quality only within the transformation, when s/he first objects to it by insisting on hir manliness. So the process not only establishes the outcome, but also its other, the material that supposedly pre-exists the procedure, the "original" to be transformed. In the transformation from man to woman, Schreber's manliness, associated with his being a *Senatspräsident*, his rationality and "manly ambition" is created as the other and transformed material of the process. In a sense, it is only by becoming feminine that she *will have been* a full-blown lawyer or judge, a "person of calm nature, without passion, clear-thinking and sober," whose individual "gift lay much more in the direction of cool intellectual judgment than in the creative activity of an unbounded imagination."[154] This seems accessible only in hindsight, where she says, "I have wholeheartedly inscribed the cultivation of femininity on my banner.... The pursuit of my previous profession, which I loved wholeheartedly, every other aim of manly ambition ... are now closed to me."[155]

(2) The *writing* about this transformation works in a similar way, yet reintroduces into the realm of law the very process of transformation that had led Schreber beyond the law. It is a writing that evokes the transformation as its material and only thereby posits and establishes it as something that is itself being transformed – into the subject matter of a coherent text, a paralegal writing, constituting a legal and scientific case. Like Schreber's transformation, hir writing has a material that it selects, isolates, transforms, records, examines, and re-constitutes, in a very specific and distinct manner. Through hir writing, the excess and outlandishness of hir transformation within the *Ordnung der Welt* is being transformed into a legal and scientific case. The clinical and technical character of this procedure – the legal vocabulary, the careful, scientific language, the meticulous diligence with which everything is noted, assessed, and evaluated – displays a stark contrast to the transformation it is evoking and that it establishes as its material – an other that takes many guises, be it religious vision, system of lunacy, or female *jouissance*. As can be seen in Schreber's case, the procedure is always tied to its other and prone to be haunted by it. The writing is in an uncanny way close to its object, the transformation, and contaminated by it. It reverses the direction insofar as it returns to the law, but it also maintains this otherness within

the legal, scientific, and societal order it reintroduces this otherness into.

What is the purpose, one could ask, the point, the intervention of Schreber's *Memoirs of My Nervous Illness*? First, it is quite literally Schreber's appeal against the decision to have hir declared mentally incompetent (*entmündigt*) and committed into the asylum. Yet, at the same time, this appeal was also an intervention going beyond this particular case and even this particular subject matter. With their performative procedure, the *Memoirs* are transforming the law's understanding of its own procedural character, its own subjectivizing techniques, and let the law's other re-enter the law. Schreber's double process challenges the binary opposition of law and non-law by ultimately reintroducing it on the side of the law. The *Memoirs* subvert the notion of the person that is the basis of the law, as in the course of the process Schreber hirself is constantly split, becomes many, many enter hir, and ultimately s/he becomes another and many, without ever arriving at one stable identity.[156] That is, I would claim, the contribution of Schreber to the law, and perhaps hir connection to a queer legal theory.[157] The double-edged process forces the law to open itself up to its other that leaves behind not only the posited woman as other, but therefore also masculinity, and ultimately the binary opposition itself, revealing instead a potential of another use of legal, literary, and bodily processes, that are open, plural, and inherently dynamic.

NOTES

1 Daniel Paul Schreber, *Memoirs of My Nervous Illness*, trans. and ed. Ida Macalpine and Richard A. Hunter (Cambridge, MA: Harvard University Press, 2000), 60.
2 Schreber, *Memoirs*, 60.
3 Which pronoun to use for Schreber in any given moment of the transformation poses an unanswerable question. To emphasize the transformation, I will begin writing of "him"/"his" and keep doing so where I point to the specific instance undergoing the transformation into a woman; of "her" where Schreber seems to positively identify with that woman; and continue with "s/he" and "hir" in the later part of the chapter, where the transformation has evolved to a point that Schreber manifests, or even insists, on hir inherent diversity. This will result in a certain messiness and confusion, but such was the experience and the stance the *Memoirs* articulate.
4 Schreber, *Memoirs*, 61.

5 Among other things, Schreber's delusions have been interpreted as a manifestation or allegory of Schreber's conflicts with his repressed homosexuality, his response to a crisis of investiture following his appointment as *Senatspräsident*, as a perceptive reflection of the new technological and media dispositive of his time, or an expression of the theological-political crisis at the turn of the century. See Sigmund Freud, "Psycho-Analytic Notes on an Autobiographical Account of a Case of Paranoia (Dementia Paranoides)," in *The Standard Edition of the Complete Psychological Works of Sigmund Freud*, ed. and trans. James Strachey (London: Hogarth, 1958); Jacques Lacan, *The Seminar of Jacques Lacan: The Psychoses* (Book III), ed. Jacques-Alain Miller, trans. Russell Grigg (New York: W.W. Norton, 1993); Friedrich Kittler, *Discourse Networks 1800/1900*, with a foreword by David E. Wellbery (Stanford, CA: Stanford University Press, 1990), 291–347. For the most comprehensive account, see Eric Santner, *My Own Private Germany: Daniel Paul Schreber's Secret History of Modernity* (Princeton, NJ: Princeton University Press, 1996).

6 Peter Goodrich, "The Judge's Two Bodies: The Case of Daniel Paul Schreber," *Law and Critique* 26 (2015): 117.

7 In this sense, Schreber resists a certain politicization of the law that Goodrich characterizes in the following terms:

> Lacking any artistic training or compass, the ultra-modern lawyer succumbs to the ultra-modern demon of efficiency. Law submits to politics or more accurately to political economy, and the solo lawyer, the "good professional," Posner's parsee is equipped only to declaim either market interests or private causes. Law, pure law, nomocon jurisprudence is in practice an erasure of legal history, of the artistic reason of law, and we find in its place an inculcation of a finely honed and infinitely abstracted training in virtual instrumentalities that pay no attention to philology, literature, or the interpretations that require attention to what is relayed sub auditio or through the text. (Peter Goodrich, "The New Casuistry," *Critical Inquiry* 33 [2007]: 707)

8 On the notion of *Verfahren* in its legal, scientific, and literary contexts see Katrin Trüstedt, "Der Fluch des Verfahrens: Karl Kraus und die Akten zum Fall Kerr," *Modern Language Notes* 131, no. 3 (2016): 701–23; Trüstedt, "The Fruit Fly, the Vermin, and the Procurist: Operations of Appearing in Kafka's Metamorphosis," in *Cultural Techniques*, ed. J. Dünne, K. Fehringer, and W. Struck, 295–315 (London: Bloomsbury, 2020). See also Werner Gephart, "Schreber's Cases: Escaping from Rational Law," in this volume.

9 Fritz Sander, "Die transzendentale Methode der Rechtsphilosophie und der Begriff des Rechtsverfahrens," *Zeitschrift für öffentliches Recht* 1 (1919/20): 468–507.

10 Hans-Jörg Rheinberger, *An Epistemology of the Concrete: Twentieth-Century Histories of Life* (Durham, NC: Duke University Press, 2010).
11 Friedrich Hölderlin, "Über die Verfahrungsweise des poetischen Geistes," in *Sämtliche Werke. 6 Bände, Band 4*, ed. F. Beissner, 241–65 (Stuttgart: Kohlhammer, 1962); Victor Shklovsky, "Art as Technique," in *Russian Formalist Criticism: Four Essays*, trans. and ed. Lee T. Lemon and Marion J. Reis, 5–22 (Lincoln, NE: University of Nebraska Press, 1965).
12 Niklas Luhmann, *Legitimation durch Verfahren* (Frankfurt a.M.: Suhrkamp, 1989), vii, 11.
13 According to Foucault's analysis of ancient probative techniques, they were thinking of duels as a way to assess a given higher will; cf. Michel Foucault, "Truth and Juridical Forms," in *Power: The Essential Works of Michel Foucault 1954–1984*, ed. James D. Faubion, 1–89 (New York: New Press, 2000).
14 Luhmann, *Legitimation*, 40.
15 Cf. Rheinberger, *Epistemology of the Concrete*.
16 Cf. the classic study on late modern physics: Peter Galison, *How Experiments End* (Chicago, IL: University of Chicago Press, 1987).
17 Paul G. Kaupers, *The Frontiers of Constitutional Liberty* (Ann Arbor, MI: University of Michigan Press, 1956), 146; cited according to Luhmann, *Legitimation*, 19.
18 On the role of participation in litigation and its consequences for democracy, see Alexandra Lahav, *In Praise of Litigation* (Oxford: Oxford University Press, 2017); for a comprehensive overview of the legal discussion of the challenges and intricacies of civil procedure more generally, see Geoffrey C. Hazard (Jr.), John Leubsdorf, and Debra Lyn Bassett, *Civil Procedure* (Eagan, MN: Foundation Press Thomson/West, 2011).
19 Luhmann, *Legitimation*, 40.
20 Cf. Jacques Derrida, "Before the Law," in *Acts of Literature*, ed. Derek Attridge, 181–220 (New York: Routledge, 1992).
21 See Jacques Derrida, "Force of Law: The 'Mystical Foundation of Authority,'" *Cardozo Law Review* 11, no. 5–6 (1990): 920–1045.
22 Cf. Rheinberger, *Epistemology*.
23 Cf., e.g., the procedure of purification, "*Läuterungsverfahren*," Daniel Paul Schreber, *Denkwürdigkeiten eines Nervenkranken* (Berlin: Edition Holzinger, 2013), 18.
24 Freud takes up this mode of talking in his famous remark that Schreber's delusions "sound almost like endopsychic perceptions of the *processes* [*Vorgänge*] whose existence I have assumed in these pages as the basis of our explanation of paranoia" (Freud, "Psycho-Analytic Notes," 79).
25 Schreber, *Denkwürdigkeiten*, 49.

26 Schreber, *Denkwürdigkeiten*, 71: "Nur der Eindruck ist mir geblieben, daß es bei diesem und ähnlichen Vorkommnissen, wenn wirklich Visionen in Frage gewesen sein sollten, Visionen waren, in denen *Methode* lag" (Schreber's emphasis).

27 For instance, he writes about a "process of purification" (*Läuterungsverfahren*). "The souls still undergoing the process of purification were" – according to their stage in the process – "variously graded as 'Satans,' 'Devils,' 'Assistant Devils,' 'Senior Devils,' and 'Basic Devils'" (Schreber, *Memoirs*, 26). The process of a "transmigration of souls" also seems to have served the purpose of "purifying human souls and was widespread, as a number of experiences lead me to believe" (Schreber, *Memoirs*, 27).

28 Schreber, *Memoirs*, 53.

29 Schreber, *Memoirs*, 121.

30 Schreber, *Memoirs*, 60–1. Another description of this transformation goes as follows:

> Most nearly in consonance with the Order of the World were those miracles which were somehow connected with a process of unmanning to be carried out on my body. To them belonged especially the various changes in my sex organ: several times (particularly in bed) there were marked indications of an actual retraction of the male organ; frequently however, particularly when mainly impure rays were involved, of a softening approaching almost complete dissolution; further the removal by miracles of single hairs from my beard and particularly my mustache; finally a change in my whole stature (diminution of body size) – probably due to a contraction of the vertebrae and possibly of my thigh bones. The last-mentioned miracle which emanated from the lower God (Ariman), was always accompanied by him with the announcement "I wonder whether to make you somewhat smaller"; I myself had the impression that my body had become smaller by about 6–8 cms, that is to say approximating the size of the female body. The miracles enacted against the organs of the thoracic and abdominal cavities were very multifarious. (Schreber, *Memoirs*, 142)

31 To what precise extent the medical and physical "treatment" Schreber received in the asylum was understood by him as an integral part of the overall process of transformation remains ambiguous. It is noteworthy, however, that even the manly resistance here seems to be induced by outside forces: "Those rays which were intent on 'forsaking' me and which for that purpose wanted to destroy my reason, did not fail to make a hypocritical appeal to my sense of manly honor; some of the phrases, since repeated innumerable times whenever soul-voluptuousness appeared, were: 'Are you not ashamed in front of your wife?,' or still more vulgarly:

'Fancy a person who was a Senatspräsident allowing himself to be f…d'" (Schreber, *Memoirs*, 164).

32 Schreber, *Memoirs*, 246.

33 Schreber, *Memoirs*, 55.

34 Schreber, *Memoirs*, 136.

35 Schreber, *Memoirs*, 136; emphasis mine.

36 Schreber, *Memoirs*, 90; emphasis mine.

37 Regarding the threat of an endless process and the surprising attraction of an execution without verdict, see Katrin Trüstedt, "Execution without Verdict: Kafka's (Non-)Person," *Law and Critique* 25 (2015): 135–54.

38 Schreber, *Memoirs*, 60–1. Other instances of differentiation of instruments enabling opposite directions of process are those between "'searing' and 'blessing' rays; the former were laden with the poison of corpses or some other putrid matter, and therefore carried some germ of disease into the body or brought about some other destructive effect in it. The blessing (pure) rays in turn healed this damage" (Schreber, *Memoirs*, 95).

39 Schreber, *Memoirs*, 30.

40 Schreber, *Memoirs*, 61.

41 Schreber, *Memoirs*, 55.

42 Schreber, *Memoirs*, 61. Schreber writes about *the institution* of "'fleeting-improvised-men in the Order of the World." On the enormous implications of the figure of the "Eternal Jew," see Santner, *My Own Private Germany*, esp. chap. 3.

43 Schreber, *Memoirs*, 55.

44 "Six years of uninterrupted influx of God's nerves into my body has led to the total loss of all the states of Blessedness which had accumulated until then and made it impossible for the time being to renew them; the state of *Blessedness* is so to speak suspended and all human beings who have since died or will die *can for the time being not attain to it*" (Schreber, *Memoirs*, 41).

45 Schreber, *Memoirs*, 231.

46 Schreber, *Memoirs*, 60.

47 Schreber, *Memoirs*, 56.

48 Schreber himself writes about experiments, such as when he describes the reaction to the "middle Flechsig" using "this form of fastening for the first time": "It was felt in God's realms that behavior so contrary to the Order of the World could not be tolerated. The 'middle Flechsig' was therefore forced to untie himself again. But when the *experiment was later repeated* there was no longer sufficient energy for such measures" (Schreber, *Memoirs*, 122; emphasis mine).

49 Schreber, *Memoirs*, 62; emphasis in the original.

50 Schreber, *Memoirs*, 62; translation modified.

51 Schreber, *Memoirs*, 34; translation modified.

52 Schreber, *Memoirs*, 58–9.

53 Schreber, *Memoirs*, 115. Cf. Luhmann's observation that one essential way in which procedures operate is through attrition, by wearing and tiring its participants down: "Die Interaktionsform des Verfahrens hat deshalb nicht nur die Funktion, brauchbare Entscheidungsgesichtspunkte herauszufiltern; sie dient auch ganz unmittelbar der Konfliktdämpfung, der Schwächung und Zermürbung der Beteiligten" (Luhmann, *Legitimation*, 4).

54 Schreber, *Memoirs*, 35.

55 Schreber, *Memoirs*, 138.

56 Schreber, *Memoirs*, 164.

57 Schreber, *Memoirs*, 38.

58 Schreber, *Memoirs*, 41–2.

59 Schreber, *Memoirs*, 67n35 (added November 1902) explains this relation further: "The above may seem somewhat obscure, insofar as 'the Order of the World' may appear as something impersonal and higher, more powerful than God or even as ruling God. In fact there is no obscurity. *'The Order of the World'* is the lawful relation which, resting on God's *nature and attributes, exists between God and the creation called to life by Him.*"

60 Schreber, *Memoirs*, 68n35.

61 Schreber, *Memoirs*, 46.

62 Schreber, *Memoirs*, 69.

63 Schreber, *Memoirs*, 164.

64 Schreber, *Memoirs*, 165.

65 Schreber, *Memoirs*, 70.

66 Schreber, *Memoirs*, 96.

67 Schreber, *Memoirs*, 239.

68 Schreber, *Memoirs*, 239.

69 "madmen who themselves add to all sorts of mad things happening" (Schreber, *Memoirs*, 240). On the relation of femininity and madness see Shoshana Felman, "Women and Madness: The Critical Phallacy," *Diacritics* 5, no. 4 (1975): 2–10.

70 Felman, "Women and Madness."

71 Schreber, *Memoirs*, 91.

72 Schreber, *Memoirs*, 91.

73 Schreber, *Memoirs*, 113.

74 Schreber, *Memoirs*, 290.

75 Schreber, *Memoirs*, 291.

76 Schreber, *Memoirs*, 291.

77 Schreber, *Memoirs*, 112.

78 Friedrich Kittler, *Aufschreibesysteme 1800/1900* (München: Fink, 1985); Trans.: *Discourse Networks 1800/1900*, foreword by David E. Wellbery

(Stanford, CA: Stanford University Press, 1990), 369. In this regard, Kittler has also stressed the procedural character of these systems.

79 Schreber, *Memoirs*, 123.
80 Schreber, *Memoirs*, 128.
81 Schreber, *Memoirs*, 127.
82 Schreber, *Memoirs*, 127.
83 Schreber, *Memoirs*, 127.
84 Schreber, *Memoirs*, 123.
85 Schreber, *Memoirs*, 123.
86 Schreber, *Memoirs*, 132.
87 Schreber, *Memoirs*, 132n64; emphasis mine.
88 Schreber, *Memoirs*, 136.
89 Schreber, *Memoirs*, 138.
90 Schreber, *Memoirs*, 154.
91 Schreber, *Memoirs*, 154.
92 Schreber, *Memoirs*, 166.
93 Schreber, *Memoirs*, 168.
94 Schreber, *Memoirs*, 158.
95 Schreber, *Memoirs*, 154.
96 Schreber, *Memoirs*, 197.
97 Schreber, *Memoirs*, 199.
98 Schreber, *Memoirs*, 199.
99 Schreber, *Memoirs*, 155.
100 On the implications of this judging, see Goodrich, "Judge's Two Bodies," 127–9.
101 Schreber, *Memoirs*, 189.
102 Schreber, *Memoirs*, 189.
103 Schreber, *Memoirs*, 220.
104 Schreber, *Memoirs*, 170.
105 Schreber, *Memoirs*, 170.
106 Schreber, *Memoirs*, 171.
107 Schreber, *Memoirs*, 172.
108 Schreber, *Memoirs*, 172.
109 Schreber, *Memoirs*, 211.
110 Schreber, *Memoirs*, 250.
111 Schreber, *Memoirs*, 249.
112 Schreber, *Memoirs*, xxii.
113 Another representation of Schreber in the Order of the World functions rhetorically as a measure of personification of an abstraction:

> In my opinion the expression "Prince of Hell," which was only erroneously applied to me, was originally based on an abstraction. The realms of God may always have known that the Order of the World however great and magnificent, was yet not without its Achilles' heel,

inasmuch as the human nerves' power of attracting God's nerves constituted some danger for the realms of God.... In order to form a clearer picture of these dangers the souls had apparently adopted a kind of *personification*.... The phrase "Prince of Hell" was probably meant to convey the uncanny power inimical to God that could develop from moral decay among mankind or a general spread of nervous over-excitement in consequence of over-civilization. As my nerves' power of attraction became more and more irresistible, the "Prince of Hell" appeared suddenly to have *become reality in my person*. (Schreber, *Memoirs*, 153; emphasis mine)

On the general notion of person as proxy, cf. Katrin Trüstedt, *Stellvertretung. Zur Szene der Person* (Konstanz: Konstanz University Press, 2021).

114 Schreber, *Memoirs*, 228.

115 As a case of the fantastic genre of literature, Edgar Allen Poe's "The Facts in the Case of M. Valdemar" would be interesting to read in this context, with the interconnected layers of science and the irrational.

116 Schreber, *Memoirs*, 180.

117 Schreber, *Memoirs*, 171n37.

118 Schreber, *Memoirs*, 171n37.

119 Schreber, *Memoirs*, 173n80.

120 Schreber, *Memoirs*, 141.

121 Schreber, *Memoirs*, 173n80.

122 Schreber, *Memoirs*, 180.

123 Schreber, *Memoirs*, 46; emphasis mine.

124 Schreber, *Memoirs*, 185.

125 Schreber, *Memoirs*, 169.

126 Schreber, *Memoirs*, 235n105; emphasis mine.

127 Schreber, *Memoirs*, 129.

128 Cf. Claude Lévi-Strauss, *The Savage Mind* (Oxford: Oxford University Press, 2004), chap. 1; compare also Roland Barthes's account of what he calls "the structuralist activity" in "The Structuralist Activity," in *Critical Essays*, 213–20 (Evanston, IL: Northwestern University Press, 1972).

129 Schreber, *Memoirs*, 238.

130 Schreber, *Memoirs*, 353.

131 Schreber, *Memoirs*, 354.

132 Schreber, *Memoirs*, 356.

133 Schreber, *Memoirs*, 368. Schreber also argues that "a person can be placed under tutelage only in his own interest." Schreber, *Memoirs*, 373.

134 Schreber, *Memoirs*, 373.

135 Schreber, *Memoirs*, 373.

136 Schreber, *Memoirs*, 477.

137 Goodrich, "Judge's Two Bodies," 119.
138 Schreber, *Memoirs*, 369.
139 Schreber, *Memoirs*, 370.
140 Schreber, *Memoirs*, 362.
141 Schreber, *Memoirs*, 82.
142 Schreber, *Memoirs*, 363.
143 Schreber, *Memoirs*, 226.
144 Schreber, *Memoirs*, 238–9.
145 Schreber, *Memoirs*, 245.
146 Schreber, *Memoirs*, 361.
147 Schreber, *Memoirs*, 303.
148 Schreber, *Memoirs*, 303.
149 Schreber, *Memoirs*, 307.
150 For Derrida's concept of a double-bind structure, see Jacques Derrida, *Glas* (Paris: Galilée, 1974).
151 This is true even for his sexual fantasies in which he himself plays both the male and the female part.
152 *Verwandlung* is the German term Schreber uses to describe the process, which is the title Kafka will give to his story usually translated as "The Metamorphosis."
153 On the blurring of the border between the material and the techniques and instruments manipulating the material in biological procedures, see Rheinberger, *Epistemology*.
154 Schreber, *Memoirs*, 63.
155 Schreber, *Memoirs*, 178.
156 Giorgio Agamben, *The Use of Bodies* (Stanford, CA: Stanford University Press, 2016).
157 See, for instance, Martha Albertson Fineman and Michael Thomson, eds., *Exploring Masculinities: Feminist Legal Theory Reflections* (London: Routledge, 2013). See as well, for example, the work of Noa Ben-Asher, "Laws of Sex, Changed," in *The Oxford Handbook of Law and Humanities*, ed. Simon Stern, Maksymilian Del Mar, and Bernadette Meyler, 601–18 (Oxford: Oxford University Press, 2020); Ummni Khan, "Hot for Kink, Bothered by the Law: BDSM and the Right to Autonomy," *Law Matters* (2019) https://www.cba-alberta.org/Publications-Resources/Resources/Law-Matters/Law-Matters-Summer-2016-Issue/Hot-for-Kink,-Bothered-by-the-Law-BDSM-and-the-Rig. For a lengthy examination of the precarity of sexual normativities, see Joseph J. Fischel, *Screw Consent: A Better Politics of Sexual Justice* (Oakland, CA: University of California Press, 2019).

5 Address without Signature: Schreber's *Memoirs* and the *Manning-Lamo Chat Logs*

LUDWIG SCHMITZ

In this chapter I will read one document of paranoia, the *Manning-Lamo Chat Logs*, together with another, the thoroughly interpreted and psychoanalyzed *Memoirs* of Daniel Paul Schreber. My intention with this juxtaposition is to suggest that the paranoid position could be construed as a contradictory insistence on simultaneously refusing a particular subjectivation and on requesting to become recognized as such a symbolically valid subject. Schreber's and Manning's texts can then be read not so much as paranoid texts, but in the first case as a response to, and in the second case as a reaction against a process of subjectivation that is itself intrinsically paranoid – a constitutive suspicion that is conditioned not on the presence of corresponding experiences but on their absence: not knowing what is normal, or who is determining the norm, is what coerces one to act normal. Taking up Trüstedt's analysis in the previous chapter of the rewriting of legal categories that the judge paradoxically achieves in his *Memoirs*, reading them both as an existential text but also as a legal intervention, I will attempt to conceptualize the contradictory and recalcitrant discursive position that both Schreber and Manning, naturally with more differences than similarities, inhabit as both an excess of address in relation to signature – a failure to speak as someone but an insistence on speaking to everyone – and an excess of signature in relation to address; a request to be recognized as someone but without being able to address anyone. The experience that Schreber and Manning share of something being deeply wrong in the world could then be seen as originating with their most intimate experience of being unaddressable in it; the very position from which they lose the authority to address the problem becomes the only one from which it can be addressed.

Self-Revelation and Global Conspiracy: Two Positions

(11:36:12 AM) bradass87: still gonna be weird watching the world change on the macro scale, while my life changes on the micro.

– Chelsea Manning, *Manning-Lamo Chat Logs*

In both Schreber's *Memoirs of My Nervous Illness*, written in 1900, and the *Manning-Lamo Chat Logs*, written in May 2010 and published online by *Wired*, we encounter a subject who has lost everything, yet possesses a secret knowledge that, once revealed and made public, seems to have an immense restorative capacity. Both are experiencing, in Manning's own vocabulary, a transformation taking place on both the macro- and micro-scale: Something has happened to the world that is still kept secret; something has happened to the most proximate and intimate sphere of experience, their bodies, which has already been revealed.

In the very beginning of his *Memoirs*, Schreber writes that, although he cannot be certain of everything that he claims in his book, "one thing I am certain of, namely that I have come infinitely closer to the truth than human beings who have not received divine revelation."[1] In a Kantian register he goes on to pre-emptively placate the reader's scepticism by separating the sphere of the sensible from the super-sensible, the phenomena from the noumena, and by resolving the antinomy that his revelations seem – at least when one is speaking in the public voice of an author introducing his work – both highly unreasonable and absolutely real, by placing them in the realm of the latter: "Where intellectual understanding ends, the domain of belief begins; man must reconcile himself to the fact that things exist which are true although he cannot understand them."[2] The situation in which Schreber finds himself is, however, one in which phenomena and noumena have become exceedingly difficult to separate.[3] The inner and the outer have, with the discovery of the nerves that connect his human body to God, become intricately confused. God used to remain distant from humans, maintaining the distinction between belief and reason that Schreber asks his readers to remember before they refute his revelations. Those were the conditions of the Order of the World: "Within the Order of the World, God did not really understand the living human being and had no need to understand him, because, according to the Order of the World, He dealt only with corpses."[4] Now, however, God's otherwise only exceptional "nerve-contact" with humans has become the rule.[5] In the relations between humans themselves, this new grotesque immediacy in

God's relation to humans seems to have its correlate in the phenomenon of a "transmigration of souls," which allows for "the possibility of a partition of souls which would make it possible for certain nerves of mind belonging to a person still living (which would, as mentioned above, retain the *full knowledge of his personal identity* if only for a short time) to play some different role when outside his body."[6] Identities are thus composites of parts. One soul can both transmigrate partially and remain in its place. Instead of identity as a matter of either/or – of either being Daniel Paul Schreber or not being him but someone else – identity has become a matter of degree, a decision, an unstable choice in the face of exigent or hostile circumstances.[7]

The secret conspiracy that Schreber discovers and that he must reveal to the public – Professor Flechsig's and God's plan to murder his soul, destroy his reason, unman him, and transform his body into that of a woman in order to then rape him – is eventually seen as only partially against the Order of the World. What remains contrary to the Order of the World is in fact only the immediate contact that has been established between Schreber and God – not the gender transition, and the pleasures it entails, that are generated through that exceptional relation. He gains control of his femininity, feigns it actively with a clean-shaven face.[8] Yet even at this point, when his "unmanning" has become his own project rather than someone else's conspiracy against him, Schreber is sure that there is "*something rotten in the state of Denmark* – that is to say in the relationship between God and mankind."[9] However, what is rotten in this relationship seems to be precisely what allows for the now desirable process of unmanning. Schreber needs the illegal "nerve-contact" with God, contrary to the Order of the World, to experience his "Voluptuous enjoyment" or "Blessedness" of a woman. God's illegitimate nerve-contact hence enables "soul-voluptuousness" but, conversely, it is only by always being in this state of a woman that God's withdrawal from him can be avoided: "God would never attempt to withdraw … but would follow my attraction without resistance if only I could *always* be playing the woman's part in sexual embrace with myself."[10] The crime is also a blessing: the criminal overreach of God's power makes possible the lawful generation of a fluid and ambiguous gender position. However, that gender transition is at the same time what sustains God's illegitimate nerve-contact. On the one hand, the illegitimate contact between God and Schreber, between power and subject, makes his legitimate transition possible; on the other, his gender transition makes his exceptional contact with God possible. Schreber seems to have discovered that his transition is not a transgression and that he, in his transition, generates a new norm without contradicting an existing one.[11] In incessantly thinking and talking, in his continuous address as someone who is unmanning himself, he is the one who sustains the permanence of God's castrating act; he is the one allowing his unmanning to remain in progress, which lets him be neither definitively man nor definitively unmanned. In the last chapter of his *Memoirs*, Schreber concedes that it is possible that the process of becoming a woman may be one without an endpoint. He writes that it is "possible, indeed probable, that to the end of my days there will be strong indications of femaleness, but that I shall die as a man."[12]

The secret rottenness in the relation between God and humankind that Schreber reveals to the public with his *Memoirs* is never really located by that revelation. Schreber's interpretation of his gender transition changes from it being the result of a conspiracy against him to it being a contradictory but desired necessity, both in accordance with the Order of the World and contingent on an exceptional and immediate nerve-contact between himself and God that is conflicting with that order. As this interpretation shifts, there is a conflation and separation of two events, one concerning only Schreber himself that is already revealed – his gender transition – and the other concerning the whole of humankind that remains concealed. Schreber's own gender transition is, according to himself, already known, it is already there to be examined, revealed, and offered to the public. However, the overreach of divine power, both enabling and enabled by his private yet fully disclosed gender transition, is still concealed from the public, indiscernible from any other position than his own.

Chelsea Manning, in her own words at the time "an army intelligence analyst, deployed to eastern Baghdad, pending discharge for 'adjustment disorder' in lieu of 'gender identity disorder,'" initiates her conversation with the hacker Adrian Lamo by setting the scene: after having lived an "opaque life" she is now "kind of coming out of a cocoon." She, then he, has lost everything; she "is a mess," trapped in the limbo of the army base, and is already in trouble for having revealed her gender dysphoria, waiting to be discharged. The only "safe place" left for her is the satellite internet connection through which she secretly can address her supposed confidant, who would later turn her in to the authorities. Her transition is already revealed, but circumstances prevent her from completing it – "I wish it were as simple as 'hey, go transition'..." – and the possibility of a restoration of herself and the world seems foreclosed by the absolute loss that has precipitated that possibility. A second transformation, one with global impact, is coinciding with her own, both prompting and obstructing it, and remains as a spectre of her ruinous past self, a catastrophe in the world prohibiting her private restitution. She has released secret information about "incredible things, awful things" that explains how "the first world exploits the third, in detail, from an internal perspective" and it is still in the process of being released to the public domain in which it belongs. "bradass87," the screen name of then–Bradley Manning writes that she must "figure out how on earth im going to transition" and in the next message, "all while witnessing the world freak out as its most intimate secrets are revealed." The "awkwardness" of her situation seems to arise out of a series of imbalances: she has come out as transgender but has not yet initiated her transition, she is "super-intelligent" yet works as a supply guy, she is isolated at an army base in eastern Baghdad yet has changed the world by revealing its most intimate secrets. The solace she finds in the secret chat with Lamo is equally an imbalanced discourse, in which "bradass87" reiterates her apologies, lamentations, and cries for help with "info@adrianlamo.com" replying laconically or his computer filling in for him with a generic auto-response, reminding his interlocutor of the communicative frailty and distance that are separating her from him: "<AUTO-REPLY> I have more messages than resources allocatable to action them." "bradass87" finds herself in a triadic imbalance between what she knows and what people see on the one hand, and on the other between this imbalance and who she is – the nexus necessary to hold the first imbalance in place and initiate its repair by revealing it: there is a "disconnect between myself, and what I know … and what people see."[13]

From the outset, the exchange between Manning and Lamo appears to be conditioned on a possible sexual desire between the interlocutors, with flirtation being a consistent fallback register: Manning is talking to Lamo in the capacity of someone whom she has, as an initiation of the conversation, confirmed as a possible source of recognition and desire of her in her new gender identity. The fact that Lamo identifies as bisexual and that his former partner was "MTF" appears to be important for how trust is bypassed and replaced with desire as a clearance to speak freely and confide in the other, without there appearing to be any conventionally good reasons to do so. "bradass87" notes early in the conversation that "im pouring my heart out to someone i've never met, and i don't exactly have a lot of proof of anything."

This discourse of desire becomes the medium of a symbolic disordering, in which norms are vacated of their capacity and force, and signifiers like "good" and "bad" reveal themselves to be mere functions of competing self-interests; "the political" in Carl Schmitt's sense has reasserted itself as a delimitation of one's own sphere against the existential threat of another.[14] Manning recounts the genesis of this weakening of her sense of a normative order: after having inquired into the crimes of fifteen detainees arrested by the Iraqi federal police, and having found that their offence consisted only in printing a critique of the Iraqi government, she took the information to her superiors, who dismissed her concerns: "everything started slipping after that … i saw things differently." While she had always been critical, she now found herself complicit in the very thing she was critical of: "i was actively involved in something that i was completely against." This traumatic experience of complicity and, as an effect of that complicity, of there being no outside of the corrupt system, triggered a crisis in which the revelation of the secrets of the self and the secrets of the world must coincide: "i just … couldnt let these things stay inside of the system … and inside of my head." A second crisis came when, in response to the first one, she watched the "Collateral Murder" video of the 12 July 2007 Baghdad airstrike, which she would later leak to the press. She recounts that she at first felt unmoved by it: "i was like … ok, so thats what happened … cool," but that after she had read in the *New York Times* that alongside eleven insurgents, two journalists had been killed. She now felt "connected to everybody" and unable to separate herself from others. She elaborates further on, now in the present tense, that the reaction to the video, the global secret that she has revealed, poses an ultimate test to humankind: either react to it, with "worldwide discussion, debates, and reforms" or be "doomed … as a species." The public criticism of the U.S. military that the video prompted has in fact given back some hope to her that there could still exist a normative order in the world, but all she can do is "watch the whole thing unfold … from a distance." The disclosure to the world of its brokenness does not seem to have removed the guilt of having been complicit in that brokenness. Instead of restoring her position as firmly outside of the disorder of the normative order, free of complicity in it, the revelation of that dis-order seems to have further isolated her. She becomes a necessarily absent, god-like figure on whom the restoration of the order in the world depends, yet whose own restoration, her transition, cannot take place until she again has become present within that restored order. Toward the end of the chat logs, Manning contrasts herself with such a god: She is not "playing 'god' or anything," because her investment in the fate of humankind is, in contrast to that of a god, only temporary, a necessary measure to make reparations to the damaged world and through that reparation gain a new identity, Chelsea Manning, who has come out of the normative dis-order in which Bradley Manning had been complicit. However, she seems to be able to make this reparation – to blow the whistle and show the world what is happening to it – only by abstaining from realizing her new identity, from fully coming out.

Both Manning and Schreber find that the disorder in the world is intricately related to themselves. Both possess a secret knowledge of the world's disorder, its decay, and disarray. For both, this knowledge appears inseparable from a new knowledge of their gender identities and bodies. Schreber's "gender identity disorder" seems to be both the premise and result of the disorder in the relation between God and humankind, i.e., himself, which – along with his other divine experiences – must be made public. Manning's transition, on the other hand, is in her confessional and self-revelatory discourse rhetorically intertwined with a global conspiracy; the signifiers "breakdown" and "mess" expand their reach from the most private and intimate to the most public and global. Her revelation to the world of the global conspiracy in which she unwillingly has taken part and the normative dis-order that it has caused is precipitated by and resulting in her own lack of a stable identity. Furthermore, the completion of her transition, which would yield a new stability, seems obstructed by that same revelation, since it requires her self-sacrifice and absence from the normative order to which she makes reparations. However, the contradiction that she faces is that the completion of this reparation requires not only her absence – the whistle-blowing vacuum left by no-longer-Bradley Manning – but also her participation, as Chelsea Manning, necessarily held accountable for a necessary crime. In revealing their secret truths, both Schreber and Manning thus come up against contradictions that appear necessary for their revelations to take place.

Insisting on the Contradiction

"The Court is in no doubt that the appellant is insane," begins the section "Grounds of the Judgment" of the Royal Superior County Court of Dresden's judgment in 1902 to allow Daniel Paul Schreber's appeal to have his tutelage rescinded. The former *Senatspräsident*, whose command of the legal code is admitted by his former colleagues to be untainted by his deliriums, his cross-dressing, and purported physical transitioning from man to woman, is asking the law for permission to leave the asylum in Sonnenstein and have his legal capacity as a person restored. From the beginning, the procedure is caught up in presuppositional gymnastics: his *Memoirs*, containing a defamatory accusation against his former doctor, Professor Flechsig, of soul murder, has been submitted to the court to support his appeal, putting him in a contradictory position of asking the court for permission to be held accountable for what the judges have already read and acknowledged as his, the plaintiff's, words. Schreber is asking the law to recognize him and to give back to him a legal name with which to sign and take responsibility for his psychotic and paranoid revelations – but in responding to his request, the court seems to have already granted it.

It is true, the court admits, that the plaintiff still holds his hallucinations to be reality. In fact, they are for him an "irrefutable certainty," standing above human knowledge. But the fact that a legal subject's sense of reality is not that of her community is not reason enough, according to § 6, No. 1 of the Civil Code, to deprive that subject of her legal capacity and personhood. To keep Schreber in tutelage, the prosecution would have to demonstrate that he is incapable of managing his affairs, because to place someone under tutelage "is only permissible if such dangers to the person concerned are present which can be successfully countered by abjudication of his legal capacity (§ 104 of the Civil Code)."[15] In other words, abjudication of legal capacity does not depend on fixed criteria for what it means to be a legal subject, but is relative only to the law's ability to prevent harm to the person. Tutelage does not mean being denied the attention of the law, but to receive its care most directly and immediately; it is the social and legal position corresponding to that of the paranoiac in the symbolic order. Eric L. Santner notes, following Jacques Lacan, that Schreber's foreclosure of the primal signifier, that would have given the symbolic order its stability, puts him in an "excessive proximity" to an unmediated, unsymbolized power. In other words, to have the full attention of power is to cease being recognized as a determinate subject of it, at the same time as one is more individuated and determined by it than ever.[16]

Elaborating on Michel Foucault's analysis of disciplinary power,[17] Santner refers to Schreber's crisis as one that reflects a crisis of symbolic investiture in modernity, a chronic dysfunction in the symbolic authorization of subject positions that emerges when authority becomes split as, on the one hand, symbolic and legal and, on the other, immediate and disciplinary – as both normative and exceptional to that norm, the one contained within the other. Santner writes, "The domain of juridical power in the broad sense used by Foucault is structured around laws of *symbolic causation* (e.g., one's becoming a *Senatspräsident* is 'caused' by an official act of nomination). When this symbolic or pseudocausality, on which all acts of symbolic investiture depend, becomes chronically dysfunctional, we have crossed the threshold into a psychotic realm of extreme literalization. Foucault's Schreberian point would seem to be that disciplinary power fosters this chronic dysfunction."[18] The specific historical situation that Santner refers to is one in which power is split into a legal and a disciplinary element. With the primal signifier foreclosed, the authority granting existential legitimacy is felt as both too distant from bodily human life and too close to it, as an incursion on one's most bodily experiences. Disciplinary power is then a "literalization" of the symbolic authority of the law – it reveals the performative tautology of symbolic power, compresses the distance between violence and law, and becomes visible as a direct material control. As such it entangles the subject in the Real. It prevents the subject from fully symbolizing the body. It reveals to the subject that there is no licence for symbolic power that is external to the symbolic order, but rather only a violence internal to it. However, this disciplinary power also produces an imperative to limit that direct and immediate power and "clear a space for the rule of law" in which someone like Schreber can regain his legal accountability and personhood; the juridical subject and the disciplinary subject emerge dialectically, simultaneously facilitating and foreclosing each other. There can be no one held under tutelage as long as there is no one who also asks for the legal rights of a juridical person.

The court finds that tutelage is not the right position for someone like Schreber, who – even if he has no access to the communicative community – still, through his command of the legal code, has access to the legal community. Schreber may be partially mad, but not in that part over which the law rules. The delusions of accusing one's doctor of soul murder, of wanting to repopulate a world in ruin together with God, of a man becoming a woman – these are experiences that are not recognized as belonging to *"ordinary civil life."* For Schreber, it is enough to be part of the limited symbolic community defined by the law, of having a command of the law of "ordinary civil life," in order to regain a minimum of his lost symbolic stability: his ability, not to be held accountable in the abstract, to humankind itself, but to be held accountable as Daniel Paul Schreber to someone in particular, Professor Flechsig, his wife, and the judges of the Superior Court. In the Civil Code, Schreber finds a stable common symbolic order that can include him as a legitimate subject – although only as a subject in a partial, narrow, and exclusively legal sense – while at the same time allowing him to write his *Memoirs* from a discursive position where language has lost its communicative capacity, where the foreclosed symbolic order has already reappeared in the Real, indifferent to the linguistic community that Lacan calls "the big Other," which could have yielded a recognition beyond that of the legal code.[19]

Submitted as a legal document, and as such asking for the legal recognition of its author, the paranoid-psychotic discourse of Schreber's *Memoirs* is positioned on both sides of the limit of a symbolic order: it is at once a refusal of signature within that order, addressing everyone without having a point from which – "man" or "woman" – to do so, and a request to regain such a position, by insisting on addressing someone – Dr. Flechsig, Miss Schreber, the Superior Court, etc. – within the community of symbolically distributed identities.[20]

Peter Goodrich understands Schreber's *Memoirs* as formulating a juridical theology in which it is Schreber's sacrifice of himself, his abandonment of the juridical institution, that gives back a divine authority to the human law that has lost its symbolic resources and force, but in doing so also separates the two realms and rids the human law of any further divine intervention. Schreber's juridical act is thus an inversion of investiture, an abstention from the weak powers of the juridical institution that serves to strengthen them.[21] Schreber is seen as actually working against the court's recognition of him as juristically competent. Instead, his own juridical theology requires him to withdraw from that competence, insofar as that withdrawal restores the capacity for such competence within the juridical institutions. This reading of the jurisprudence of the *Memoirs,* taken in isolation from the discourse in which it appears, seems to emphasize only one of the two directions in which Schreber's discourse moves. Schreber's abstention from symbolic investiture and his withdrawal from the legal institution seem to correspond with an inverse movement of renewed investment in those symbolic resources. What Goodrich's isolation of a jurisprudence in Schreber's *Memoirs* seems to have to put into parenthesis is that the withdrawal from law is part of a dialectical movement, going in opposite directions at once: on the one hand a withdrawal from the symbolically distributed particulars of the law; on the other, a request to be recognized by the law as one of those particulars. The one only seems possible through the other.

The chat logs share a similar imbalance between address and signature, and a similar conflation of seeking and refusing symbolic recognition. "bradass87" writes about the possibility of being held accountable for her release of classified materials that, "i just … dont wish to be a part of … at least not now … im not ready … I wouldn't mind going to prison for the rest of my life, or being executed so much, if it wasn't for the possibility of having pictures of me … plastered all over the world press … as boy." There is, she says, a "'visible' mess" – the mess of losing a partner, of losing one's social safety net, of a suddenly changing gender-identity – and then there is "the mess i created that no-one knows about yet." The two are interconnected: the secret diplomatic cables must be released, and the heroic crime recognized, for her transition to be possible. Yet that same revelation is also what will forever preclude that transition, since it will not be Chelsea Manning but Bradley Manning who revealed himself. "bradass87" is in a double-bind in which she must reveal the conspiracy in order to be herself, and in which she cannot reveal the conspiracy because it will not be she who will be able to account for the act of having revealed it; the visible mess and the invisible mess are intrinsically intertwined. Manning knows that she exceeds her symbolically recognized position. She needs to repair this discrepancy in the symbolic order. But the repeated variation on "im a total mess" interrupts any solution to the contradiction: there is no way for *her* to intervene in a symbolic order in which she is *he*, but she is only *she* if she intervenes in it. Manning both recognizes the impossibility of addressing someone – there seems to exist no "third" between Lamo and the other "6.7 billion people" – yet insists on the necessity of doing so. In the face of having no stable position from which to make interventions, no legitimate name with which to sign, or underwrite, accept liability in case damage occurs when one's secrets are revealed, and of having no one who would accept one's address as one's own in particular, legitimately, and recognized as such – Manning's "im a total mess" refuses a resolution to the biopolitical and paranoid contradiction of being able to be *someone* only as long as one accepts that one is also potentially *no one*.

Universal and Particular Address; Being No One and Someone at Once

Both Schreber and Manning expect the publications of their secret revelations to be absolutely relevant to an abstract everyone. The former's secret knowledge would give "mankind" an opportunity to gain "more correct ideas about the beyond that might never occur again" and the latter's would "have an impact on 6.7 billion people."[22] For both, this public revelation, addressing the whole of humankind, is intrinsically and contradictorily connected with a private one. The writer of the *Memoirs* is adamant that he will publish his work once his tutelage is rescinded. But Schreber's intention to publish the text that contains the theory of the conspiracy against his soul and body produces a number of contradictions. In the text that must be made available to the whole of humankind, his transition from man to woman is both unequivocally announced and concealed, relativized, and censured by demands of decorum that seem diametrically opposed to his wish to make the same account available to the public. This is further complicated by the already noted dilemma of address that permeates Schreber's discourse: who is Schreber speaking to? Is it the Superior Court that by reading his *Memoirs* can be convinced to rescind his tutelage, Professor Flechsig who can verify at least some of his claims, his wife whose hardships could be eased a little by a deeper understanding of her husband's predicament, or, on the other extreme, humankind itself?[23] The two first sentences of the *Memoirs* are instructive of the first kind of address: "I have decided to apply for my release from the Asylum in the near future in order to live once again among civilized people and at home with my wife. It is therefore necessary to give those persons who will then constitute the circle of my acquaintances, an approximate idea at least of my religious conceptions, so that they may have some understanding of the necessity which forces me to various oddities of behavior, even if they do not fully understand these apparent oddities."[24]

In the penultimate chapter of the *Memoirs*, Schreber both admits and asserts that "I venture to assert flatly that anybody who sees me standing in front of a mirror with the upper part of my body naked would get the undoubted *impression of a female trunk* – especially when the illusion is strengthened by some feminine adornments."[25] Schreber assures the reader, whoever that may be, that his body has become that of a woman. He continues by inviting a scientific examination of his body, although with the always added comment that he would never himself "instigate such an examination."[26] In the postscripts from 1902 he again offers his person *"as object of scientific observation for the judgment of experts"* and adds that his *"main motive in publishing this book* is to invite this," and that, short of such an examination, he hopes that a dissection of his body eventually will provide proof of his transition. However, in another register, perhaps that at which Schreber is speaking directly to the Superior Court, he adds one of the addenda that this kind of exhibition of his femaleness "happens only when *I am alone*, never as far as I can avoid it within sight of other people."[27] Absolute publicity – addressing his transition, and the events related to it, to the whole of humankind – coexists with a relative privacy: offering but not instigating a physical examination, doing in secret what is announced with complete transparency. The conflict between a universal address to everyone and a particular address to someone in particular could then be seen as the recipient side of a communicative short circuit, for which the corresponding conflict on the sender side is one between insufficient and excessive signature. Universal address is without sufficient signature: to address everyone, to attract the interest of the whole of humankind, seems possible only from a position of symbolic ambiguity. It is only as signed by *no one* that his *Memoirs* will be interesting to *everyone*. It is, however, only through a particular address – addressing the court, the scientists, his wife, Professor Flechsig – that the universal address without signature becomes possible. This particular address, however, requires a particular and recognized signature – a signature that Schreber cannot fully yield, since

Daniel Paul Schreber is not a woman's name. At the risk of being too formulaic, this schema seems to point to how Schreber's transition, and the miraculous conspiracy against him that precipitates it, must become known to everyone in order for Schreber the woman to enter into, and reassign, the symbolic order so that it can accommodate her – yet she cannot do so without rejecting the very ambiguity that she is, and that she seeks to be recognized as.

For Manning, the global address to humankind seems generated by her lack of a stable position from which to be held accountable for both her complicity in the normative dis-order that she has revealed and the criminal revelation of that dis-order itself, which, once restored as a normative order, again must be allowed to acknowledge the illegitimacy of telling the secrets of the state. However, while she must address everyone in order to restore the order of the world, she, like Schreber, sacrifices herself in that address and withdraws from the communicative community to which she has made reparations. Echoing her fear of being broadcasted as a male whistle-blower, she writes to Lamo at a later point in their conversation that she is "not so much scared of getting caught and facing consequences" as she is of "being misunderstood, and never having the chance to live the life i wanted to." She remains caught in "an awkward limbo" in the symbolic order. The only possible address that can be signed by this particular woman, Manning, is to a reluctant interlocutor, almost unnoticeably switching places with an <AUTO-REPLY>, on a satellite internet connection from an army base in eastern Baghdad.

The aporia of both Schreber's and Manning's restorations of a ruined world and a ruined self is that they will never be completed until *she* enters into the world as the ambiguity that the restored order must reject; the woman Schreber is the witness of God's overreach, the woman Manning is the witness of her own complicity in a corrupt world order. Each in their way succumbs to the other sex so as to overcome the rigidity of an insouciant law. She, Schreber or Manning, must therefore insist on the contradiction that the only way to restore order in the world is to address her revelation to the whole world without having a name to sign it with: eventually the tutelage will be rescinded, the thirty-five-year sentence commuted.

NOTES

1 Daniel Paul Schreber, *Memoirs of My Nervous Illness*, trans. Ida Macalpine and R.A. Hunter (New York: New York Review of Books, 2000), 16.

2 Schreber, *Memoirs*.

3 That this problem of epistemological separation anticipates its counterpart in jurisprudence and the articulation of a "minor jurisprudence" appears to support Rajgopal Saikumar's interpretation of the latter as establishing a new foundation of law, rather than merely offering a critique of ones already given. See chapter 3.
4 Schreber, *Memoirs*, 23, 62.
5 German lacks the language of "exception" (*im einzelnen Falle*) and "rule" (*Regel*) of the translation, which resonates more with political and juridical theology. The text does, however, utilize the theological trope of miracle (*Wunder*) to present an immediate relation between God and humans, sovereign and subjects. Schreber, *Memoirs*, 23; Daniel Paul Schreber, *Denkwürdigkeiten eines Nervenkranken* (Frankfurt am Main: Syndikat, 1985), 14; cf. Carl Schmitt, *Political Theology: Four Chapters on the Concept of Sovereignty* (Chicago: University of Chicago Press, 2006), 31ff.
6 Schreber, *Memoirs*, 28.
7 For one version of this argument, see the lengthy elaboration in Judith Butler, *Undoing Gender* (New York: Routledge, 2004).
8 Schreber, *Memoirs*, 66ff., 164.
9 Ibid. 186.
10 Ibid. 252.
11 Ibid. 188ff., 235.
12 Ibid. 225.
13 Evan Hansen, "Manning-Lamo Chat Logs Revealed," *Wired*, 13 July 2011.
14 Cf. Schmitt, *Political Theology*, 26: "The specific political distinction to which political actions and motives can be reduced is that between friend and enemy."
15 Schreber, *Memoirs*, 423.
16 Eric L. Santner, *My Own Private Germany: Daniel Paul Schreber's Secret History of Modernity* (Princeton, NJ: Princeton University Press, 1996), 92.
17 Foucault notes in *Discipline and Punish* that "Judge Schreber" is a more interesting account of individuality than Lancelot when the individual no longer is only a juridical fiction but "a reality fabricated by this specific technology of power that I called 'discipline.'" Power is not only negative, delimiting, abstracting, and repressive, it is also positive and productive, intervening most directly and immediately in the fabrication of a specific body. The one who appears to be most individual is the one who is the most privileged object of a disciplinary control, surveillance, and calculation. Michel Foucault, *Discipline and Punish: The Birth of the Prison*, trans. Alan Sheridan (New York: Vintage Books, 1995), 194.
18 Santner, *My Own Private Germany*, 92.

19 It is, however, the constitutive element of the symbolic order that has been foreclosed, not the order in itself. The paranoid subject is skilled in utilizing the particular signifiers of the symbolic order taken in isolation, but the whole order, and the communicative community it holds together, is for that subject without a reliable structuring principle; it looks sane and reliable from any one point of her discourse, but as it progresses and must rely on a structuring principle for its meaning production, it collapses and reveals its fundamental disorder. In Lacan's words, for the psychotic-paranoid, something that should be symbolized has been denied that symbolization and thus reappears as "real"; it is rejected, "*verworfen*": "Prior to all symbolization – this priority is not temporal but logical – there is, as the psychoses demonstrate, a stage at which it is possible for a portion of symbolization not to take place.... It can thus happen that something primordial regarding the subject's being does not enter into symbolization and is not repressed, but rejected." Jacques Lacan, *The Psychoses 1955–1956: The Seminar of Jacques Lacan, Book III*, ed. Jacques-Alain Miller, trans. Russel Grigg (New York: W.W. Norton, 1993), 12ff., 80ff.

20 This seems to correspond to Katrin Trüstedt's insightful analysis of Schreber's "double process," his turning the legal procedure against itself and, at the same time, revealing law's other and entering it into law, through the very mechanism of positive law's procedure. See chapter 4.

21 Goodrich writes, "The investiture crisis is resolved for Schreber by the inversion of investiture, abandonment of the institution, of the Appeals Court, in favor of a self-sacrifice that will cleanse the law by restoring the proper 'Order of the World.'" Peter Goodrich, "The Judge's Two Bodies: The Case of Daniel Paul Schreber," *Law and Critique* 26, no. 2 (2015): 117–33.

22 Schreber, *Memoirs*, 384.

23 W.J.T. Mitchell reflects on similar "publications" by other gifted schizophrenics, noting, to my understanding, how the grandiosity of a unifying symbolization of everything – perhaps similarly presupposing what I call a universal address – that only a "normal," "sovereign subject" could be capable of, coincides with an incapacity to speak and "be normal" when the stakes seemingly are not as high, thus exaggerating what it is to be recognizable as "normal" to the extent of revealing normalcy's inherent, incurable madness, through the curse of the mental illness. See chapter 8.

24 Schreber, *Memoirs*,15.

25 Ibid. 248.

26 Ibid.

27 Ibid. 369.

6 Thoughts Worthy of Being Thought

DANIELA GANDORFER

Daniel Paul Schreber – this peculiar character, expressive body, scattered mind, and mad judge – is "sick of law." As history has demonstrated time and again, this is rather surprising, as judges – considered men of honour and decisive power – are rarely the ones who are brought to their knees by law. In Heinrich von Kleist's "The Broken Jug," Judge Adam, a filthy man as Eve reported, escaped the law simply by rising from his bench and running away. And in the United States, Judge Kavanaugh rose from being a United States circuit judge to associate justice of the U.S. Supreme Court, despite the testimony of Professor Christine M. Blasey Ford. Judge Schreber, however, finds himself in a rather different position. Under the impression of becoming a woman, of enduring the process of becoming-woman, and driven by the desire to think creative thoughts – thoughts worthy of being thought – he fell, per Goodrich, ill of law. Indeed, nearly every single part of Schreber's body is in pain. His perceptual apparatus is playing tricks on him, his motor functions are severely compromised, his digestive system disobedient, and his sleep disturbed. No wonder he cannot *think*. All that comes to mind are broken phrases, nonsensical clichés, and disembodied voice commands, forcing his mind to sense and to become senseable to the pains and wounds miraculously left and inflicted upon his body. Schreber is, as we learn, *verrückt* – "mad of and with law."[1]

There are protocols for such cases. It is not long before his mind is declared mad, and his body is placed in a mental institution. Undoubtedly, the judge's condition is serious. Questions are plenty, but there is no remedy in sight. What to do with an unruly body, how to think what cannot be thought, how to cure law, save humanity, and, time permitting, even restore the order of the world without losing either body or mind? Schreber's head is hurting, but he is far from surrendering – he has big thoughts, *denkwürdig* (worthy of being thought). Somewhere in his process, oscillating between speculative investigation and meticulous self-examination, unable to find sane answers to mad questions, Schreber makes a decision: in order to help his fellow human beings overcome an understanding of law that does not do bodies well, he writes his own patient and case history, his *Denkwürdigkeiten*, thoughts worthy of being thought, or, as I propose, a matterphorical expression testifying against a law that deals best with corpses and strives to efface the body and the ability to *think* alike.[2]

This proposition rests on two important assumptions, both of which shift analysis away from interpretation towards a *synaesethics* of sense-making, which exceeds the text and its time. First, Schreber, vanishing as a judge and man of law, writes not to represent, but to become something else, precisely because it is in writing – not in representing – that "one becomes-woman, becomes-animal or vegetable, becomes-molecule to the point of becoming-imperceptible," constantly containing "a component of flight that escapes its own formalization." It is, as Goodrich states, a mode of ontographically expressing "through corporeal sensibility, through a theory of knowing as a physical phenomenon"[3] that, qua its being *in* and *of* the world, is implicated in and becomes-with what it expresses. As such, writing means writing-*with* and becoming-*with* – in the case of Schreber *with* contortions, wounds, transitions, sensations, desires; *with* histories, presents, and futures of a body – of many bodies – unwilling to exist under the confines of mindless minds and nonsensical sensibilities. Accordingly, writing does not aim to represent life or "impose a form (of expression) on the matter of lived experience." This is also why one does not become Man as "the dominant form of expression that claims to impose itself on all matter," and why there is no better reason to write than, per Deleuze, "the shame of being a man."[4]

Second, and following this understanding of writing as a non-representational practice of sensing and sense-making, the *Denkwürdigkeiten* is not to be confused for an autobiography – despite its having been translated into English as "Memoirs" – as Schreber is not an author but a writer, who, again per Deleuze, "invents assemblages starting from assemblages which have invented him," making "one multiplicity pass into another."[5] Put differently, the *Denkwürdigkeiten* is not a stable object of inquiry but is closer to a "mobile entity" and is as such "a relay point between different moments in space and time, as well as different levels, degrees, forms and configurations of the *thinking process*."[6] It constantly shifts with its external relations, expressing thought – and, as we will see, even the very question of what thought *is* and of how it matters and excludes from mattering – differently and *in* difference. The question is thus not what the *Denkwürdigkeiten* means, but what it functions with, and in "which other multiplicities its own are inserted and metamorphosed."[7] The approach I take here is perhaps not dissimilar to Donna Haraway's mad gardener, who is "chipping and shredding and layering" in order to "make a much hotter compost pile for still possible pasts, presents, and futures,"[8] and also not to Deleuze's notion of being "a traitor to one's own reign," which requires to create and to experiment.[9] I do so in order to sense and make-sensible some of the onto-epistemological assumptions underlying legal thought that are hiding in plain sight, be it as black letters or as binary code. Concretely, I am picking up on Goodrich's claim according to which the *Denkwürdigkeiten* ought to be read as legal theory that critiques a philosophy of law that has yet to find its body, and I am keeping in mind the words of Antonio Negri during his imprisonment in Italy, namely that when it comes to thinking philosophical alternatives the "liberation of a cumbersome past" is not worth anything "if not carried through to the benefit of the present and the production of the future."[10] Consequently, my loyalty is not with the text as a representational unit, let alone the judge as author, or even patient. Rather, it is with the madness, the inability to conform to the norm, the resistance against a representational image of thought (and of law) that predetermines what thoughts can be thought, and with a body losing its mind. For such are the conditions that allow different thoughts to become-*denkwürdig* and create the possibility for alternative futures (as well as pasts and presents) to come into being. Finally, the question I pursue here by thinking-with both Goodrich and Schreber (as well as with the *Denkwürdigkeiten*) is less whether law is reasonable, or whether machines can think law, even though I may touch upon such concerns. Rather I am seeking to sense thoughts worthy of *being thought* for a legal theory desperately in need of finding its body, and for an understanding of law that acknowledges its being co-constituted by bodies as differential materializations.[11]

Corpus of Law

A lot has been said about Schreber's *Denkwürdigkeiten*, about Schreber himself (as a text, patient, figure, official, son, mindful lunatic, and embodied insanity), and also about the text, whether deemed a patient history, a memoir, or a testimony of a legal mind going insane.[12] What is more, it has been observed that law and language are "a little mad," both even being the "unique place and first condition of madness."[13] And, as law and legal theory are assumed to be addressed mainly in and as language, law and literature studies have emphasized the complicities between not only madness and law, but also between order words and the order of words. All of this together has set up the *Denkwürdigkeiten* to at least being considered a potential object for inquiries into the entanglement of law, language, and madness. However, what the *Denkwürdigkeiten* has not been considered to be, at least not before Goodrich's intervention, is an ontographic and juris-literary expression of a mad judge's body – shifting, aching, desiring, transforming, potentially transitioning – and by doing so, articulating both a radical critique and a transhumusian legal theory.[14] Indeed, what has escaped the theorist's attention is the possibility of approaching the *Denkwürdigkeiten* as the articulations of an ontological crisis sensed by a judge, who became sick of law and is constantly struggling between what seems incommensurate – losing his mind and giving in to becoming-women. Importantly, such an approach requires its own mode of reading and sensing the *Denkwürdigkeiten* – a written expression rendered contradictory, nonsensical, and indicative of insanity. The challenge is to make sensible, if not sensical, what has remained unrecognized, perhaps even unrecognizable by critical and uncritical modes of analysis and reading, and to do so while, or even despite, being faced with pages over pages, phrases over phrases, words over words, letters over letters. Rather than reiterating what has been recognized, identified, and determined, how can we, as the scholars and readers we imagine ourselves to be, engage in the task of *jurisliterary thought*, developing and fostering "an *aesethics of sense-making* attentive to how, amidst onto-epistemological cacophony, the silent dance of *as ifs* and *what ifs* draws the lines, all too real, that separate being from knowing, fiction from fact, matter from meaning, Life from Non-Life, law from literature: case by case, letter by letter, point by point, pixel by pixel, particle by particle – or wave?"[15]

For once, picking up on the last part of the question, nothing should be taken for granted or as an already given – not even the assumption of which thoughts, and which kinds of thoughts, are worthy of being thought. Goodrich demonstrates as much when he attests in *Schreber's Law* that the reason Schreber's *Denkwürdigkeiten* has not been approached as a legal theory, let alone a critique of law, is that the verdict on what the text is, and what it refers to, has already been issued on the basis of what has been previously said about it. Goodrich further attests that the text has become secondary to those scientific and academic projects that have only considered secondary accounts – mediated interpretations – which thereby rely only on what has been considered to be already known about the mad judge. The result is that Schreber himself "has, postmortem, been analyzed to death."[16] According to Goodrich, attention ought to be paid to the text, which must be read "not as madness but as theory," as a "radical critique of law."[17] And indeed, traces of law, let alone of a mad judge, are plenty in the *Denkwürdigkeiten*. It speaks, for example, of justice (at least once or twice), mentions a "domestic right" (*Hausrecht*) to one's mind, and a "natural right" to a non-thinking-thought.[18] It also contains references to legal letters and is teeming with legal terms. Goodrich makes an intriguing case for a different mode of analysis, emphasizing that there is no point in continuing to "cure the dead judge"[19] and thereby facilitates the opening of both critical legal theory and the field(s) of law and literature to matterphorical and jurisographical approaches to sense-making.

In thinking with Goodrich, I wish to extend the focus away from the body of text to how the text, as a matterphorical expression, makes sense-able a specific *body* suffering from an all too familiar image of thought – upheld by reason, enforced by law, and grounded in Cartesian dualism. Given the history of the body not only in Western philosophy – as quite simply that which is inferior to the mind – but also in legal thought, it is not surprising that in addition to the unresolved question of the text's genre, and the fact that it lent itself to the increasing interest in psychoanalysis, the significance of the body (its differential materializations, monstrosity, unruliness, and desires) and the possibility of it articulating, or even co-constituting, a legal theory have not been detected – even despite Samuel Weber's verdict on the *Denkwürdigkeiten*, which states that it is the body that "constitutes the ultimate goal."[20]

Schreber's body hurts, is tortured, wounded, exhausted, and prevented from sleeping. It is not a stable body, but one shifting, transforming, metamorphizing, expressing, as well as one being pathologized, described, diagnosed, and gendered. Its organs are being messed around with, its brain functions are interrupted, and its perceptual apparatus confused. While certainly thoroughly uncomfortable, such conditions might not yet register as too peculiar. We could argue that Schreber's body does what bodies do and endures what is done to them. As a monstrous and unruly body, it is represented and approached in precisely the same manner as throughout the history of rigidly practised Enlightenment thought – as either an inconvenient yet necessary carrier of a thinking (judging) subject to be fixed or disciplined, or as a fleshly object for exploitation and eventual disposal.[21] Certainly, these conditions are not new, and for as long as the Cartesian dualism can hold its strictly enforced ontological hierarchy in place, the image of thought (determining what it means to think and to make sense), and with it the order of the world according to which the body and its materializations paradoxically do not *matter*, remains intact. Consequently, any theory, let alone any embodied and materializing expression of a different mode of doing theory that undermines this dualism, must register as the most monstrous transgression and perverse touch imaginable – one that throws the world out of order and into a deep crisis. This, of course, is not a novel condition either. Adam's and God's fingers are purposely not touching in Michelangelo's painting, and it is not simply by chance that Spinoza's "Deus, sive Natura" unleashed (and unleashes still) a strong backlash across centuries, territories, and institutions of thought.

Whether novel or not, it is precisely this perversion undetected by psychoanalytic readings that Schreber exposes when stating that the "order of the world" came into disarray through an internal rupture (*Riss*), that is, through a *crisis* (*Krisis*) engendered by the fact that God, who is not supposed to interfere with the living and with living organisms in general, suddenly touches life on earth.[22] Schreber's explanation of this perversion departs from a Christian theological narrative, but conveys the severity and consequentiality of the mind aiming to get a hold on matter, including the body as specific materialization. Schreber's wounded, transforming body is supposed to be far distant from God, who himself is not body, but nerves, vibrations, and rays, and in the business of dealing only with corpses.[23] Indeed, according to the order of the world (which is the "lawful relation" between God and the living), "God did not know and had no need to know the living human being,"[24] for the bodies he deals with were either already dead or asleep, dreaming. God created everything "out of the void" – which for Schreber denotes emptiness and nothingness – and inhabits the space of the immaterial.[25] Divine sense-making – or knowing – and expressing is conditioned on the mind/matter dualism. God's words are clichés, his language is meant for corpses, and his law – phrases over phrases – cannot be endured by living beings. God interfering with the living, or, in other words, mind (supposed to be ontologically separate from materializations and not concerned with what is living, desiring, breathing, hurting, laughing, bellowing) touching the body, throws the world – its law of reason, its conception of reasonable law, of what is thinkable and thoughtful – into crisis.

That Western conceptions of law and normativity are rooted in Enlightenment concepts such as reason, rationality, consciousness, and the thinking subject has been argued and problematized amply before. Feminist, postcolonial, and legal scholars have also done important work in exposing the inferior role the body (in its differential materializations) is assigned to in contrast to that of the superior mind. Law, as part of the larger Western philosophical tradition, "has always been predicated as a function of the mind and therefore in a hierarchical opposition to materiality which law serves to order and govern."[26] The dominant form of Western rational abstractionism at the core of law and legal reasoning, Anna Grear states, is inextricable from the separation of the mind from the body.[27] This is why, as legal scholar Ngaire Naffine writes, "the idea of a potentially disruptive body, which must be contained and managed so as not to interfere with the exercise of reason" inhabits the dominant concept of law.[28] Informed by classical humanism, law has been and still is conceived as "a discourse of reason," and as such "functions as both product and producer of this disembodied rationalism."[29] This does not mean that there is no concern for the body in law; quite the opposite, as bodies are regulated, disciplined, and problematized, but that it is not considered co-constitutive of what is considered law and legal thought. The latter determines how legal thought deals with bodies – by restricting the concept of the body to its ideal: a self-contained and self-enclosed, bounded, immutable, healthy, able, heterosexual, white, male body.[30] The further a body departs from this fiction, the less likely it is that its existence is acknowledged and protected by law. Indeed, the assumption that "sovereign minds are housed in appropriate bodies" prevents what departs from it from occupying the subject position. Consequently, "those bodily forms – the monstrous, the physically vulnerable, the disabled, the congenitally different like conjoined twins or hermaphrodites" – are those that "most clearly challenge the distinctions both between mind and body and between body and body."[31] Despite the existence of a multitude of lived forms diverting from the ideal body described, morphological difference, as Shildrick argues, continues to figure the monstrous. This proves true for law, too, where it not only represents the monstrous – what doesn't fit the form of law – but also gives shape to the madness (*Verrücktheit*) in the construct of a law that promises all too pure objectivity, certainty, and predictability.[32]

What these arguments make clear is that the image of thought and the legality of disembodied reason, which determine both what it means to think and what is thinkable, underlie law and legal thought, too. Consequently, a legal theory that can attend to bodies and their differential materializations must challenge the very notion of what it *means* to think. Following Goodrich's argument on how to approach the *Denkwürdigkeiten*, namely by acknowledging that "the initial question is not that of madness but of thought," I hold that it is this question that needs to be attended to further, precisely because it is assumed to precede any questioning. It is in this sense that my engagement with Schreber – the judge, text, patient history, onto-epistemological expression of desiring difference – also remains attentive to the title, that is, the announcement of thoughts worthy of being thought. For the *Denkwürdigkeiten* is indeed concerned with thinking – with how thinking becomes impossible as a result of a compulsion to think pre-given thoughts, how inventive and new thoughts are stifled and actively fought by acousmatic voices, how the body responds to compulsive, disembodied thoughts with pain, wounds, and bellowing, and how the very modes of thought described in the *Denkwürdigkeiten* register a crisis in legal thought that now – as well as at the time of its writing and even before – determines the possible future(s) of law, and with it, of the bodies, that is, the bodily materializations subjected to what law will be. As such, my approach is not too far from that of Goodrich, who writes in a recent text on the future of legal theory and the matters of critique that "it is the body that notices, senses, responds, thinks, and knows" in a sense "legal dogmatics has since the enlightenment been at war to exclude." It is this "corporeality as thought, as the cognitive state of being in the world," that legal theory must become aware of in order "to begin to understand the social process of theory and the possibilities of the community of thought." In thinking *with* Goodrich's diagnosis of a written expression that has always also been expressing a judge's falling ill of positive law – commonly understood "as interpretable text, as constellations of propositions, categories, syllogisms, rules, as linguistic expressions of thought"[33] – I wish to attend to how "thoughts worthy of being thought" (the *Denkwürdigkeiten*) articulate an onto-epistemological crisis of a law that is understood mainly "as the product of the positional power of the mind," and as such detached from matter and bodies.[34]

Thinking Thoughts

As the author, and writer for that matter, is not only dead but has post-mortem been analysed to death, the question is less what Schreber thought, and instead what thinking means when it comes to deciding which thoughts are worthy of *being thought*. Here, a particular *symptom* Schreber is expressing – namely the compulsion to think a thought that prevents the act of thinking-with what matters – functions as productive entry point. If the *Denkwürdigkeiten* is to be considered a legal theory, as Goodrich suggests, then it is born out of a legal subject – a judge, to be precise – falling ill of law, falling away from what constitutes it and, in an almost perverse manner, falling together with what it is not supposed to touch: a body. In this sense,

I use "symptom" not as something that refers to and is indicative of something else, but rather understood in its etymological sense as a *falling together* of law and madness, mind and body, meaning and matter, past and future. This is not an easy task.[35] But, to be fair, Schreber's fall (or *Fall*, which is German for "case") is not to be taken lightly either. As becomes clear quite early in the *Denkwürdigkeiten*, Schreber feels shitty, not only because of the peculiar bowel movements and the painful miracles inflicted on his intestines, but because he cannot think. Put more precisely, he is forced by talking voices to engage in a particular practice of thinking that rests on a structural formalism, linear causality, and predictability, and that impedes any possibility of not only an understanding of thinking as embodied, but also of what Deleuze calls the "genesis of the act of thinking in thought."[36] Thinking, for Judge Schreber, is reduced to the compulsion to complete started, fractured clauses (*irgendwelche angebrochene Phrasen*), which are given to him by so-called talking voices: "In particular, for years single conjunctions or adverbs have been spoken into my nerves – repeated a thousand of times; these ought only introduce clauses, but it is left to my nerves to complete them in a manner satisfactory to a thinking mind."[37] This strict causality and structural formalism is further expressed by his complaint that he feels forced to complete "certain fragments of formally complete phrases" that get senselessly thrown into his mind, such as "Now I shall," "now, this was," "you were to."[38] The reduction of the judge's practice to think to a banal form of data processing, bestowed onto him by a compulsion to think only what is "satisfactory to a thinking mind," a phrase certainly resonating with Cartesian dualism and indicative of the denial of thought as an embodied practice, is for Schreber nothing less than "a violation of the most original human rights."[39] Schreber's thoughts on thinking are certainly contradictory. He is constantly struggling to come to terms with embodied, creative thoughts that desire to be thought, in conflict with his desperate desire to prove himself overseeing a mind that, to his great dismay, can digest only the reproduction of structurally predetermined representations. His reflections uphold the optics of reason while his meditations are all but Cartesian. It is also the former that restricts the latter. The archive, or database, of thinkable thoughts is produced and curated by the "mechanically" executed writing-down system. [40] He explains that the writing down aims to record every thought he is thinking, building a database of already-thought thoughts, which then, Schreber complains, are thrown back at him and thereby force him to think what has been thought in precisely the way it has been done before.

Schreber cannot clearly determine what forces him to think, but we do learn that it is especially in moments when he gives himself over to a specific activity, namely to non-thinking – that is, a practice of non-thinking thought – that the system, capable of not only recording but also reading Schreber's thoughts, confronts him with the collected writing-down material (*Aufschreibematerial*). The indeterminacy of this process and its operators is furthermore expressed by Schreber's mentioning of "fleeting-improvised-men," who presumably conduct data collection by the writing-down and query system. These men are just "*gesetzt*" (put in place) and are constantly also dissolving. How to grasp what denies thought the activity of thinking? Schreber's mode of sense-making is held hostage, arrested, unable to escape predetermination. Both the process of his thoughts being written down and also the frequent intrusion of the voices stating that "we've already got," signalling a potential limit and exhaustion of what can be thought is tellingly described by Schreber as "mental torture."[41] No wonder the judge's condition is dire. Having been professionally occupied with legal sense-making prior to his falling ill of law, Schreber is now arrested by a formalism of and in thought. He is forced to think what has already been thought in precisely the manner it has been done before, complying with what Deleuze terms an image of (representative) thought that makes reason a tribunal and demands judges to be reflective, that is, engaged in bouncing back and forth thoughts whose representations do not threaten the image and its assumptions of what it means to think.[42]

However, despite his increased sense of exhaustion, Schreber insists that the capacity to think cannot be fully exhausted. In fact, he claims that the writing-down system relies on an "utter misjudgment of human thinking,"[43] for it was believed, he states, "that my store of thoughts could be exhausted by being written-down."[44] He desires, and he desires to *actually think*, to put thought to action, and to actualize thought that is inseparable from his body, even his environment – be it fellow patients, birds, insects, the sun, the weather, noises and music, or objects that surround him. This kind of thinking is hard, sometimes almost impossible, given that most of the time Schreber is tormented by thoughts and questions that are not his authentic (*ächte*) thoughts but are spoken into his mind in the course of what he calls "falsification of thoughts" (*Gedankenfälschung*).[45] The consequences of Schreber's failure to drown out the talking voices and their commands, and his inability to escape the compulsion to think, are first and foremost "significant bodily pain or persistent bellowing."[46] The rare moments in which Schreber manages to perform the non-thinking-thought are those involving the body, letting it unfold its physical capacities and its potential to create.[47]

Either way, Schreber's resistance to an arresting image of thought, his refusal to repeat nonsensical linguistic orders, empty phrases, clichés, and falsified thoughts, or, put differently, his critique, is embodied. In doing so, Schreber – the figure, written expression, mad phenomenon, judge, thoughts worthy of being thought – is struggling with a core pillar of Western philosophy, namely the assumptions about what it means to think and, precisely because of the particular history of that concern in Western thought, how it allows for some modes of existence and prevents others from mattering. What is at stake is nothing less than the future of humanity and the order of the world.

Of course, Schreber is neither the first nor the last to express, in his own way, this question. This can be said also about René Descartes, despite being widely considered to be the philosopher who articulated the beginning of philosophy (literally, the love for thinking). However, as Deleuze cautions, even Descartes' "I think therefore I am," the credo that paradoxically established and upholds still the very separation between mind and matter, already assumes everything that there is to assume, namely, that "everyone knows ... what is meant by self, thinking, and being."[48] The *Denkwürdigkeiten* is neither the beginning nor the end of the ongoing questioning of what it means to think. It comes from the middle, revealing the onto-epistemological assumptions of thought and being, as well as what such assumptions mean for the past(s), present(s), and future(s) of law and for legal thought. As such, they are still present, carrying the potential for interrupting the order of the world, exposing the dualism and the power of representationalism as the deliberate detachment of representation from what is represented, and of what is represented from the modes of representation.

To emphasize the contemporaneity of the *Denkwürdigkeiten* – both taken literally as thoughts worthy of being thought and understood as articulating the pervasiveness of the image of thought – consider a recent call to "actually think" by the posthumanist science and technology scholar Donna Haraway. In *Staying with the Trouble*, Haraway seeks to understand thoughtlessness in relation to both Hannah Arendt's definition in *Eichmann in Jerusalem* and the Anthropocene as a specific geopolitical juncture that threatens for different, yet related reasons to reiterate genocide and foster unprecedented ecological devastation. In doing so, thoughtlessness is, for Haraway, inextricable from immateriality precisely because "the world does not *matter* in ordinary thoughtlessness."[49] Her reference to Arendt and, by extension, to the convicted Nazi war criminal Josef Eichmann, aims to emphasize the stakes of questioning modes of thinking and sense-making: "Revolt! Think we must; we must think. Actually think, not like Eichmann the

Thoughtless."[50] The reference is not one simply to thoughtlessness, but also to its close ties to language and law, and their shared complicity in eradicating bodies and modes of existence. Indeed, Arendt's *Eichmann in Jerusalem* offers insightful and complicated contemplations on what it means to think (although Arendt stays close to the Kantian understanding) and how thoughtlessness relates to the horrendous encounters between stigmatized bodies and blindly (yet consciously and deliberately) applied positive law. It is, as Judith Butler points out, a condemnation of Eichmann's failure to be critical of positive law, of denying obedience to a legal system that orders the systematic killing of millions of racialized bodies, diagnosed by Arendt as the "inability to *think*, to think from the standpoint of somebody else."[51] Attending closely to this formulation reveals that to speak and think, the law means being specifically embodied, having a *standpoint* and at least *some body*, that is related and relatable to other bodies, somewhere else. Indeed, it means thinking as and *with* that body, as well as with other bodies as entangled materializations. Arendt emphasizes the links between law, language, and the potential risk of unrelatability. Eichmann's language is "officialese" (*Amtssprache*), that is, nothing but a repetition of a language and a law without bodies, or, as Shoshana Felman writes, "a sort of robot-language."[52] No communication, with Eichmann, no thinking-*with*, was possible, "not because he lied," Arendt states, but because he was "surrounded by the most reliable of all safeguards against the words and the presence of others, and hence against reality as such."[53] The "language rules" that Arendt discusses purposely increase the distance between word and world, language and body, as they are ordered to replace words like "killing," "liquidation," or "extermination" with words and phrases digestible to those who apply and execute them, so that "order and sanity" amidst the madness of mass extermination would be maintained. The constructed distance between word and (physical) reality is already indicated in the term "language rule" (*Sprachregelung*), for it is itself, as Arendt writes, a "code name" and "meant what in ordinary language would be called a lie."[54] Seen from this perspective, Arendt's text exposes not only the problematic relation between bodies and (German positive) law, but also of law as a representational system, in this case, as thoughtless repetition of language in the form of clichés, stock phrases, and sayings that have no ground in reality yet actively exclude modes of existences from being. It reveals the danger of citing a law without bodies, of thought as disembodied process, of repeating phrases that have lost touch with reality or, even worse, have bereft the bodies they touch from any possibility of existence, and of meanings that have gained lethal force.[55] It is a warning against the grammar and language of representationalism articulated most clearly, yet not exclusively, by positive law as normative mode of sense-making in denial of its being co-constituted by the bodies and matters it excludes, effaces, explodes, and evaporates.

Thinking Matters

Thought and language are historically interwoven, at times so closely that those rendered unable to speak the right language, or to speak it correctly, were said to be, by nature, unable to think and thus prevented from breathing. Hanging from trees, lying on the ground, being blown up, sinking into deep waters: *Cogito ergo sum*, written in Latin, translated into French, English, German, Spanish, excluding the thoughtless as well as the unthinkable from existing.[56] As Luce Irigaray rightfully attests, "Our linguistic tool is elaborated for mastering more than for cultivating and sharing life," and, she adds, the question thus is "to rethink our language in order that it expresses life."[57] Law, too, rests on the powerfully constructed alliance between thought and language, that is, of the conscious mind and its use of language as normative expression of its cognitive superiority. Delaney, for example, emphasizes that "law sees only what language permits it to see and is blind to what language occludes," and that "'real' law, positive law, is commonly understood primarily as interpretable text, as constellations of propositions, categories, syllogisms, rules, as linguistic expressions of thought."[58] Consequently he insists on the necessity to *re-think* "what law and life have to do with each other" and of how "we can *think* the life of law differently."[59]

In addition to the close relation between law and language, which has been endorsed and critiqued abundantly, most prominently by various strands within law and literature studies, the question of what it *means* to think is also intimately tied to the humanistic Enlightenment tenets of reason and rationality. To give an example of how underlying humanistic notions of what it means to think – or, in this case, which thoughts are worthy of being thought – reiterate exclusive notions of what it means to be human and to establish normative societies, consider an article, titled "Thoughtfulness and the Rule of Law," by Jeremy Waldron, a law professor at NYU Law School teaching legal and political philosophy. In this article Waldron argues that "we want to be ruled thoughtfully," and characterizes "thoughtfulness" as "the capacity to reflect and deliberate, to ponder complexity and to confront new and unexpected circumstances with an open mind," and thus as related to human dignity. Waldron's text seeks to parse out "legalistic thoughtfulness" and focuses on three "thoughtful aspects" of the Rule of Law, namely standards, procedures, and precedents, which carry with them traditional notions of objectivity. What reveals the underlying assumptions here most clearly, however, is his conclusion, which cites Aristotle's argument according to which "law is reason unaffected by desire." Waldron is intrigued by the connection between law and reason, which is, he writes, the connection "between law and the god-like activity of reasoning."[60]

The conglomerate of law and language and, most importantly, its rootedness in reason and a predetermined understanding of what it means to think and, consequently to *be*, has important implications for contemporary discussions on emerging modes of legal sense-making, including those pertaining to shifting notions of law and normativity resulting from technological developments such as (but not exclusively) artificial intelligence, machine learning, distributed-ledger-technologies (i.e., blockchain), and hashing technology. Mireille Hildebrandt's preface to *Human Law and Computer Law: Comparative Perspectives* serves as a good example. Hildebrandt argues that any comparative analysis of how human and what she terms "computer law" relate, ought to understand the role (natural and computer) language plays in the articulation of legal norms. For Hildebrandt, the question of the relation between human and computer law can be best approached by turning to law and literature, more concretely to the notions of *law as code* and *law as literature*, not least because both modern law and literature are "affordances of the printing press" and are thus ontologically inextricable from text and natural language. This, however, is changing with the influence of information and communications technologies, affecting also what law will be. Whereas the "bookish mind," she writes, "requires and generates sequential thinking, the digital mind nourishes parallel processing and this has major consequences for the articulation of the law."[61] What remains unaddressed in the preface, yet structures much of the phenomena correctly analyzed by Hildebrandt, is the shared assumptions on which both computational thinking and (what is considered) human thinking rely, most importantly representationalism, reason, and the subject as consciousness preceding and superior to the body. It is thus not surprising, yet important, that she mentions, even if only in passing, the future possibility of "a law that addresses computing systems as legal subjects."[62]

The implications of such tacit acceptance of the fact that, at the core, we already know what it means to think, and that the question of sense-making ought not go "all the way down,"[63] can be witnessed when turning to transhumanism, a philosophical stance that not only fully embraces the ontological and epistemological assumptions bequeathed to thought from Enlightenment humanism but, with the help of new technologies, pushes for its actualization. A proponent of such a stance is Nick Bostrom, an Oxford University–based philosopher who is widely celebrated for pointing out the possible (future) dangers of artificial intelligence (AI). In his bestseller *Superintelligence: Paths, Dangers, Strategies* – abundantly praised by, among others, Bill Gates, Elon Musk, and MIT professor and transhumanist Max Tegmark – Bostrom imagines a future governed by AI and expresses his concerns about the treatment of digital workers. He coins the term "mind crimes" and states that the erasure and destruction of simulated humans and (digital) sentient minds – the future workers – "might be equivalent to genocide."[64] Bostrom even intensifies his concern by saying, "The number of victims might be orders of magnitude larger than in any genocide in history."[65] New digital technologies bring about different legal concepts (such as "mind crimes") to which legal theory and practice must attend carefully. Such concepts are also evolving in the vicinity of synthetic biology and artificial life, blockchain and digital twins, non-fungible, and utility tokens, and are shifting not only understandings of normativity and value, but also the conditions for certain modes of existence to matter.[66] It is thus not my interest to render technologies inherently good or bad. Rather I hold that what technologies *are* in the world, and what they can *do*, is determined by what they function *with*, how they are mobilized, which modes of existence they render possible, and which ones they exclude from mattering. With this in mind, what to make of the fact that Bostrom's thoughts are first and foremost with a potential "genocide" of digital minds when imagining future implications of new technologies for law and governance? And further: What allows the analogy that brings together genocide with mind crimes and, even further, introduces comparability by elevating the potential concept of mind crimes to "orders of magnitude larger than any other genocide in history"? As emphasized elsewhere, comparison, a mode of binary and oppositional meaning production, and analogy, a levelling out of what is not sufficiently adaptable or applicable to the contexts in question, are representational devices of sense-making.[67] As such, they are rooted in the ontological separation between mind and body, and consequently, meaning and matter. Put differently, meaning might matter (language is performative, discourse materializes, legal norms have material effects), but matter does not co-constitute meaning (the specific material constitution of a tree does not affect the signifier; matter is not discursive and materialization, such as bodies, is not co-constitutive of norms).

Bostrom's argument is all the more curious, considering that Article II of the "Convention on the Prevention and Punishment of the Crime of Genocide" defines genocide as "acts committed with intent to destroy, in whole or in part, a national, ethnical, racial or religious group," which are (as listed exhaustively) the act of "killing members of a group"; of "causing serious bodily or mental harm to members of the group"; of "deliberately inflicting on the group conditions of life calculated to bring about its physical destruction in whole or in part"; of "imposing measures intended to prevent births within the group"; and of "forcibly transferring children of the group to another group."[68] In order for Bostrom to analogize and compare the erasure of digital minds with the extermination of racialized, stigmatized, and targeted bodies, the specific physicality of the bodies at stake (which are most certainly constitutive parts of that norm) is considered negligible in the act of legal reasoning. Here also, the question is not only what Bostrom was thinking, but how the notion underlying thinking – more precisely, the thinking mind (he did not speak of "brain crimes") – threatens to deny bodies and their material-discursive specificity, render them unthinkable for the computational mind, and make them ungraspable by digital reason.

In large part, this can be answered by looking more closely into the transhumanist mindset, which differs, depending on its geopolitical manifestation, yet displays common traits across them.[69] Put concisely, transhumanism is a futuristic, philosophical, and political movement, guided by technology optimism, infused by a "Promethean ambition" to overcome and dominate the physical world, working towards the realization of the Cartesian subject as reproducible, immortal digital self, unconcerned with biological bodies and substrates. It rests upon a particular mixture of European Enlightenment humanism (with its emphasis on rational thought, progress, reason, individualism), on what this since has become in its specific geopolitical manifestations (for example. U.S. transhumanism or Northern European transhumanism), as well as on human speciesism. Bostrom, a prominent representative of the British transhumanists, describes transhumanism as an "extension of humanism," with its emphasis on the centrality of humans, individuals, and the promotion of "rational thinking," which thereby leads towards a stronger focus on the possibility of enhancing the human organism, not only through educational and cultural means, but also with technological ones.[70] Max More, speaking from the perspective of the U.S. American strand of transhumanism and for decades invested in realizing the transhumanist project, similarly argues that humanism relies "exclusively on educational and cultural refinement to improve human nature," whereas transhumanism aims to "apply technology to overcome limits imposed by our biological and genetic heritage."[71] In the cases where the thinking, in transhumanist scenarios, remains embodied in some way (let alone entangled with the biological or non-machinic world), it is considered an obstacle to overcoming. The biological body, an undesired conglomerate of matter, is, in the words of Max More, a "flawed piece of engineering."[72] For transhumanists, the body is a machine, and the mind a functional process of the brain that can be recreated in any other suitable matter.[73] For advanced rational thought (i.e., intelligence) to be possible, the mind, as transhumanist and roboticist Hans Moravec puts it, has to be "freed from the bondage of a mortal body."[74] For this to happen, however, some technical details (at the very least) need to be addressed. For example, how can the brain be removed from the body, and even more intricately, how to find "a way to get our mind out of our brain"?[75] In Moravec's 1988 book *Mind Children*, a cornerstone publication for the transhumanist movement and certainly outdated by contemporary standards in terms of available technologies, he imagines it as follows: "Layer after layer the brain is simulated, then excavated. Eventually your skull is empty, and the surgeon's hand rests deep in your brainstem. Though you have not lost consciousness, or even your train of thought, your mind has been removed from the brain and transferred to a machine. In a final, disorienting step the surgeon lifts out his hand. Your suddenly abandoned body goes into spasms and dies. For a moment you experience only quiet and dark. Then, once again, you can open your eyes. Your perspective has shifted."[76] In the more contemporary public sphere, such ideas are cultivated by, for example, Elon Musk's insistence on how the merger of machine and human intelligence will lead to the possibility of digital consciousness and how brain-machine interfaces are an important step towards this aim. Another example are cryonic facilities (among them the Alcor Life Extension Foundation, led by Max More), whose procedures are claimed to best preserve the brain, and with it memory, mind, and consciousness.

The term "transhuman" speaks to the struggle against the body and denotes the interim state between mortal human (Anthropos, Man) and the post-biological, immortal posthuman. Proponents of this line of thinking admit that it will take a while before humanity reaches the desired "post-biological condition" wherein posthumans will live in digital eternity as non-biological existences and as computational mind power. Emphasis is thus placed upon the importance of perfecting technologies such as human enhancement, mind scanning, mind uploading, brain-computer interfaces, and whole-brain simulation, to eventually bring about a new species of beings that are "completely synthetic artificial intelligences," or "enhanced uploads."[77] Once this state is reached, transhumanists argue, there will be no limits for the digital mode of human existence – a claim possible precisely because thinking, in the transhumanist imagination, eventually will reach its ideal by becoming high-speed digital computation, capable of grasping a world fully translatable into bits and other representational units. This also refers back to the beginnings of transhumanism, as it developed alongside the rise of computer and information technology studies, cybernetics, and cognitive science, all of which equate the rational mind to information processing and thus as a constantly improvable entity that defines the essence of human existence. As Katherine Hayles argues, the risk is that when "information loses its body," then "equating humans and computers is especially easy, for the materiality in which the thinking mind is instantiated appears incidental to its essential nature."[78] The roots of this line of thought lie as much in ideas of the liberal and autonomous self, as in information and computer technologies. This makes it possible to understand intelligence as "a property of the formal manipulation of symbols rather than enaction in the human lifeworld," and to conceive of thinking as disembodied.[79] What this means concretely for how transhumanists imagine the (or, rather, their) future of humanity, which is considered distinct from the future of the earth and non-human beings, can be grasped from the words of an extropist (the Californian predecessors of transhumanists) stating, "I am no more than a particular pattern of information, a set of data and processing rules," with the ultimate goal (and possibility) of reaching "the singular, perfect, omnipotent power of God."[80]

Outlook into the Future

What – and *how* – would Schreber think? What – and how – would the Schreberian body, desiring, aching, transitioning, becoming-woman think? And how would it negotiate the matterphorical struggle between somehow remaining answerable to a "reasonable mind," while at the same time eagerly and ontographically resisting God, this "intelligent cause" that remains disembodied nerve, "did not know and had no need to know the living human being," and cannot learn by experience (*Erfahrung*)?[81] On the one hand, this question is of course rhetorical and signals the (omni)presence of an image of thought that permeates past(s), present(s), and future(s). On the other hand, if we were inclined to look for hints expressed by the *Denkwürdigkeiten*, it is noteworthy that Schreber is most threatened by the miracles that attack his mind, which means, according to him, first and foremost the head, and second the spinal cord, which, together with the head, marks "the location of the mind."[82] In a manner not unsimilar to Moravec's "transmigration" scenario, Schreber describes the miracles conducted against his head in order to access and modulate his mind:

> The miracles directed against my head and the nerves of my head happened in manifold ways. One attempted to pull the nerves out of my head, for a time even (during the nights) to transplant them into the head of M. who slept in the next room. These attempts caused (besides the fear of an actual loss of my nerves) an unpleasant tension in my head.... Serious devastation was caused in my head by the so called "flights of rays," a phenomenon difficult to describe, the effect of which was that my skull was repeatedly sawn asunder in various directions. I frequently had – and still have regularly daily – the sensation that my whole skull had temporarily thinned; in my opinion this was brought about through the bony material of my skull being partly pulverized by the destructive action of the rays.[83]

Aside from his concerns about losing his mind, Schreber also fears that his ability to think could be reduced to repetitive patterns and automated computation. Consequently, he is constantly concerned with both proving that he is bestowed with reason, that he has not yet lost his mind, and exercising his "natural right" (*natürliches Recht*) to the non-thinking-thought, which means an intellectual or mental activity that neither feeds the writing-down system nor consists of a compulsive response to input offered by a machine. Other than what might be understood as reason, which assumes particular notions of objectivity, rationality, and causality, the non-thinking-thought is usually accompanied or made possible by another creative activity, mainly playing the piano, but also "sticking together, filling in pictures with paints," and "those jobs which count as feminine occupations, for instance sewing, dusting, making beds, washing up."[84] As mentioned, the non-thinking-thought is challenged by yet another symptom: the "compulsion to think" (*Denkzwang*), which is also inflicted on Schreber and aims to display a certain pattern: the "causal relation" (*Kausalitätsverhältnis*).[85] "It is often not at all easy, particularly in the case of sensations and feelings," Schreber notes, "to account for reasons ('But why') satisfactorily; indeed most often the question why is inept, as for instance in such sentences as 'This rose has a nice smell' ... or 'This is a magnificent painting' or 'This piece of music is particularly melodious.'"[86] In a more contemporary setting, however, the matterphorical thoughts, ontographically expressed and deemed worthy of being thought by Schreber, are excluded from legal sense-making. As the legal scholar and proponent of legal singularity Benjamin Alarie remarks, it is all but clear whether "human empathy and moral sentiments" (that is, emotions, sentiments, creative thoughts, which are the result of an embodied and relational existence) are "required for legal acumen."[87]

While Schreber, long before the possibility of AI governance has entered legal discourse, expresses concerns about the reduction of thinking to representational modes of computing and reasoning, Alfred North Whitehead is probably too enthusiastic in his lectures *Modes of Thought*, published thirty-five years after the *Denkwürdigkeiten*, when he states, "The legal profession can never be superseded by automata," as "complete codification" is neither possible nor desirable.[88] Even looking at how legal futures are currently conceptualized, and even if only in regard to algorithmic law and governance, portrays a rather different image. In "Law's Algorithm," for example, McGinnis and Wasick argue that what's at stake when algorithms find their way into law and legal practice is how this will "affect the form of law." Confidently, they claim that because of technological developments, our legal age is in fact an age of "computable realism"[89] and that algorithms will eventually be able to create law without human intervention or intelligence. The search itself, they predict, "will become the law."[90] This coincides with what Benjamin Alarie, Anthony Niblett, and Albert H. Yoon see as the "future of law" – "a world of self-driving law" and of the reign of a "legal singularity."[91] Alarie argues that the legal singularity "will arrive when the accumulation of a massive amount of data and dramatically improved methods of inference make legal uncertainty obsolete." It will, therefore, he writes, "contemplate complete law" and "affect all areas of the law."[92] Finally, he foretells, legal singularity will eliminate legal uncertainty and cause the emergence of "a seamless legal order."[93] The underlying idea that data processing will bring about a more just and less biased application of law – in other words, that computation needs to fully replace what is considered human thinking and legal reasoning – stems from the same Cartesian and Enlightenment informed tradition that feeds transhumanism, too. It is not surprising then that Max Tegmark, transhumanist and professor of physics at MIT, holds that "robojudges" could finally ensure that, "for the first time in history, everyone becomes truly equal under the law," since they, if correctly programmed, would apply the law "in a truly unbiased fashion."[94] Because he views the legal process as abstract and nothing more than "a computation, inputting information about evidence and laws and outputting a decision," the idea of robojudges and robolegislators strikes him as a desirable future scenario.[95] And, despite the justified criticism against Bostrom, the idea of digital and machinic personhood (legal subjectivity) is not only referenced by Hildebrandt. In fact, a report issued in 2015 by Mady Delvaux, discussed by the EU Parliament, states that there is ultimately "a possibility that, in the long-term, AI could surpass human intellectual capacity"[96] and concerns the bestowing of legal personhood to robots.

The vision of an approaching occurrence of an intelligence explosion, which will ultimately lead to a singularity, and even a singleton – a form of AI governance that is free of any human interaction – is both contested and embraced. It is a futuristic vision that builds on the emerging corpus of academic and public transhumanist legal imaginations and does not remain restricted to cyberspace and virtual realities, but seeks to govern what John P. Barlow calls the "civilization of the Mind" on Earth – and even beyond.[97] It is a future that has been contested and challenged in the past and yet manages to dominate the present; a future built on the representational image of thought, including legal thought, neatly detached from matters of bodies and bodily materializations. There is still a long way to go before human as well as non-human bodies will have fully disappeared, when, as John Harris predicts, new types of creatures that are "created by synthetic biology or by mixing the elements of different species or, indeed, through multiple forms of technology," will have joined or replaced what we conceive of as humans.[98] It will most likely take even longer until the uploading of minds to exclusively "non-biological substrates" will have become feasible.[99] However, such visions signal, and have signalled for centuries, the present and future implications of the Cartesian onto-epistemological assumptions about what it means to think and, consequently (per Descartes) to *be*, including what it means to *be* before and after the law. If, as Goodrich argues, Schreber fell ill of an "inhuman law," which is "operated by automata, machines, rather than a material and embodied law" and is based on a pure and lifeless theory as a "philosophy of law that has yet to find a body,"[100] then understanding how legal theory and, consequently, thought can *matter* differently is the precondition for crafting liveable alternatives. This is precisely what the *Denkwürdigkeiten* offers as it exposes, if read by mad gardeners and loyal traitors, that it matters which "thoughts think thoughts" and that the thoughts desiring to *be thought*, worthy to be considered long after the judge's death, are not born from the mind of a thinking subject, but are matterphorical expressions, as such of the body (of many bodies), neither reducible to bits, nor expressible in bytes, let alone representable in language or structured by grammar. It is, in other words, "an attack on the hermeneutic institution of legalism and its exclusion of diversity of thought and feeling."[101]

Haraway, in her call to actually think, reads Eichmann's thoughtlessness – his inability to think – as the inability to entangle, to "track the lines of living and dying," to "cultivate response-ability," and consequently as a surrender to immateriality and inconsequentiality.[102] Thoughts matter and there are still thoughts worthy to be thought, all the way down to "that which must be thought and that which cannot be thought," to the "non-thought within thought," the thought that unthinks the image of thought with all its underlying assumptions. While thinking might provoke general indifference, it is, as Deleuze argues, precisely when the dangers become obvious that the indifference, which has been inherent in the enterprise all along, ceases.[103] Schreber's compulsion to think, his being torn between proving himself capable of reasoning, his engagement with his desire for a different mode of (non-)thinking, and his bodily expressions are, to him, a threat to his existence. The judge is forced to think, to think from some-*body*-else, and to embody thinking differently. He writes, expresses, and transforms. His fear of losing his mind, his embodied thoughts, the miracles and desires, and his becoming-women articulates an embodied theory or a theory of a law that continues sensing its body and acknowledges its being co-constituted by monstrous, indeterminate modes of being embodied in the world. Legal thought, too, is a process. For Deleuze and Guattari, as mentioned before, all becomings "have to begin with and pass through becoming-woman," since it is "the key [*clef*] of all becomings."[104] Perhaps it is less a mistake than a slip that Elizabeth Grosz, when quoting this passage in *Volatile Bodies*, replaces "key" with "law," inscribing law in the becoming of the text and the concept.[105] There is no becoming-man, and even becoming-women is a provisional stage, a line of flight that is, as the "breakdown or shrinkage of all identities, molar and molecular," a "process whose end is achieved only with complete dissolution, the production of the incredible ever-shrinking 'man.'"[106] Perhaps this is why those new human beings created from Schreber's spirit are of significantly "smaller stature than our earthly human beings."[107] And perhaps, by matterphorically approaching the *Denkwürdigkeiten*, synaesethically sensing thoughts worthy of *being thought*, they can be shrunk even further, so that, one day, life, even existence, and law can relate differently.[108]

The last chapter of the *Denkwürdigkeiten* is entitled "Concluding Observations, Outlook into the Future." The *Denkwürdigkeiten* is not a verdict. It offers no decision but contains observations, seeks – for better or worse – to counter-actualize different futures. It is neither a manifesto nor a manual. Rather than diagnosing and prescribing remedies, it is a matterphorical expression of the attempt to sense law synaesethically and to register such sensings *jurisographically*. How to think a legal philosophy that has yet to find its body, and, not only that, whose body has yet to legitimately co-constitute thoughts, including legal thoughts, considered worthy of being thought? How to express such thoughtful materializations and material thoughts, rather than representing them in writing? And, to articulate yet another challenge for those willing to think-with the *Denkwürdigkeiten*, how to approach such expressions synaesethically? Indeed, how to think what cannot be thought, and how to do so without falling into the habits representational modes of thinking that eventually are incapable of preventing a future that threatens to seamlessly connect to a past that has already reached its verdict on what thinking, reason, and law *is*?

In all its madness, the *Denkwürdigkeiten* with its Gods and nerves, rays, wounds, and sound explanations for unsound scenarios provides ample thoughts with which many possible futures are thinkable. Not every actualization is desirable. For once, the text is driven by the anxiety of a former judge about losing his reason and thereby his power to rule, and by his limitless hubris, which leads him to believe that he is the one chosen to not only transcend earth and heavens, but also to outsmart God and eventually become immortal. All of this would fit perfectly well in transhumanist ideas of what it means to become posthuman. It does so because it relies on the same philosophical assumptions, drawing a straight line from humanism to the posthuman (though not posthumanism!) via transhumanism. It is the actualization of the Cartesian privileging of the mind over the body and the fantasy of rational Man as "the sun, the nucleus, the fulcrum, the unifying force, the glue that holds it all together."[109]

However, the future that Schreber envisions is different from transhumanist imaginations. It is influenced by an offspring resulting from his physical transformation and his subsequent impregnation by God, that is, a reunification of law and living body, a reintroduction of the body into the realm of law, not as its object but as its subject. His body transforms in degrees, depending on how it is affected by divine miracles. The more his mind is rendered mad, the more the body transforms. Schreber fell sick of a law that denies bodily materializations their role in constituting what law is, and that nevertheless determines whose existence is thinkable. All in all, whether he admits it or not, the Cartesian tradition, and therefore also transhumanism, is not Schreber's cup of tea. To begin with, he has already ruled out self-disembodiment (*Selbstentleibung*). Schreber himself can imagine only two possible ways out of this mess, that is, two ways towards a possible "solution of the conflict in accordance with the Order of the World," whereas both underscore the centrality of the body: unmanning (*Entmannung*) or cure (*Heilung*).[110] The latter seems improbable to him. It is not he who needs a cure, it is our notion of law, and that, given the state in which it is in, seems even less feasible. Schreber is left with *Entmannung*. Becoming-woman as unmanning, as moving away from and becoming-imperceptible of Man, the rational master subject of law, seems the solution "most in accordance with the inner essence of the Order of the World."[111] The aim is a renewal of humanity (*Erneuerung der Menschheit*), and as such requires the renegotiation of what it means to be human.[112] Schreber states that it is possible that, even if to the end of his days he will be traversed by femaleness, he might "die as a man."[113] In other words, while he can imagine dying as a man, the process of becoming-woman as such is not affiliated with an end point. It is the death of man that interrupts his becoming-woman and makes Schreber wonder whether the unmanning, the un-becoming of man, will ever be fully achieved. The fact that Schreber, ill and mad of law, speaks of a continuous process of becoming-woman, imagines dying as man, and at the same time questions (and even leans towards denying) his mortality (*ob ich überhaupt sterblich sei*) indicates the complexity of a living, transforming, and becoming subject in law. According to the *Denkwürdigkeiten*, humanity has experienced multiple renewals already: "Unmanning for the purpose of humanity's renewal has in all probability actually occurred several times in earlier periods in the history of the universe," Schreber claims.[114] In a way, this makes the *Denkwürdigkeiten* a posthuman, if not yet posthumanist, expression, which bears, as I have attempted to show, the potential to be mobilized as a creative critique of humanist (liberal) legal theory. As such, it draws our attention to an enduring crisis in legal thought, constantly creating rifts and cracks in the structure of law, engendering thoughts that are out of joint and often utterly mad (*verrückt*), and leaving wounds on bodies that can or would prefer not to bend to codified and encoded notions of humanism. As a nineteenth-century German judge, Schreber ultimately remains anthropocentric in his critique of both law and legal thought, pushing for embodied modes of thinking, yet focusing on "human thinking" and reason (*Verstand*). While there certainly is a limit to what Schreber can think, the *Denkwürdigkeiten*, if read with the tools of a mad gardener and loyal traitor, offers possibilities to think further and perhaps even leave the framework of humanism and anthropocentrism. This is precisely where the power and potential of the *Denkwürdigkeiten* (thoughts worthy of being thought), coming from a particular canon and expressing difference from within, reside, and why Goodrich chooses it as a jurisliterary entry point into a practice of legal theory that matters. For it is "in the body, in our sensibility" that "we can feel the beginnings of a style, the stirring of thought, the distant rhythm of a tune we cannot hear."[115] The task for legal theory, expressed through the *Denkwürdigkeiten*, is to develop a *"synaesethics of thought*, neither taking for granted that we already know what it means to think, nor that thought already knows how to encounter relationality."[116] The judge has never left us – at least not for good. She will be back.

NOTES

1 Peter Goodrich, *Schreber's Law: Jurisprudence and Judgment in Transition* (Edinburgh: Edinburgh University Press, 2018), 30.
2 Daniela Gandorfer, *Matterphorics: On the Laws of Theory* (Durham, NC: Duke University Press, forthcoming).
3 Peter Goodrich, *Advanced Introduction to Law and Literature* (Cheltenham, UK: Edward Elgar Publishing, 2021), 92.
4 Gilles Deleuze, "Literature and Life," *Critical Inquiry* 23, no. 2 (1997): 225.
5 Gandorfer, *Matterphorics.*
6 Rosi Braidotti, *Transpositions: On Nomadic Ethics* (Cambridge: Polity, 2008), 166. My emphasis.
7 "We will never ask what a book means, as signified or signifier; we will not look for anything to understand in it. We will ask what it functions with, in connection with what other things it does or does not transmit intensities." Gilles Deleuze and Félix Guattari, *A Thousand Plateaus: Capitalism and Schizophrenia*, trans. Brian Massumi (Minneapolis: University of Minnesota Press, 2014), 4.
8 Donna J. Haraway, *Staying with the Trouble: Making Kin in the Chthulucene* (Durham, NC: Duke University Press, 2016), 57.
9 Deleuze and Guattari, *Thousand Plateaus*, 44.
10 Antonio Negri, *The Savage Anomaly: The Power of Spinoza's Methaphysics and Politics*, trans. Michael Hardt (Minneapolis: University of Minnesota Press, 1991), xxi.
11 As my analysis is bound by the *Denkwürdigkeiten* and by the degree to which it pushes conceptions of mind and body, the notion of bodies in this chapter is limited. However, my broader work argues that bodies are entangled onto-epistemological expressions. In doing so, my understanding of bodies is informed by process philosophers such as Baruch Spinoza, Gilles Deleuze, Henri Bergson, as well as Karen Barad, who argues that bodies, "not merely 'human' bodies," are not to be understood as already existing and fixed entities, but are "integral

'parts' of, or dynamic reconfigurings of, what is." Karen Barad, *Meeting the Universe Halfway: Quantum Physics and the Entanglement of Matter and Meaning* (Durham, NC: Duke University Press, 2007), 152, 70.

12 For a detailed and nuanced overview of the field, see Goodrich's work, such as Goodrich, "Screening Law," *Law and Literature* 21, no. 1 (2009): 1–23; Goodrich, *Schreber's Law;* Goodrich, *Advanced Introduction to Law and Literature* (Cheltenham, UK: Edward Elgar Publishing, 2021), 90–108.

13 Jacques Derrida, *The Monolingualism of the Other: The Prosthesis of Origin* (Stanford, CA: Stanford University Press, 1998), 10.

14 Peter Goodrich, "Transhumusians: On the Jurisography of the Corpus Iuris," *Theory & Event* 24, no. 1 (2021): 117–30.

15 Daniela Gandorfer, "Introduction: What Is Your Power?," in *Research Handbook on Law and Literature*, ed. Peter Goodrich, Daniela Gandorfer, and Cecilia Gebruers (Cheltenham, UK: Edward Elgar Publishing, forthcoming).

16 Goodrich, *Schreber's Law*, 10.

17 Goodrich, *Schreber's Law*, 3, 21.

18 Daniel Paul Schreber, *Denkwürdigkeiten Eines Nervenkranken: Nebst Nachtraegen Und Einem Anhang Über Die Frage: Unter Welchen Voraussetzungen Darf Eine Fuer Geisteskrank Erachtete Person Gegen Ihren Erklaerten Willen in Einer Heilanstalt Festgehalten Werden?* (Leipzig: Oswald Muke, 1903), 182, 224. For convenience I mainly use the English translation by Ida Macalpine and Richard A. Hunter, except in cases where I suggest a different translation and thus cite the original German text.

19 Goodrich, *Schreber's Law*, 5.

20 Samuel Weber, "Introduction," in Schreber, *Memoirs of My Nervous Illness* (Cambridge, MA: Harvard University Press, 1988) xlvii.

21 See, for example, Alexander G. Weheliye, *Habeas Viscus: Racializing Assemblages, Biopolitics, and Black Feminist Theories of the Human* (Durham, NC: Duke University Press, 2014), chap. 5; Stephen Michael Best, *The Fugitive's Properties: Law and the Poetics of Possession* (Chicago: University of Chicago Press, 2004).

22 Schreber, *Denkwürdigkeiten*, 10–11, 22.

23 Schreber, *Denkwürdigkeiten*, 7–8.

24 Schreber, *Denkwürdigkeiten*, 55.

25 Schreber, *Memoirs*, 42.

26 Elisabeth A. Grosz and Pheng Cheah, "The Body of the Law: Notes toward a Theory of Corporeal Justice," in *Thinking through the Body of the Law*, ed. Judith Grbich, David Fraser, and Pheng Cheah (St. Leonards, Australia: Allen & Unwin, 1996), 3.

27 Anna Grear, *Redirecting Human Rights: Facing the Challenge of Corporate Legal Humanity* (Basingstoke, UK: Palgrave Macmillan, 2010), 114.

28 Ngaire Naffine, *Law's Meaning of Life: Philosophy, Religion, Darwin and the Legal Person* (Oxford: Hart, 2009), 147.

29 Grear, *Redirecting Human Rights*, 42.

30 Ngaire Naffine, "The Body Bag," in *Sexing the Subject of Law*, ed. Ngaire Naffine and Rosemary Owens (North Ryde, NSW [u.a.]: LBC Information Services Sweet & Maxwell, 1997), 84; Naffine, *Law's Meaning of Life*, 144.

31 Margrit Shildrick, *Embodying the Monster: Encounters with the Vulnerable Self* (London: Sage, 2002), 51.

32 On "morphological difference," see Shildrick, *Embodying the Monster*. Especially literature on disability and transgender studies contribute indispensable work on how to challenge the idea of the inherent value of the fixed, white, male, and able body. Although it might prove useful to read Schreber's transformation through this work, I would be able to perform a reading based only on the *Denkwürdigkeiten*. Therefore, to a large degree, it would remain detached from a situated and embodied account and run counter to many attempts to re-inscribe the embodied and positioned subject in theoretical thought.

33 David Delaney, "Afterword: Lively Ever After: Beyond the Cult of Immateriality," in *Animals, Biopolitics, Law: Lively Legalities*, ed. Irus Braverman (New York: Routledge, 2016), 215.

34 Elisabeth A. Grosz and Pheng Cheah, "The Body of the Law: Notes toward a Theory of Corporeal Justice," in *Thinking through the Body of the Law*, ed. Judith Grbich, David Fraser, and Pheng Cheah (St. Leonards, Australia: Allen & Unwin, 1996), 3.

35 I have shown the differential meanings of falling elsewhere in more detail. See Gandorfer, *Matterphorics*.

36 Gilles Deleuze, *Difference and Repetition*, trans. Paul Patton (New York: Columbia University Press, 1994), 139.

37 "Ganz besonders häufig werden seit Jahren in tausendfältiger Wiederholung nur einzelne Konjunktionen oder Adverbialwendungen, die zur Einleitung von Relativsätzen bestimmt sind, in meine Nerven hineingesprochen, denen dann die Ausfüllung der Relativsätze mit irgendwelchem, dem denkenden Geiste genügendem Inhalt überlassen bleibt." Schreber, *Denkwürdigkeiten*, 217.

38 Schreber, *Denkwürdigkeiten*, 217.

39 Schreber, *Denkwürdigkeiten*, 223n96.

40 Schreber, *Denkwürdigkeiten*, 126.

41 Schreber, *Denkwürdigkeiten*, 219.

42 Gilles Deleuze and Félix Guattari, *What Is Philosophy?*, trans. Janis Tomlinson and Graham Burchell III (New York: Columbia University Press, 1994), 72.

43 Schreber, *Denkwürdigkeiten*, 131.
44 Schreber, *Memoirs of My Nervous Illness* [Denkwürdigkeiten eines Nervenkranken], trans. Ida Macalpine and Richard A. Hunter (Cambridge, MA: Harvard University Press, 1988), 132.
45 Schreber, *Denkwürdigkeiten*, 287; Schreber, *Memoirs*, 153.
46 Schreber, *Denkwürdigkeiten*, 224.
47 Schreber, *Memoirs*, 144.
48 Gilles Deleuze, *Difference and Repetition* (New York: Columbia University Press, 1995), 130.
49 Haraway, *Staying with the Trouble*, 36. My emphasis.
50 Haraway, *Staying with the Trouble*, 47.
51 Judith Butler, "Hannah Arendt's Death Sentences," *Comparative Literature Studies* 48, no. 3 (2011): 280; Hannah Arendt, *Eichmann in Jerusalem: A Report on the Banality of Evil* (New York: Penguin, 2006), 49.
52 Arendt, *Eichmann in Jerusalem*, 48; Shoshana Felman, "Theaters of Justice: Arendt in Jerusalem, the Eichmann Trial, and the Redefinition of Legal Meaning in the Wake of the Holocaust," *Critical Inquiry* 27, no. 2 (2001): 204.
53 Arendt, *Eichmann in Jerusalem*, 49.
54 Haraway, *Staying with the Trouble*, 85.
55 See also Lynne Tirrell, "Genocidal Language Games," in *Speech and Harm: Controversies over Free Speech*, ed. Ishani Maitra and Mary Kate McGowan (Oxford: Oxford University Press, 2012).
56 Gandorfer, *Matterphorics*.
57 Luce Irigaray and Michael Marder, *Through Vegetal Being: Two Philosophical Perspectives* (New York: Columbia University Press, 2016), 90.
58 Delaney, "Afterword," 215.
59 Delaney, "Afterword," 213. My emphasis.
60 Jeremy Waldron, "Thoughtfulness and the Rule of Law," *British Academy Review* 18 (2011): 1–11.
61 Mireille Hildebrandt and Jaenne Gaakeer, *Human Law and Computer Law: Comparative Perspectives* (Dordrecht: Springer, 2013), 2.
62 Hildebrandt and Gaakeer, *Human Law and Computer Law*, 5.
63 Karen Barad and Daniela Gandorfer, "Political Desirings: Yearnings for Mattering (,) Differently," *Theory & Event* 24, no. 1 (2021): 18.
64 In mind crimes, Bostrom writes, "The side effect is not external to the AI; rather, it concerns what happens within the AI itself (or within the computational processes it generates)." Bostrom, *Superintelligence* (Oxford: Oxford University Press, 2014), 125.
65 Bostrom, *Superintelligence*, 126.
66 See, for example, SingleEarth, which aims to tokenize nature (https://www.single.earth) or Decentraland, a virtual real estate market (https://decentraland.org).

67 See especially Daniela Gandorfer and Zulaikha Ayub, "Introduction: Matterphorical," *Theory & Event* 24, no. 1 (2021): 2–13.
68 UN General Assembly, "Convention on the Prevention and Punishment of the Crime of Genocide, Art II," 1948, https://www.refworld.org/docid/3ae6b3ac0.html.
69 For a more comprehensive analysis of transhumanism, see chapter 1 of *Matterphorics*.
70 Nick Bostrom, "The Transhumanist FAQ: A General Introduction: Version 2.1," 2003, 4, https://nickbostrom.com/views/transhumanist.pdf.
71 More, "Philosophy of Transhumanism," in *The Transhumanist Reader*, ed. Max More and Natasha Vita-More (Chichester: Wiley, 2013) 4.
72 More, "Philosophy of Transhumanism," 15.
73 Gudrun Frommherz, "Memetics of Transhumanist Imagery," *Visual Anthropology* 26, no. 2 (2013): 147– 159.
74 Hans Moravec, *Mind Children: The Future of Robot and Human Intelligence* (Cambridge, MA: Harvard University Press, 1988), 4.
75 Moravec, *Mind Children*, 109.
76 Moravec, *Mind Children*, 110.
77 Bostrom, "Transhumanist FAQ."
78 N. Katherine Hayles, *How We Became Posthuman: Virtual Bodies in Cybernetics, Literature, and Informatics* (Chicago: University of Chicago Press, 1999), 2.
79 Hayles, *How We Became Posthuman*, xi.
80 A, "Arch-Anarchy," *Extropy: Vaccine for Future Shock*, ed. Max More and Tom Bell (Winter 1990): 13, 17.
81 Schreber, *Denkwürdigkeiten*, 55, 155.
82 Schreber, *Memoirs*, 135.
83 Schreber, *Memoirs*, 135–6.
84 Schreber, *Memoirs*, 202.
85 Schreber, *Memoirs*, 179.
86 Schreber, *Memoirs*, 179.
87 Benjamin Alarie, "The Path of the Law: Toward Legal Singularity," *University of Toronto Law Journal* 66, no. 4 (2016): 443–55.
88 Alfred North Whitehead, *Modes of Thought* (New York: Free Press, 1968), 13.
89 John O. McGinnis and Steven Wasick, "Law's Algorithm," *Florida Law Review* 66, no. 3 (2015): 1049.
90 McGinnis and Wasick, "Law's Algorithm," 1022.
91 Benjamin Alarie, Anthony Niblett, and Albert H. Yoon, "Law in the Future," *University of Toronto Law Journal* 66, no. 4 (2016): 428.
92 Alarie, "Path of the Law," 445.
93 Alarie, "Path of the Law," 443, 445, 446.

94 Max Tegmark, *Life 3.0: Being Human in the Age of Artificial Intelligence* (New York: Alfred A. Knopf, 2017), 105.
95 Tegmark, *Life 3.0*, 105.
96 "Civil Law Rules on Robotics – European Parliament Resolution of 16 February 2017 with Recommendations to the Commission on Civil Law Rules on Robotics (2015/2103(INL))," European Parliament, 2015/2017, https://www.europarl.europa.eu/doceo/document/TA-8-2017-0051_EN.html.
97 John Perry Barlow, "A Declaration of the Independence of Cyberspace," in *Crypto Anarchy, Cyberstates, and Pirate Utopias*, ed. Peter Ludlow (Cambridge, MA: MIT Press, 2001), 30.
98 John Harris, "Taking the Human out of Human Rights," *Cambridge Quarterly of Healthcare Ethics* 20, no. 1 (2011): 17.
99 In his introduction to the *Transhumanist Reader*, Max More responds to the critique according to which transhumanists are dualists by pointing to the transhumanist commitment to "functionalism." Mental states such as beliefs and desires, More argues, "consist of their causal role. That is, mental states are causal relations to other mental states, sensory inputs, and behavioral outputs. Because mental states are constituted by their functional role, they can be realized on multiple levels and manifested in many systems, including nonbiological systems, so long as that system performs the appropriate functions." In other words, whatever the material form of the body is, it functions only as what sustains the functionality of mental states, which are in turn what produce thought and meaning. That is to say, when More states that currently many transhumanists "accept some form of functionalism" and would agree that the "self has to be instantiated in *some* physical medium but not necessarily one that is biologically human – or biological at all," then this physical medium is inherently different from what we understand as body. Not only as a result of its material make-up, but, most importantly, in the fact that for transhumanists the body is a machine that sustains and, as they hope, even improves the capacity and power of the intelligent mind. More, "Philosophy of Transhumanism," 7.
100 Goodrich, *Schreber's Law*, 87, 100, 30.
101 Goodrich, *Advanced Introduction*, 96.
102 Haraway, *Staying with the Trouble*, 36.
103 Deleuze and Guattari, *What Is Philosophy?*, 41.
104 Deleuze and Guattari, *Thousand Plateaus*, 277.
105 Elizabeth Grosz, *Volatile Bodies* (Bloomington: Indiana University Press, 1994), 173.
106 Grosz, *Volatile Bodies*, 178.
107 Schreber, *Memoirs*, 112.

108 Examples for important contemporary feminist philosophy that focus on embodiment and matter are, among others, the works of Karen Barad, Rosi Braidotti, Donna Haraway, Elizbeth Grosz, Erin Manning, and Stacy Alaimo. In regard to Western legal theory, the works of, for example, Andreas Philippopoulos-Mihalopoulos, David Delaney, and Margret Davis are important contributions to a more post-anthropocentric and materialist approach to law. The works of many Indigenous scholars, or scholars working on Indigenous legal thought – such as Christine Black or Val Napoleon – push against the rigid Cartesian and exclusively human-centred approach Western legal thought has established.

109 Karen Barad, *Meeting the Universe Halfway: Quantum Physics and the Entanglement of Matter and Meaning* (Durham, NC: Duke University Press, 2007), 134.

110 Schreber, *Denkwürdigkeiten*, 124.

111 Schreber, *Denkwürdigkeiten*, 289.

112 This is indicated by the German suffix "*-heit*" in *Menschheit*, which translates as "-ness" (humanness) or "-tiy" (humanity). Schreber, *Denkwürdigkeiten*, 289.

113 Schreber, *Denkwürdigkeiten*, 289.

114 Schreber, *Memoirs*, 134, 212.

115 Peter Goodrich, "The Pure Theory of Law Is a Hole in the Ozone Layer," *University of Colorado Law Review* 92 (2021): 1007.

116 Gandorfer, "Introduction: What Is Your Power?"

7 Schreber's *Grande Bellezza*

PATRICIA GHEROVICI

Freud's study of Schreber can be considered the first psychoanalytic inquiry on transsexualism. Schreber's paper, however, is an oddity in Sigmund Freud's case studies – he never met the person he analysed. In fact, Freud indulged in what might be an egregious example of the "wild analysis" he advised against: he read the *Memoirs* and then wrote a detailed analysis of the author's delusions, in which he recognized an exemplary case of paranoid dementia. For Jacques Lacan, the situation was clear from the start: "The Schreber case is for us also Schreber's text."[1] He noted that the text is "no doubt exceptional, but it is certainly not unique."[2] As Trüstedt's analysis of Schreber's rewriting of the laws of legal procedure shows (see chapter 4), his success in litigating his own release by means of the *Memoirs* might contest Lacan's view of lack of uniqueness, but Lacan wanted to highlight something paradigmatic in the singular circumstances of the case and speculated that what made the *Memoirs* unique was that they got published, even in a censored version, and that Freud took an interest in them. Nevertheless, Lacan admits that "Schreber was *exceptionally gifted*, as he himself puts it, at observing phenomena of which he is the center and at searching for their truth, makes his testimony incomparably valuable."[3]

Schreber had spent six years in a private psychiatric clinic and, as soon as he felt he had sufficiently recovered, he wrote a thorough account of his illness to argue in court for his discharge from the asylum. It secured Schreber's freedom and made him into an *avant-la-lettre* anti-psychiatry advocator. *Memoirs of My Nervous Illness* is also the first-person account of psychosis most often discussed in psychiatric literature as well as one of the first sex-change memoirs. *Memoirs of My Nervous Illness* was published in 1903 and became a sort of best-seller. Both Freud and Jung were intrigued by the book and its author to whom Freud referred to as "my wonderful Schreber." Indeed, partly because of Freud's essay, the

Memoirs have attracted a lot of attention although, ironically, not from lawyers, and not for the significant contribution to upending jurisprudence that Rajgopal and Trüstedt both stress in their contributions to this volume.

Daniel Paul Schreber was born in 1842 to an upper-class family in Leipzig. His father was a prominent orthopaedic physician, writer, educator, and reformer endowed with endless missionary zeal, a reputed authority on hygiene and child rearing. The complex delusional world of Schreber had a centre – his body, which was the place of an astounding transformation:

> The month of November, 1895, marks an important time in the history of my life and in particular in my own ideas of the possible shaping of my future. ... During that time the signs of a transformation into a woman became so marked on my body, that I could no longer ignore the imminent goal at which the whole development was aiming. In the immediately preceding nights my male sexual organ might actually have been retracted had I not resolutely set my will against it, still following the stirring of my sense of manly honour; so near completion was the miracle. Soul voluptuousness had become so strong that I myself received the impression of a female body, first in my arms and hands, later on my legs, bosom, buttocks and other parts of my body.[4]

Beset by persecutory delusions about his doctor, Schreber had been dominated by the conviction that he was going to change into a woman; then, he would become God's bride, a consenting prey to God's voluptuous pleasures. Following some catastrophe, together they would engender a new race of Schreberian creatures and repopulate the earth.

Lacan's highly original interpretation of the Freudian Oedipus complex was buttressed by his careful reading of the *Memoirs*. Lacan started the study of Schreber in the first two terms of the 1955–16 seminar *The Psychoses*.[5] After returning systematically to his 1932 doctoral thesis on paranoia, the seminar moved to explore hysteria by addressing the question "What is a woman?" The thematic progression of the seminar confirmed that psychosis opens the way to a new formulation about hysteria and feminine sexuality. Above all, Lacan found in Schreber an exemplary case to explore what a father means, precisely because Lacan argued that Schreber lacked what makes paternity possible – the signifier. The function of being a father, which Lacan argues is dependent on language, and thus is "absolutely unthinkable in the human experience without the signifier."[6]

This father deficit in Schreber was the key: "President Schreber lacks this fundamental signifier called *being a father*. This is why he had to make a mistake, become confused, to the point of thinking of acting like a woman. He had to imagine himself a woman and bring about in the second part of the path that, when the two are added together, was necessary for the function of *being a father* to be realized."[7]

Lacan offered an almost line-by-line reading of Freud's essay alongside Schreber's *Memoirs*. Both Freud and Lacan centre their analyses of the psychosis on the function of the father. Freud's thesis has the merit of simplicity. For him, Schreber's transformation into a woman implied a feminine position toward the father, that is, a castration. According to Freud, Schreber's repressed homosexual relationship to his father was reawakened by his relationship to his doctor, Professor Flechsig. Schreber developed a massive transference that led to his persecutory delusion, which centred on his eventual transformation into God's wife.[8] In this view, Schreber's evolution showed first a rejection, then an acceptance of his transformation into a woman. Finally, in his cure, the cultivation of a female persona itself was to acquire a stabilizing effect.

The transformation originally experienced by Schreber as an invasion by God that caused him indignation was understood by Lacan[9] also as connected with some basic bisexuality: "In President Schreber's case this rejected meaning is closely related to the primitive bisexuality."[10] But for Lacan, homosexuality played a secondary role in the interpretation of the case: "In no way has President Schreber ever introjected any type of feminine form."[11] For Lacan, castration had not operated – Schreber was confronted with the enigma of sexual difference without a signifier to create relations of classification and filiation. The missing meaning for Schreber was related to bisexuality insofar as bisexuality "involves the feminine function in its essential symbolic meaning ... at the level of procreation."[12] Schreber had managed to navigate his life with a dormant psychosis, without the inscription of a main signifier. The breakdown took place when he was promoted to the top of the legislative structure, a position of authority that required "something of himself that he ... never symbolized,"[13] or, again, the father – here is the moment when a father as a signifier of the Law was summoned, but in the case of Schreber, it was missing.

Lacan differs from Freud's speculation that Schreber's psychosis is the result of the repression of his passive homosexual position vis-à-vis the father. Lacan insisted that what was not simply repressed, but more drastically rejected, was not a homosexual desire for the father but the Name-of-the-Father, which meant rewriting Freud's theory of psychosis by summing up the theory of the Oedipus complex in a formula hinging on the paternal metaphor: the father's function (to impose the law and regulate desire) was reduced to a signifier that intervened in the mother-child dyad and offered a substitute for the child in the desire of the mother. The father's prohibition "castrates" the child because he introduces a "no" that separates the child from the mother; at the same time, it is also a "yes" that gives the child his Name, a place in the family genealogy, a signifier of self and subjectivity that grants access to culture and civilization.

The Name-of-the-Father is thus defined as a key signifier granting access to phallic signification; it is the factor that allows the subject to bestow meaning to signifiers and adopt a position as male or female in the basic sexual division. Lacan stresses the role of the father in the promotion of the Law, which founds humanity – this signifier of the Law allows the emergence of the subject as represented by the Name-of-the-Father.

Separated from the mother, the child can become a desiring subject. By accepting the father's Law, the child moves from the pure register of being (the phallus) to the register of having (a legitimate desire). The child internalizes the Law by identification with the father. This Law is a liberating force; it puts a limit to the cruelty of the archaic superego.

However, if the father does not fulfil his function or if any representative of the Law – who may or may not be a father per se but is placed in that position – fails, then the subject is at a loss and lacks the regulation of the post-Oedipal superego. What is more, for Lacan, the failure of the paternal metaphor leaves the subject at the mercy of a superego that internalizes the voice of a persecutory, obscene, and ferocious Kantian-Sadean father: "This superego is something like the law, but it's a law without dialectic, and it's not nothing that it is recognizable, more or less correctly, in the categorical imperative."[14] This senseless law destroys the Law, because without a father who is castrated who transmits a Law that he is also subjected to, the Law loses its normative meaning. Developing the implications of the paternal failure, Lacan writes,

> The father's relation to the law must be considered in its own right, for one will find in it the reason of the paradox whereby devastating effects of the paternal figure are found with particular frequency in cases where the father really functions as a legislator or boasts that he does – whether he is, in fact, as a paragon of integrity or devotion, as virtuous or a virtuoso, as serving a charitable cause whatever the object or lack thereof that is at stake, as serving the nation or birth rate, safety or salubrity, legacy or law, the pure, the lowest of the low, or the empire. These are all ideals that

> provide him with all too many opportunities to seem to be at fault, to fall short, and even to be fraudulent – in short, to exclude the Name-of-the-Father from its position as signifier.[15]

Furthermore, the father is a function, the Law is the Law of the Father, as he is the agent and the source that gives to the Law its foundation and legitimacy. When the father fails, the reasons often exceed psychobiographical minutiae.

> That for example the father is deficient in the sense that he is too stupid, is not what is essential. What is essential is that in one way or another, the subject has acquired the dimension of the Name-of-the-Father.
>
> Of course what actually happens, and you can glean this from biographies, is that the father is often there in the kitchen doing the dishes and wearing the wife's apron. This is not sufficient to make a schizophrenic.[16]

Lacan speculated that for Schreber the Name-of-the-Father was foreclosed and the Real was summoned in place of the Symbolic. Lacan argued that Schreber was unable to substitute the signifier of the Name-of-the-Father for another signifier – the desire of the mother. Lacan's causation of Schreber's psychosis needs to be read structurally and not biographically as William G. Niederland's[17] does in his portrait of the Schreber father as an abuser, or Zvi Lothane's interpreting the illness of Schreber as a melancholic psychosis aggravated by the harassment of involuntary internment in the Asylum where he was likely subjected to sexual abuse.[18] As Damien Riggs[19] argues, both explanations are anecdotal and seem to neglect a factor that is central in this case – the role of Schreber's mother. In contradistinction to Tarizzo's brilliant theory of the judge's resistance to the real of the other's body, presented at the end of this volume, a more complex picture emerges if we address the figure of maternal mediation that plays such a crucial role in Schreber's relation to the Law.

Indeed, Schreber's mother, Pauline, plays an important role, as the mother can become the conduit to what Geneviève Morel[20] calls the law of the mother. This is a law of unbounded, unregulated jouissance from which children need to separate in order to develop their sexual identity. The "hard" Law will be introduced by the father or whomever the mother identifies as such. Thus it gives to the mother a central stake because the father is to be found in the mother's speech. A "natural" father may "recognize" a child not as the consequence of his role in procreation but as the result of the mother's attribution of this privileged function. The father's "no" that promotes the law, relies on a power bestowed by the mother, in the place she attributes to the Name-of-the-Father. It is this triad of mother, father, and child, the father has to be recognized by the mother as both a man and a representative of the law that applies to both her and the child. The father's intervention via language already constitutes a law, since language has rules and laws. If his agency is acknowledged by the mother, the father's word acquires the value of a Law. Let us note that despite the fact that Lacan reserves a privileged place for the Name-of-the-Father in the promotion of the law, the authority of the father is like the transmission of Jewish religion, which is strictly matrilineal.

Schreber's case shows a father who was an exceptional, excessive father, an apostle of child education who operated as an unbarred Other not subjected to symbolic castration – not just as a representative of the Law but rather as the Law itself. His father was not so much the bearer of the symbolic Law (hence capitalized) as the bearer of the commandments of an absurd law, which legitimated nothing. How could Schreber abide by the law of phallic signification when that Law was foreclosed? For Lacan, the Name-of-the-Father is primordial because it gives to the Law its authority. Because for Schreber the signifier of the Name-of-the-Father of the father is not available, there is no legitimate place for him in the Law.

Schreber's feminization, described in the 1950s by Lacan[21] as only imaginary, must be understood more generally as having effects at the level of the three registers of the Symbolic, Real, and Imaginary.[22] His feminization is an invention that grants him a "transsexualist jouissance." This is where we catch a manifestation of jouissance in his body, or what Lacan calls the Real. It is imaginary, as witnessed by Schreber's bliss in looking at his feminized image in the mirror, and it has also a symbolic reference: the woman as an exception, "the" woman, who will copulate with God and create a new world order by providing a new generation is a Name-of-the-Father in disguise, as we shall see.

For Lacan, in Schreber's case the paternal metaphor had failed and his transformation into a woman worked as a supplement, a stand-in for the missing phallic signifier in the Symbolic. "I consider my right and in a certain sense my duty to cultivate feminine feelings which I am enabled to do by the presence of nerves of voluptuousness."[23] Because castration does not operate, there is a gap in signification and the orientation is displaced from the signifier to the axiom of jouissance without any symbolic protection. Thus the "excess of voluptuousness"[24] that Schreber experienced as an invasion. Schreber's excessive, "inescapable" voluptuousness, "God's demands for *constant enjoyment,*" "which ... might be considered immoral,"[25] become regulated by his transformation into a woman, which frames jouissance.

In the end, Schreber was driven to become a woman, not just any woman, but God's wife, the anointed person who would give birth to a new human race. This transformation into a woman functions for Schreber as the certainty of the prospect of a future. The potential but ineluctable transformation sustains him because it makes up for the deficiencies in the Name-of-the-Father while being a correlate of his transsexual jouissance. For Marie-Hélène Brousse,[26] Lacan's reading of Freud's analysis in the Schreber case reveals that the latter's drive to become a woman is not a contingent feature but a logically and necessary structural element that one should look for in psychoses, even when it does not manifest itself clinically.

In his study of the *Memoirs*, Freud had stated that Schreber's idea of transformation into a woman was "the earliest germ of the delusional system. It also proved to be the one part of it that persisted after his cure, and the one part that was able to retain a place in his behavior in real life after he had recovered."[27] Following Freud's path, Lacan stressed the core function of Schreber's transformation into a woman and wondered whether this was a "properly psychotic mechanism, one that would be imaginary and that would extend from the first hint of identification with and capture by the feminine image, to the blossoming of a world system in which the subject is completely absorbed in his imagination by a feminine identification."[28] What should interest us at this point is that it was in his commentary of the Schreber case that Lacan presented imaginary mechanisms that he later systematized under the name of "the push-towards-Woman." Lacan used the phrase in 1972 when he referred to Schreber's transformation into a woman, which he explained as the result of the sudden, violent entrance of a father, the representative of the law of the signifier: "I could here, by developing the inscription that I made through a hyperbolic function of Schreber's psychosis, demonstrate in what it contains of the sardonic the effect of the push-to-the-woman which is specified in the first quantifier; having made very clear that it is from the irruption of One-Father as without reason that is precipitated here the effect felt as of forcing, in the field of an Other to be thought as the most foreign in every sense."[29]

The coining of the phrase "push-towards-Woman" derives from Lacan's 1957–8 text "On a Question Prior to Any Possible Treatment of Psychosis," which condenses his year-long seminar on psychoses quoted above but is used mostly in 1972. Then the phrase "push-towards-Woman" appears directly linked to the paternal function, as the result of the "irruption of *One-Father*" (italics in the original), the same *One-Father* alluded to in "On a Question…." In the earlier text, the *One-Father* was presented as being at the dramatic conjuncture that marked the beginning of each case of psychosis. This *One-Father* is not the subject's own father, but rather the signifier of paternity as a legal fiction. This real father is the agent for a metaphor, an agent represented by a signifier summoned by a contingency of life. This missing or foreclosed signifier "presents itself to a woman who has just given birth, in her husband's face, to a penitent confessing her sins in the person of her confessor, or to a girl in love in her encounter 'with the young man's father.'"[30]

Thus the *One-Father*, foreclosed in the symbolic, comes back as real jouissance, and it can also be embodied in a female form. The concept of push-towards-Woman completely refutes the Freudian hypothesis of an unconscious homosexuality as determinant for the sexual causality of psychosis but confirms Lacan's primacy given to the father as bearer of the Law. If, as Brousse claims, "the push-towards-woman is a theory of the sexual partner in psychosis, a way of thinking about the sexual partner,"[31] it is more specifically the sexual partner's jouissance that is at stake. This jouissance cannot be symbolized, because the phallic signifier the father represents has been foreclosed. Brousse identifies in the push-towards-Woman a specific way by which the subject related to the Other, not just any Other, but an Other of sensual pleasure, in other words, of jouissance. The push-towards-Woman is thus a construction that expresses an interpretation of jouissance in terms of its very feminization.

In contrast, for Catherine Millot, feminization was a sign of psychosis in primary transsexuality.[32] Other psychoanalysts have considered the push-towards-Woman as a more generalized phenomenon. Going further, Franz Kaltenbeck[33] proposed the application of the "*pousse-à-la-femme*" to all clinical structures, while always keeping in mind a differential diagnosis. Kaltenbeck[34] considers the "push-towards-Woman" in psychosis to be the opposite of the attraction toward a woman one finds in neuroses and perversions. Moreover, the push-towards-Woman has been observed both in men and in women. Kaltenbeck calls the push-towards-Woman a "clinical belvedere," that is, a vantage viewpoint for any gender and for all structures proposed by Lacan (neurosis, perversion, and psychosis). This is why Eric Laurent[35] sees it not as a phenomenological category but as a logical concept related to the drive that problematizes Freud's argument about the libido being masculine.

Lacan's term "*pousse-à-la-femme*" could be more accurately rendered in English as "driving one to become a woman," if "drive" were not already a technical concept translating Freud's *Trieb.* The concept was perfectly described by Renée Richards, the famous transgender tennis player, who created a media frenzy in 1976 when she went to court and won the right to play as a woman in the U.S. Open. She was asked at age seventy-two about the motivations for her gender transition more than thirty years before. Richards described her decision to change gender as resulting from an unyielding "pressure to change into a woman."[36] This provides an adequate translation of Lacan's expression. Richards describes the evolution as inevitable; the imperative to turn into a woman also had been a strategy to resolve a life-or-death situation: "The pressure to change into a woman was so strong that if I had not been able to do it, I might have been a suicide."[37] Schreber's description of his transformation into a woman also conveys this sense of an imposed force, of a drive pulling him into an inevitable sexual metamorphosis that eventually restores life.[38]

For Schreber the first indication of a transsexual transformation came in a thought linked to women's sexual enjoyment. Schreber indeed speculated "that after all it really must be rather beautiful to be a woman submitting to the act of copulation."[39] In Schreber's mind, this notion evolved and finally led to the voluptuous debauchery that he would not hesitate to attribute to God. What stands out, as Brousse[40] has reminded us, is that the "push-towards-Woman" is not an Oedipal phenomenon (it is not a push-towards-mother), and, moreover, that the Freudian thesis of an unconscious homosexuality fails.

As we have seen, the push-towards-Woman that he resisted with indignation but experienced as inevitable, functions for Schreber as the prospect of a future, the potential transformation still sustains him because it makes up for the deficiencies in the Name-of-the-Father and is a correlate of his transsexual jouissance. As Stijn Vanjeule[41] observes, Lacan suggests that before the construction of the delusional metaphor, "the subject has died."[42] He comes back to life by an invention that compensates for the absence of the Name-of-the-Father and restores order in the chaos. However, as we know from the whole context of the *Memoirs,* Schreber had to resort to his delusions in order to fight back against a domineering father whose desire to control his son's body could be compensated only by a wild drift away from this imposed orthopaedic normality, in the same way as his parody of a God who, despite his power, has no understanding of humanity, constitutes a rejection of the compulsive religiosity of his family.

For Lacan, as for Freud, the pattern described by Schreber nevertheless places him on the side of psychosis. Was Schreber really a "psychotic"? For me, what is important is that he was Freud's and Lacan's transsexual. The stress would fall on "trans" more than on "sexual," as Deleuze and Guattari understood it well when they stated that Schreber was "not simply bisexual, or between the two, or intersexual. He is transsexual. He is trans-alivedead, trans-parentchild."[43] Indeed, Schreber wrote that he felt his body hovering between life and death, as he was destined to be regenerated thanks to a mystical transition from man to woman. The key, then, is to underline that Schreber's conviction that he was going to become a woman is not a case of transgender "identity." What links him with the trans problematic is on the contrary his hesitation about being alive as such.[44] Hence Schreber will not become just a woman (or change his gender) but will become Woman: here is a founding exception that can function as a sort of name-of-the-father.

Note that here the name-of-the-father is not capitalized because Woman is not the Name-of-the-Father but the name of an agency of presymbolic unrestrained power, unrestricted by the Law of castration. Woman amounts to a myth similar to that of the father in Freud's analysis of the primal horde of "Totem and Taboo." According to the myth, all the sons accept the law and abide by it, in contrast to the "primal father." The primal father stands out as the exception to the law because he has access to unlimited jouissance. However, it is this same exception to the law that secures it. Such a position of exclusion can be occupied by a tyrant, by Woman, by a lawless mother, and so on. Woman as such appears as both a limit and a substitute for the paternal function while granting access to unlimited jouissance. Both the father of the primal horde and Woman are a mythical starting point of unbridled fullness whose "primordial repression" constitutes the symbolic order. By placing Woman (the one that Lacan argues does not exist) as one of the names-of-father, castration is repudiated because Woman represents a position unencumbered by any prohibition. Schreber's transformation into a Woman is his strategy of survival when the Law fails.

The main explicit motivation of Schreber's transsexual transformation is that he wanted to become a woman for aesthetic reasons above all. A dream revealed this to him: "It must be very beautiful [*recht schön*] to be a woman succumbing to the act of copulation."[45] As we have seen, according to Freud, the first indication of a transsexual delusion in progress appeared in Schreber's hypnopompic idea that it really must be rather *beautiful* to be a woman subjected to sexual intercourse. This notion evolved and finally led to the voluptuous debauchery that he would not hesitate to attribute to God. This singular phrase that is the centre of Freud's interpretation of the case has not attracted much attention among the many commentators of the *Memoirs*. As Janine

Chasseguet-Smirgel notes, Schreber does not say that it would be "amusing, pleasant or voluptuous" but rather "*beautiful* to be a woman succumbing to the act of copulation."[46] This phrase combines beauty with what Freud called the "biological bedrock," an imperative "repudiation of the feminine" common to both sexes. What is the value of beauty for Schreber? Does beauty allow him to tolerate a transformation bound to happen, assuaging what he first experienced as persecution, "a threatening ignominy"[47] a difficult and injurious process of "unmanning"?

The preoccupation with beauty ran deeply in Schreber's family. His father, Dr. Daniel Gottlieb Moritz Schreber, was not only a famous physician but an athlete who proselytized for the benefits of exercise and physical fitness. The elder Schreber popularized the pursuit of a beautiful, healthy body. His preoccupation with a perfectly erect posture, even during sleep, was combined with the use of constraining straps and belts as part of his crusade against children's masturbation. At the age of fifty still, Schreber's father, a body-builder and winner of several fitness contests, used his body as the model for the illustrations in his book *Pangymnasticom*. His biographer observes that "constant training had given his body perfect beauty," a beauty foregrounded by the title of one of his books, *Callipedia or Education towards Beauty through the Natural and Progressive Production of a Normal Body*. Schreber father's pedagogical method exposes an aesthetic preoccupation based on the classical ideals of beauty condensed in the German word *Plastik*. The word "plastic" has roots in both Greek and German. In Greek, "plastic" derives from πλαστικός (plastikos), meaning "capable of being shaped or moulded"; "plastikos" derives from πλαστός (plastos) meaning "moulded," in reference to the malleability of forms, allowing them to be cast, pressed, or extruded into a variety of shapes. In German, "plastic" derives from *Plastik*, meaning "classical sculpture," an art presenting beautiful forms and harmonious arrangement of visual stimuli.

In her groundbreaking meditation *The Future of Hegel*, Catherine Malabou pivots from Hegel's discussion, in *Aesthetics*, of Greek art and sculpture as "the plastic art par excellence." Malabou writes,

> The sense for the perfect plasticity of gods and men was pre-eminently at home in Greece. In its poets and orators, historians and philosophers, Greece is not to be understood at its heart unless we bring with us a key to our comprehension an insight into the ideals of sculpture and unless we consider from the point of view of their plasticity not only the heroic figures in epic and drama but also actual statesman and philosophers. After all, in the beautiful days of Greece, men of action, like poets and thinkers,

> had this same plastic and universal yet individual character both inwardly and outwardly.[48]

Malabou understands "philosophical plasticity" as a philosophical attitude, the behaviour of the philosopher; to her, "philosophical plasticity" applies to philosophy, to the rhythm with which the speculative content is unfolded and presented. In the *Science of Logic*, Hegel states,

> A plastic discourse demands, too, a plastic sense of receptivity and understanding on the part of the listener; but youths and men of such a temper would calmly suppress their own reflections and opinions in which "the need to think for oneself" is so impatient to manifest itself, listeners such as Plato imagined, who would attend only to the matter at hand, could have no place in a modern dialogue; still less could one count on readers of such disposition.[49]

I will not engage with the nuances of Malabou's argument; I will just note that she has chosen to emphasize the idea of a continuous productivity of forms, namely "plasticity," whereas "plastic" by itself hesitates awkwardly between a certain concept of beauty and the technical possibility to transform matter according the canons of beauty. Hence "plastic surgery."

Daniel P. Schreber followed his father's ideal of beauty, but added his own twist when he saw beauty not as a sign of health but as a source of pleasure. He found the feminine body to be the most beautiful body, a site of voluptuousness creating desire for both men and women: "Female nudes stimulate both sexes equally."[50] The female body was a superior form of embodiment to which he aspired, a "miraculous" form that could be frightening. It appeared in moments of intense pleasure, for instance, when playing the piano and "feeling aroused by the beauty of the music."[51]

I will now move on to a wonderful film about beauty in which the positioning of the subject facing the Law takes a turn similar to that experienced by Schreber. The film *La Grande Bellezza*[52] can tell us more about the articulation between beauty, death, and the law. The film begins with a quote about fiction and death from Louis-Ferdinand Céline's epigraph for *Journey into the Night*: "Our journey is entirely imaginary. That is its strength. It goes from life to death. People, animals, cities, things, all are imagined. It's a novel, just a fictional narrative."[53]

If fiction is a better compass to guide us in our journey from life to death, is beauty a mere strategy aiming to ward off death by dressing up decay and obsolescence? Both the protagonist of *La Grande Bellezza* and Daniel Paul Schreber engage in parodic dialogues with beauty, which are also dialogues with death and decay, but they are engaged in a search that can be resolved only under the auspices of a father or an equivalent.

La Grande Bellezza takes us on a travelogue through Rome that brings us from death to life by way of writing. Our guide and the movie's protagonist is Jep Gambardella, a sixty-five-year-old man originally from Naples who has spent four decades enjoying the pleasures of the high life of Rome. A cynical nostalgic, an aging socialite, he lives in subdued despair in a magnificent apartment overlooking the Coliseum. After he published one acclaimed book in his twenties entitled *The Human Apparatus*, he failed to write anything of note in forty years. Ironically, this title could have been a fitting one for Schreber's own memoirs, so concerned with describing the mechanics of his nerves and his body parts.

Now, semi-retired, Jep works occasionally as a journalist but above all enjoys the idle life of the rich. He is a charming high society parasite and drifter who has wasted his potential and spends his time with beautiful women in night-long wild parties. He is also our Virgil who unveils for us the splendour of the Eternal City with the wonder of a tourist. The journey through Rome's famous landmarks is haunted by the shadow of fleeting encounters with death.

Before we meet Jep, in the opening scene of *La Grande Bellezza,* a group of tourists is seen admiring the magnificent view from the Janiculum Hill, overlooking Rome. Suddenly, perhaps overwhelmed by the beauty of the scene, an Asian tourist falls to the ground, perhaps killed by a heart attack or perhaps simply killed by beauty. There are other deaths in Jep's searching travels. The first scene with the collapse of the tourist is followed by a woman's piercing scream. However, she is not a mourner at a funeral but a reveller at Jep's extravagant sixty-fifth birthday party. The celebration leads to a discovery: "The most important thing I discovered a few days after turning sixty-five is that I can't waste any more time doing things I don't want to do." Desire and even caprice seem to replace the social sense of obligation; moreover, with age and its attendant awareness of mortality, beauty is not felt to be a value in itself. Talking to his friend about being with a gorgeous woman, Jep comments, "At my age, beauty isn't enough." Jep has reached a point in life when the veil offered by beauty has been ripped apart, leaving room for more essential questions.

The movie is impressionistic, and its tenuous plot is maintained by a recurring question of why Jep did not write a Great Book. There is a pervasive sense of transience in the film. We can be reminded of Freud's illuminating mediation on beauty and transience. If we know that something beautiful will perish, if we accept that sense of loss, the enjoyment of its beauty may intensify.

One paradox of Sorrentino's film is that even though there are several deaths in the plot, one never feels that Jep is deeply mourning. In preparation for a funeral, he instructs his then girlfriend about the etiquette to follow at a posh burial: to be restrained and sombre, all along pretending to be totally shaken by grief. Nevertheless, when they attend the actual funeral, Jep loses his composure and sobs in public, making the social faux-pas he was cautioning against of never eclipsing the sorrow of the mourning family.

Death is a secondary character in many scenes. There is the offstage death of Jep's first youthful love, the unseen death of a middle-aged stripper, a casual lover who appears on screen asleep looking like an exquisite corpse, the almost inevitable suicide of the delusional son of a socialite, and the presence of a holy living-dead, the 104-year-old nun Sister Maria called "the Saint" because she is soon to be canonized. They are all fellow travellers in the face of beauty and death. Their deaths punctuate Jep's wandering, giving new meaning to his questions.

We can see that the cases of President Schreber and *La Grande Bellezza* are linked by a similar concern for what might be called the hidden law of beauty in its deeper relation to death. Thus one might argue that Schreber's debunking of the father's Law by replacing it with a parody of gospel in which God is a lubricious whore is similar to Sorrentino's relentless satire of Catholicism. Schreber's father embodied a Law that was also a model of aesthetics, given his preoccupation with the orthopaedic beauty of the body. In Sorrentino's film, satirical moments poke fun at Catholicism's mixture of aestheticism and perversity. All the while, these parodic attacks question the very source of beauty by wondering whether the obvious beauty of the city, its statues, monuments, works of art both ancient and contemporary, can be divorced from the theology that perpetuated a concern for beauty that lasted centuries.

Jep Gambardella is lost in a futile life of mundane pleasures, a victim of his meaningless hedonism. He is sunken in a jouissance that seems to bore him while half-heartedly searching for "The Great Beauty" that would bring inspiration for writing and meaning to his life. He tries to find in religion a reason to limit jouissance. And he searches for it in a father, fittingly called Cardinal Belluci (the name derives from the adjective *bello*, "beautiful.") When Jep first approaches the prelate who is rumoured to become the next pope, during a wedding garden party, the cardinal avoids talking to him. All he cares about is sharing elaborate cooking recipes. When on a second opportunity Jep tries again to find in the cardinal's words something of the Name-of-the-Father, the cardinal remains cold and silent before driving away, leaving Jep alone and stranded in his spiritual quest.

Beauty in *La Grande Bellezza* is what remains when you have lost your religious faith, a thin, last veil before death. Similarly, Schreber's beauty is buttressed to protect him from an apocalyptic sense of destruction of human beings compensated by regeneration through children he will bear with God. The promise of beauty after becoming a woman was for Schreber a strategy of survival.

In *The Great Beauty* there is a surrealist scene in which we see a group of people waiting to get injections of Botox and wrinkle fillers in a place that resembles a Weimar cabaret. There the young and the old, the ugly and the pretty, and even a nun, meet a guru-like aesthetician doctor who will deliver quick injections of beauty and eternity. All the clients, with the exception of the nun who wants to fix her sweaty hands, search to embody an aesthetic ideal, maybe to deny their own mortality, as if they were saying, *I know full well that I am mortal, but I am beautiful and ageless.* Cosmetic interventions can grant a new lease on life; the pursuit of beauty promises a renaissance. This resonates with what happened to Schreber after he had been able to write his memoirs and see that the text had been instrumental in obtaining his freedom.

On 29 June 1905, on the occasion of his mother Pauline's ninetieth birthday, President Schreber wrote a poem for her in which on line 15, he exclaims,

> Doch mildernd wirkt auch hier der Zeiten Lauf;
> Er lässt, was schön war, immer schön erscheinen
> [Yet the course of time works soothingly;
> it lets what was beautiful always appear beautiful].[54]

Then, the poem moves on to a self-deprecating note that reiterates the theme of beauty as a gift:

> Ist auch die Kunst gering,
> Wirst Du die Gabe doch nicht ganz verachten:
> So schön just ward's, wie nach den Kräften ging
> [Although the art is scant,
> You will not completely disdain the gift:
> It is as beautiful as my strength could shape it].[55]

Then we can note that the theme of beauty reappears at the conclusion of the rather long and elaborate poem, full of biographical references, often couched as riddles:

Hier stehts, ein Bauwerk night geringer Schöne, Das sein Namen –
hört ich – davon trägt,
Das es der ersten lernbegier'ge Söhne,
Als Musensöhne oft in sich gehegt.[56]
[Here, as always, an edifice of not little beauty
Which has its name, so I have heard,
In that it shelters the first sons
Desirous of learning as sons of the muses].[57]

The answer to this last riddle is "*Fürstenhaus*" that had been mentioned earlier, but the main goal of Schreber seems to have been to have *Schöne* (beauty) rhyme with *Söhne* (sons), whereby he calls himself not only one of his mother's sons (he had a brother, Gustav), but also a "son of the muses," as if, thanks to his mother's longevity and assiduous viduity (she had been a widow for about fifty years when he wrote the poem), he could finally come into his own as a writer. It seems almost too obvious to point to the way his own name, Schreber, can easily suggest *Schreiber,* the one who writes and triumphs.

In this remarkable poem, Schreber celebrates his mother's longevity, the resilience of beauty in spite of all, his inscription in a genealogy marked by suicide and madness (his brother Gustav shot himself in 1877, his father died in 1861 after a debilitating ailment turning into a fully fledged mental illness), and his own power as a writer at last. In this, he announces the positive turn of events that takes place at the end of *La Grande Bellezza.* Jep has finally found his inspiration after a writer's block of half a century. This comes through one of the apparently desultory and banal one-liners given by the "Saint." She is an ascetic, indifferent to the self-indulgent pursuits of pleasure of Jep's social circle. Asked why she eats only roots and disdains the wonderful food served at one lavish dinner, she throws back that "roots are important." Indeed, after years of frustration, Jep's good friend Romano, the other struggling Neapolitan writer marooned in Rome, finally reclaims his origins and decides to head back home to seek his own roots and regain his inspiration. Jep also decides that it is time he should start writing again.

This movement is accomplished only when Jep finds a signifier of the Law to limit his jouissance, an anchoring signifier that will grant him a place in the world. The movie closes with a series of sublime images of Rome and Jep's voice off-screen saying, "This is how it always ends, with death. But first there was life. Hidden beneath the blah, blah, blah. It is all settled beneath the chitter-chatter and the noise. Silence and sentiment. Emotion and fear. The haggard, inconstant flashes of beauty.

And then the wretched squalor and miserable humanity. All buried under the cover of the embarrassment of being in the world. Beyond there is what lies beyond. I don't deal with what lies beyond. Therefore, let this novel begin. After all it's just a trick. Yes, just a trick."

The traveller is no longer lost, he has found his trick – fiction. Writing helps him see life beyond beauty, which works only if there is Law limiting the lawlessness of pure hedonism, a hedonism haunted by death. That Law is to be founded in a "trick" that allows him to combine the Father of the paternal metaphor bringing a limit to jouissance and the creative *pseudos* allowing the divided subject to find a truth via fiction. The result may not be a new best-seller, as his first novel had been, for it could as well embody Flaubert's dream of a book about nothing. If it was so, Jep and Schreber would meet: both have found a certain freedom in a creative nothing. Schreber insists in the *Memoirs* of his "freedom to think about nothing."[58] Schreber has moved away from the thoughts imposed from the exterior arriving to his mind as hallucinations. He can put some distance between his subjectivity and the "inspired" or constant compulsive thinking about a terrifying God, even if he does not recant his religious system. What matters is that he has been able to argue for his release from the carceral system of the asylum in his writing. He is not totally free in his mind, but he can combine his being a son with a different appreciation of beauty. This is also what Jep tells us at the end of *La Grande Bellezza.*

NOTES

1 J. Lacan, *The Seminar of Jacques Lacan: Book III: The Psychoses 1955–1956*, ed. J.A. Miller, trans. R. Grigg (New York: Norton, 1993), 102.
2 Lacan 1993, 97.
3 Lacan 1993, 206; italics in the original.
4 Daniel P. Schreber, *Memoirs of My Nervous Illness* (New York: New York Review of Books, 2000), 163.
5 J. Lacan, 1993.
6 Lacan 1993, 292.
7 Lacan 1993, 293; italics in the original.
8 Sigmund Freud, "Psychoanalytic Notes on an Autobiographical Account of a Case of Paranoia (Dementia Paranoides): The Case of Schreber," in *The Standard Edition of the Complete Psychological Works of Sigmund Freud*, vol. 12, ed. James Strachey (London: Hogarth, 1958), 1–82.
9 Lacan, 1993.
10 Lacan, 1993, 85.
11 Lacan, 1993, 85.

12 Lacan, 1993, 86.
13 Lacan, 1993, 88.
14 Lacan 1993, 276.
15 Lacan 1993, 482–3.
16 Jacques Lacan, *Formations of the Unconscious: The Seminar of Jacques Lacan, Book V*, ed. J.A. Miller, trans. R. Grigg (Cambridge: Polity, 2017), 141.
17 See William G. Niederland, "Schreber: Father and Son," *Psychoanalytic Quarterly* 28 (1959): 151–69.
18 Z. Lothane, "Schreber's Feminine Identification: Paranoid Illness or Profound Insight?," *International Forum of Psychoanalysis* 2, no. 3 (1993): 131–8; Lothane, "Schreber, Freud, Flechsig, and Weber Revisited: An Inquiry into Methods of Interpretation," *Psychoanalytic Review* 76, no. 2 (1989): 203–62.
19 Damien RIggs, *Pink Herrings: Fantasy, Object Choice and Sexuation* (London and New York: Routledge, 2016), 113.
20 Geneviève Morel, *La loi de la mère. Essai sur le sinthome sexuel* (Paris, Anthropos, 2008).
21 Jacques *Lacan, Ecrits: The first complete edition in English*, trans B. Fink (New York: Norton, 2006).
22 Lacan, 2006, 476.
23 Schreber, *Memoirs*, 248.
24 Schreber, *Memoirs*, 249.
25 Schreber, *Memoirs*, 250.
26 M.H. Brousse, "The-Push-to-the-Woman: A Universal in Psychosis?," *Review of the London Society of the New Lacanian School* 11 (2003): 79–98.
27 Freud, 1911, 20.
28 Lacan, 1993, 63.
29 Jacques Lacan, *Autres Ecrits* (Paris: Seuil, 2001), 466. My translation.
30 Lacan, 2006, 481.
31 Brousse, "The-Push-to-the-Woman," 81.
32 Catherine Millot, "Un cas de transsexualisme feminine" et "Transsexualisme et homosexualité." *Ornicar?* (1981): 167–76; and Millot, *Horsexe: Essays on Transsexualism*, trans. K. Hylton (New York: Autonomedia, 1992), 42.
33 Franz Kaltenbeck, "Le 'pousse-à-la-femme,' un belvédère clinique," *La Lettre Mensuelle de L'École de la Cause Freudienne* 112 (1992): 9–10.
34 See Kaltenbeck, "Le 'pousse-à-la-femme'"; and Eric Laurent, "Lettre à la lettre mensuelle," *La Lettre Mensuelle de L'École de la Cause Freudienne* 114 (1992): 12.
35 Laurent, "Lettre à la lettre mensuelle."
36 Renée Richards, *No Way Renée: The Second Half of My Notorious Life* (New York: Simon & Schuster, 2007).

37 Joyce Wadler, "At Home with Renée Richards: The Lady Regrets," *New York Times*, 1 February 2007), https://www.nytimes.com/2007/02/01/garden/01renee.html.

38 See my discussion of Lacan's "push-toward-Woman" in *Please Select Your Gender: From the Invention of Hysteria to the Democratizing of Transgenderism* (New York: Routledge, 2010), 173–81.

39 Freud, 1911, 36.

40 Brousse, "The-Push-to-the-Woman."

41 Lacan, 2006, 473.

42 Lacan, 2006, 1959, 473.

43 Gilles Deleuze and Félix Guattari, *Anti-Oedipus: Capitalism and Schizophrenia* (London: Continuum, 2004), 85.

44 Elsewhere I have developed the idea that gender transition is more about mortality, the limit between life and death, than about sexuality, the limit between male and female. See P. Gherovici, *Transgender Psychoanalysis: A Lacanian Perspective on Sexual Difference* (New York: Routledge, 2017).

45 Sigmund Freud, "Psychoanalytic Notes on an Autobiographical Account of a Case of Paranoia (Dementia Paranoides): The Case of Schreber," in *The Standard Edition of the Complete Psychological Works of Sigmund Freud*, ed. James Strachey (London: Hogarth, 1958), 12:36.

46 Janine Chasseguet-Smirgel, "On President Schreber's Transsexual Delusion, in *Psychosis and Sexual Identity: Toward a Post-Analytic View of the Schreber Case*, ed. D.B. Allison, Prado de Olivera, M.S. Roberts, and A.S. Weiss (Albany, NY: SUNY Press, 1988), 156.

47 Schreber, *Memoirs*.

48 Catherine Malabou, *The Future of Hegel: Plasticity, Temporality, and Dialectic* (New York: Routledge, 2005), 9–10.

49 Malabou, *Future of Hegel*, 10.

50 Schreber, *Memoirs*, 155.

51 Schreber, *Memoirs*, 224.

52 *The Great Beauty*, dir. Paolo Sorrentino, 2013.

53 L.F. Céline, *Journey to the End of Night*, trans. R. Manheim (New York: New Directions, 1983), 1.

54 D.B. Allison, Prado de Olivera, M.S. Roberts, and A. Weiss, eds., *Psychosis and Sexual Identity: Toward a Post-Analytic View of Schreber's Case* (Albany: State University of New York, 1988).

55 Allison, de Olivera, and Weiss, *Psychosis and Sexual Identity*, 234; modified translation.

56 Allison, de Olivera, and Weiss, *Psychosis and Sexual Identity*, 267.

57 Allison, de Olivera, and Weiss, *Psychosis and Sexual Identity*, 266.

58 Schreber, *Memoirs*, 55.

8 On Gifted Schizophrenia

W.J.T. MITCHELL

If I'm going to be crazy, I want to be really good at it. I want to be the Michael Jordan of crazy.

– Gabriel Mitchell

I want to attempt a comparative study of several "gifted schizophrenics" – the canonical figure of German jurist Daniel Paul Schreber, the English artist William Blake, law professor Elyn Saks, art historian Aby Warburg, and the mathematical game theorist John Nash. I will then reframe these cases within that of my son, Gabriel, a single high-functioning individual whose illness I lived with for twenty years. Gabriel was diagnosed with schizophrenia at age twenty-one and survived the illness until his death by suicide at thirty-eight. Throughout his struggle with schizophrenia, both its symptoms and its impact as a psycho-political-juridical label, Gabe worked as an artist and filmmaker, reflecting on his condition. Like Schreber, Gabriel wanted to create a record of his "nervous illness," and he did so in a remarkable archive of films, poems, and drawings still available on his website: philmworx.com. Schreber published his memoir with a somewhat disreputable publisher of occult literature.[1] Gabriel, a child of his technological age, self-published in a combination of video and social media. I will return to the case of Gabriel after considering these other gifted schizophrenics whose cases may help us see why it is so important to engage with the singularities of schizophrenic experiences and not rest content with the generic typologies provided by psychiatric labels.

It is difficult to describe schizophrenia as a gift. It is mainly a curse, a cause of the deepest kind of suffering, when the self feels shattered and assaulted by demons, haunted by destructive voices, as if possessed by a malignant spirit. It can produce the most extreme forms of disability, including depression, paranoia, inability to work, concentrate, or function in normal society. Most people with schizophrenia live relatively short, unhappy lives and remain unknown to anyone except their immediate families. A rare few, like Ted Kaczynski, the Unabomber, become notorious for acts of violence.[2] But the rarest of all are the "gifted" schizophrenics who are highly intelligent, articulate, and skilled, who find a way to struggle with their condition and to report back on it to the "straight" or normal world. The aim of this chapter is to ask why, beyond diagnostic and therapeutic precision, it might be important to study the significance of these reports as keys to an understanding that goes well beyond individual psychology to address issues of collective mentalities and cultural history. I am, of course, going to raise the question of the meaning of schizophrenia and whether the word is properly applied to any of these cases. The word "schizophrenia" has a deeply fraught and controversial history that I won't enter into here. I will be keeping my nose out of nosology. Schizophrenia names the most extreme form of mental illness, the most intractable to cure with either talk or drugs. It is what stands in as the modern replacement for madness, the wild world of folly both tragic and comic from antiquity through the modern where it is rendered as a scientific object by psychiatry and psychoanalysis. Or, perhaps, more properly, the "sublime object of psychiatry," which defies explanation, exceeds our categories, as Angela Woods argues in her book by this title.[3]

Judge Schreber's report, his memoir of his "nervous illness," is, of course, the canonical example. He is the most famous case of schizophrenia that we know, thanks to Freud's early interest, and the sustained attention it has received throughout the history of psychiatry and psychoanalysis. There are other notable cases with a wide range of severity and recognition. At one end, we have the case of the English poet and painter William Blake, who manifested many of the positive symptoms of schizophrenia such as delusions of grandeur, paranoia, and highly elaborate hallucinations. Blake, as George Bataille noted, explored the "frontiers" of madness without succumbing; he displayed few of the negative symptoms, and although he was an "outsider artist" in his own time, he was able to lead a long, productive life creating visionary texts and images that have now become central to the canon of English art and literature.[4]

At the other end of the spectrum, we might position the case of Elyn Saks, who has suffered from all the negative symptoms of schizophrenia, including horrific delusions, deep depression, and multiple suicide attempts. Yet Saks, through a combination of extraordinary intelligence, willpower, and a lucky series of brilliant therapeutic interventions, managed to have a successful life as a law professor. More important for our present purposes, her memoir of her struggle with schizophrenia, *The Center Cannot Hold*, is among the most vivid and detailed, not to mention beautifully written, accounts of schizophrenia that we have.[5] In contrast to Schreber, who "persists in his folly until he becomes wise," as Blake would have put it, Saks's story is one of triumphing over the folly as a matter of survival and assimilation to "straight" society. Interestingly, both Schreber and Saks had law careers, his as an eminent judge whose memoir introduced a legal brief arguing for his release from confinement, hers as a legal advocate who has contributed to case law defending the rights of the mentally ill in the face of confinement. If Schreber is the first great hero of the anti-psychiatry movement, establishing the basic criterion of "danger to oneself or others" as the standard for confinement, Saks is a strong contemporary contributor to that argument. Her narrative, moreover, is a vigorous protest against the ultimate horror she suffered, the imposition of physical restraints such as straitjackets. What links Schreber and Saks, then, is the ability to tell the story of schizophrenia from within and to assert a position within the political and legal framework of mental illness. But the contrasts are equally important. Unlike Schreber, Saks was not in the grip of a cosmic fantasy and grandiose world picture in which she would play a central role in the redemption of the human species. Saks's delusions took the form of a massive guilt complex and sense of utter worthlessness, probably initiated by her parents' early decision to subject her to a rather harsh regime of forced "therapy."[6] Schreber affirmed his delusional cosmology to the end, while arguing for the harmless and private character of his nervous illness; Saks resigned herself to a life of managing her delusions and self-destructive symptoms in order to participate in a normal life. In both cases, as Katrin Trüstedt says of Schreber in this volume (see chapter 3), a significant deepening of our understanding and critique of law is an ironic by-product of the brilliance of the jurist's madness. Is this what Derrida meant when he told us "the law is mad, is madness"?[7]

The two other cases I wish to consider before returning to Gabriel are those of the art historian Aby Warburg and the mathematician John Nash. If we think of Blake and Schreber as defining the spectrum of intense immersion into the world of schizophrenia, Warburg and Nash exemplify what we might call episodic or intermittent immersion. Both underwent intense and repeated psychotic "breaks" followed by prolonged hospitalization. Both emerged from their involuntary confinement to resume productive but somewhat precarious lives. Warburg, widely regarded as the single most important founder of modern art history, described himself as incurable and as a "revenant" or ghost.

He achieved his release from confinement, not with a legal brief, but with a brilliant lecture, "Notes on the Serpent Ritual of the Hopi Indians," which ranged over the symbolism of the serpent in both ancient and modern, Western and non-Western cultures. In the last five years of his life after his release, he promulgated the massive project of a "Bilderatlas" that was to provide a global survey of images. Centred on the representations of passions or what he called "Pathosformel," the *Bilderatlas* was a Herculean project that sought a comprehensive representation of world pictures, including the entire realm of cosmological and diagrammatic renderings of the universe, as well as contemporary events such as the coronation of Mussolini and the flight of the Zeppelin.

Nash's mathematics had similarly grandiose ambitions, aiming at nothing less than a comprehensive model of human behaviour grounded in non-cooperative game theory. Nash depicted human beings as fundamentally selfish, isolated individuals, like poker players, driven by nothing more than self-interest. The good news of this theory was that it predicted an equilibrium that would emerge from unbridled competition and prove to be a benefit to all the players in the long run. Needless to say, this theory was music to the ears of neoliberal economists and other "market fundamentalists" who transformed the global economy in the late twentieth century, ushering in a global regime of deregulated finance capital and the destruction of the welfare state. Adam Smith on steroids, non-cooperative game theory provided a mathematical rationalization of a new theology: the "wisdom of the market" would take care of the poor, the sick, and the homeless, who would (in the long run) be safe in the warm embrace of "the invisible hand" known as capitalism.

It was hardly surprising that this theory earned Nash the Nobel Prize for Economics, and that it turned him into a Hollywood icon in the film about his life, *A Beautiful Mind*, winner of the Academy Award for Best Picture in 2002. What is interesting is that Nash's actual illness, the real story of his schizophrenia, was almost completely erased in the film in favour of a depiction of him as the victim of Cold War delusions of the dangerous game called "Mutually Assured Destruction" (appropriately acronymed "MAD") in the nuclear standoff between the United States and the Soviet Union. The movie portrays Nash as haunted by imaginary friends – a college roommate, an orphaned girl – with special emphasis on a shadowy intelligence operative played by Ed Harris who recruits Nash to engage in pointless searches for hidden Soviet messages in wall atlases of ads, news, and images taken from magazines and newspapers.

Nash's great gift, the ability to see patterns in any random array, is turned into the curse known as "apophenia," the tendency to project patterns where there aren't any. Coupled with his hallucinations and paranoid delusional system, his game theories recede into the background of the film.

The actual content of Nash's delusions, as documented by his biographer, Sylvia Nasar,[8] is much more complicated and interesting. Although Nash did work as a game theorist for the Rand Corporation where Cold War scenarios of first strikes, deterrence, and rapid responses were being studied, when he fell ill, it was into quite a different world. Instead of the Manichean structure of the Cold War, Nash turned into a peacenik, a "one worlder" who set out for Europe, where he repeatedly tried to renounce his American citizenship and turn in his passport at U.S. embassies. None of this survives in the film version of *A Beautiful Mind*. Instead, he is portrayed as a wounded but recovered Cold Warrior whose genius is finally being acknowledged in the new post–Cold War era of "globalization" and the final victory of capitalism. We might ask ourselves, Who or what is crazy in this scenario? Could it be that Nash's brilliant but narrow non-cooperative game theory provided the perfect mathematical rationalization for two rather demented world systems, the madness of total self-destruction threatened by the Cold War, and the destruction of the environment and human civilization promised by neoliberal globalization? Could it be that Nash's schizophrenic delusion of a pacifist international world order is, in the long run, the better picture of a sane planet?

So far I have been talking about a few of the famous cases of gifted schizophrenia. I turn now to one that is scarcely known, but that I can describe in intimate detail. The first sign of Gabriel's schizophrenia occurred when he was a freshman at NYU, and he telephoned me to say that he had discovered the authentic way of life. This authentic way turned out to be a firm resolution to become homeless and to join the community of beggars he was hanging out with in Washington Square. When I tried to steer the discussion toward a possible career of social work and helping the homeless, he firmly rejected this alternative. He assured me that I was completely missing the point; he needed to become homeless in order to experience the reality of the human condition, a reality that he was quite sure I was completely ignorant about.

This episode passed, and Gabe returned to being a relatively normal college freshman: idealistic, confused, ambitious, and subject to rapid changes. But over the next three years the number of bizarre and disturbing episodes began to increase. He had to withdraw from school, and it was clear that he was becoming increasingly angry, depressed, and delusional. When he began to act out violently, we had to hospitalize him. He was diagnosed with schizophrenia and we began to deal with the usual prescribed course of partially effective medications and mainly ineffective psychotherapy. He had to move into supervised housing where a social worker saw him regularly and his medication was administered. It was, of course, a deep trauma for his family, as we watched our formerly bright, lively, and affectionate son sink into apathy and depression. There were episodic bursts of creativity and enthusiasm, but by and large this was a very dark time for him. He was filled with anger at us for, as he saw it, "throwing him out" and betrayed a deep resistance to psychotherapy as a form of thought control that threatened his freedom. We tried to keep him as close to us as possible without having him live with us, and over a period of years he began slowly to improve. He took a job as a produce clerk and began to write autobiographical screenplays documenting his struggle with schizophrenia. Ultimately, he improved enough to move out of supervised housing into rather nice subsidized housing in the centre of downtown Chicago, and his life began to improve measurably. He taught himself video editing and began to make films, ultimately settling on an ambitious project of making a film that would show schizophrenia "from inside and outside," as he put it, and "transform schizophrenia from a death sentence into a learning experience."

If we were to construct a comparative table of Gabriel's symptomatology with Schreber's, a whole list of similarities would emerge: Acute paranoia accompanied by a persecution complex in which a formerly trusted person becomes a traitorous enemy. Gabe experienced auditory hallucinations remarkably similar to Schreber's, but without the visual component of "speaking rays." Voices filled with accusations, or boring repetitions that seem to write themselves down, mechanical storage, crowding out the possibility of mental silence. Terrible nightmares in which one's body becomes the prey of devouring creatures, a Hobbesian nightmare of nature red in tooth and claw. An ability to stare into empty space for very long periods without getting bored, but on the contrary, watching in wonder as miracles unfold that are visible to no one else. Gabe stared out windows from an early age, and Schreber was famous for his catatonic staring intently in order to keep the universe stabilized.

Labels are, of course, always controversial, especially in cases of gifted schizophrenia. Schreber was officially a case of dementia praecox in the psychiatric lingo of his time. Gabe was diagnosed a number of times, increasingly pessimistic in character. Especially disturbing was the way the sedative effects of medication dulled his keen intelligence.

He described it as a thought disorder without any thoughts, like living underwater. Gabe often rejected the schizophrenic label, preferring to trace his illness to a singular traumatic event involving brain injury and betrayal. Schreber's narrative ranges over his entire environment: the political character of late nineteenth-century Germany; the rise of anti-Semitism; the emergence of psychiatric power in its alliance with the law; the new sciences of forensic psychiatry and neuroscience, the world of nerves and rays; Schreber's family, especially his disciplinarian father who subjected his children to strict exercises and hygienic practices.

But the most important similarity between their cases is what psychiatrists might call "delusions of grandeur," or simply "grandiosity." Both men created what might be called "world systems" that aimed to comprehend all time and space and to produce an apocalyptic transformation in human life. One might use Schreber's term, a "private religion" with a membership of one, or (in Gabriel's case) a "private science" that would unite mysticism and mathematics, and astound the professional scientists that Gabe corresponded with. "I've never seen anything quite like it," was the tactful remark of one mathematician at the University of Chicago. Schreber's narrative of his transformation into a woman had the ultimate goal of engendering a new, improved version of the human species; Gabriel was aiming for a "unified physics of peace" that would gather the history of human thought into a grand new synthesis linked to Ray Kurzweil's idea of "the singularity," an event to come with the perfection of artificial intelligence.

The grandiosity or, more generously, the grandeur of these ambitions is a recurrent feature of gifted schizophrenia. It reflects the tendency of psychoses to defy reality testing in favour of the creation of an encyclopedic fantasy world. Aby Warburg's *Bilderatlas* might be seen as a borderline phenomenon, partly symptomatic and partly therapeutic, in which the parts added up to become the defining, if impossible agenda of an ambitious global iconology. William Blake's grand plan aimed at an epic and mythopoetic rewriting of a human history in which all religions are one, and Blake himself is designated as the prophet of a new age of emancipated humanity. The fact that he was writing his encyclopedic poems in the era of the French Revolution helped to convince him that history was on his side, and that in the future age he was prophesying, war, capitalism, and the "dark religions" would be replaced by a "Sweet Science" of visionary awareness.

One sharp contrast between Gabriel and Schreber is their attitude toward other people. Schreber, perhaps because he was hospitalized for so long in degrading environments, retreated deeply into himself and tended to see others as "improvised" men and women, phantoms who had only a fleeting existence in his consciousness. Gabe, who was hospitalized only once, had a rich social and family life, complete with adoring grandmothers who talked to him regularly. He had an endearing openness and innocence when encountering other people. This made him highly vulnerable to con artists, and part of our task as his caregivers was to head off his entrapment by monitoring his acquaintances. Gabriel saw the eyes of strangers as windows into infinite depths of personhood. At social events I would sometimes watch in wonder as he "worked the room" like a skilled politician, greeting every new acquaintance as an occasion for profound curiosity and discovery. This could sometimes be off-putting, since it meant that the small talk of socializing would, in his case, quickly give way to an intense discussion of the meaning of life. Many people did not realize that he had a diagnosis of schizophrenia and simply regarded him as a charming, intense, and somewhat eccentric young man. Not that he made any attempt to conceal his status; almost any prolonged conversation would lead to him volunteering to complete strangers that he was suffering from a mental illness. When people would remark on how normal he seemed, he would sometimes laugh and say, "That is because I am heavily medicated."

On a scale of observable severity, Schreber's mental disorder was much more serious than Gabriel's. On the other hand, Schreber's illness had a relatively late onset, when he was established as a prominent jurist in Saxony, whereas Gabe's condition commenced while he was a student, and for the first ten years it seemed to arrest his emotional development at about age nineteen. In contrast to Schreber's multiple suicide attempts, Gabriel attempted it only once, at a time when it seemed to some of us as if he was on the verge of defeating schizophrenia and moving forward as an experimental filmmaker. It is possible that he was experiencing an "Everest moment," feeling on top of the world, and tapered off his medication in order to go even higher, with fatal consequences. It became clear to us in retrospect that he was too strong for his own good and had become increasingly skilled at concealing his suffering from us, and from himself.

One key question in cases of gifted schizophrenia is how the case is mediated. As Friedrich Kittler has shown, Schreber's writing of his memoir involved the outering of the discourse network of nineteenth-century neuroscience and forensic psychiatry, coupled with an uncanny foreshadowing of psychoanalysis.[9] Schreber's Doctor Flechsig becomes, in his imaginary world, the persecuting God who cannot understand living beings and so must commit soul murder against them in order to perform post-mortem analysis of the brain and nervous system. Schreber's endo-psychic reports on the complex of nerves and rays that assail him on all sides becomes the answer of a living soul who refuses to lose his reason despite his "nervous illness." This picture of the embodied psyche was anticipated in Blake's image of "nervous fibres that run from man to man," and elaborated as the ensnaring of the body in a media system by Jakob Mohr, whose drawings in the Prinzhorn collection provide a fundamental icon of psychotic consciousness.[10] Freud concluded, famously, that Schreber's memoirs had managed to provide a "concrete representation and projection outwards of libidinal cathexes; and they thus lend his delusions a striking conformity with our theory."[11] He also pondered a profound question about the whole relation of scientific theory to paranoia: "It remains for the future to decide whether there is more delusion in my theory than I should like to admit, or whether there is more truth in Schreber's delusion than other people are as yet prepared to believe."[12]

Schreber's memoir was published by Mutze in Leipzig, an easily dismissed theosophical publisher in Leipzig.[13] Gabriel's memoirs were self-published in the form of Philmworx.com, a website containing links to his films, writings, and other artworks. Schreber became a central figure in the anti-psychiatry movement of the late nineteenth century. Like Elyn Saks, his brief arguing for his release from involuntary confinement established the fundamental separation between psychiatric and legal authority in terms of the "danger to oneself or others" criteria. Gabriel, by contrast, was immersed in the literature of the anti-psychiatry movement of the 1960s and the whole cultural revaluation of madness that went along with it. He read Deleuze and Guattari, R.D. Laing, and Michel Foucault, and participated in my own seminars on madness and visual culture. Needless to say, this did not make him an especially tractable candidate for psychotherapy. He was fond of mimicking the clichés of the talking cure, and (as he told us) generally used therapeutic sessions as an opportunity for grandiose filibusters. If Schreber was immersed in a world of heavy sedation and bleak imprisonment, Gabe was the beneficiary of contemporary antipsychotic medications such as Zyprexa, which he was free to take or not.

The question of freedom is central to the contrast between Gabriel and Schreber. The latter's childhood has famously featured lengthy discussions of his authoritarian father, who invented strict disciplines of physical exercise and posture that made him famous in the nineteenth century. Freud emphasized Moritz Schreber's toxic role in providing his son with a classic Oedipus complex, but subsequent studies have suggested that, if anything, it is the oppressive, soul-killing doctor Flechsig who is most relevant to Schreber's case.[14] For Gabriel, the freedom to go crazy was a mixed blessing. He liked to blame his parents for giving him too much freedom and for failing to provide him with a definite identity. As his father, I found myself caught between a sense that it was my responsibility to provide a reality check on his delusions, and exactly the opposite impulse, to give free reign and enthusiastic support to his most grandiose ambitions as an artist. The latter impulse became more and more prevalent the longer he survived schizophrenia, and the more proficient he became as a filmmaker. Indeed, by the end of his life, Gabe and I had undergone a dramatic transference of roles. He had begun to take responsibility for me both physically and spiritually, serving as my consigliere on the stresses of aging, and happily pushing me around in a wheelchair when I suffered a crippling back injury. He had transformed the valences of our relationship, graduating from being a beloved but wounded son to the role of best friend and future caregiver. And he had put me to work as the research assistant for his most ambitious film project. Inspired by Godard's *Histoire du Cinema*, Gabe was sketching out a cinematic *Histoire de la Folie* that was to provide an encyclopedic, global overview of madness across cultures and time periods. That was the motivation for my taking up the project of "Seeing Madness," which has generated a series of seminars over the last six years, and of which this chapter is a part.

What is the point of studying cases of gifted schizophrenia? One obvious answer is the possibility of improving therapeutic approaches that combine medication with psychotherapy. Elyn Saks's autobiography is a perfect case study in the successful management of dangerous symptoms with this double approach, and the particular efficacy of Kleinian efforts to engage psychosis with talk therapy.[15] But there is another way of thinking about this: what can we learn about ourselves as implicated in these cases? And when I say "ourselves," I mean ourselves as a species, i.e., *Homo sapiens*, the dominant animal group on this planet. What can gifted schizophrenia teach us about individual and collective psychology?

Another way of describing "gifted schizophrenia" would be to adopt R.D. Laing's term: "schizophrenics who have come back to us." That is, persons afflicted with psychoses who have struggled with that condition and who have managed to produce compelling, articulate reflections on it, whether in memoirs, works of art, or (like Warburg) enduring projects of knowledge production. Laing suggests that these rare persons "deserve no less respect than the often no less lost explorers of the Renaissance."[16] I do not think that Laing was romanticizing schizophrenia in saying this. He knew as well as anybody the extraordinary suffering that goes with schizophrenia and was well aware that most people who suffer from it live blighted, unhappy lives. Even the lucky ones who survive and manage to produce work undergo terrible ordeals. Schizophrenia is not the gift; it is the curse, and the gift is an independent variable, the luck of those explorers who survive the voyage on strange seas of thought. "If the human race survives," Laing predicts, "future men will ... look back on our enlightened epoch as veritable Age of Darkness" for its failure to grasp these reports from the frontiers of madness, and to reduce them to generic labels.[17] As Tarizzo notes in detail in this volume (see chapter 9), there is an impasse, the psychotic hits a wall, a boundary he cannot cross, the foreclosure that turns the subject back upon himself as a double form. Therein lies the curse but also potentially, as Gherovici elaborates it, the improvisation of an aesthetic cure.

What will they say about schizophrenia from that standpoint? Perhaps one answer is already anticipated by Aby Warburg: "All mankind is at all times schizophrenic."[18] They will understand, as psychotherapists from Melanie Klein to Gilles Deleuze have suggested, that schizophrenia is not merely a deviation from normality, but itself a kind of foundation for many different kinds of normality in many different cultures. The "schizoid position" for Klein is not an aberration, but a necessary phase of infantile development, one that some individuals find themselves recapitulating in later life.[19] For Deleuze and Guattari, schizophrenia is a reaction formation to the invention of capitalism.

A second answer is suggested by the most common symptoms of schizophrenia, the sense that the self has been shattered into parts that can no longer be integrated. The experience of being beset by voices and visions from all sides is the sensuous manifestation of this shattering, as if the self were surrounded by, or even more disturbing, *inhabited by* a quarrelling, contentious crowd. And this inversion of the individual/group relationship suggests a decisive rethinking of the whole constitution of the psyche as primarily an individual matter. We know from Freud's *Group Psychology and the Analysis of the Ego* that the boundary between the individual and mass psychology is not nearly as clear as one might suppose. We suppose, however, that as a science, psychology literally is concerned only with individuals, and its extension to groups is, as we say, "merely metaphorical." But suppose the message of schizophrenia turns this assumption upside down? Suppose it is the group mind, along with all its disorders, that is the literal foundation of human psychology, and the individual is to be regarded as the site of convergence and assemblage of that group, whether it is as small as the family or the couple, as large as the culture or society, as ephemeral as the crowd or the queue?

One thing this might help to explain at the individual level is the tendency of those with gifted schizophrenia to report it as a religious experience, one in which they feel themselves to be in a godlike sovereign position, exercising the omnipotence of their thoughts; or contrarily, in a position of damnation or demon possession. Gabriel and William Blake had visions of God and thought that it was a lot like looking in the mirror, or into the face of another human being.

Elyn Saks looked in the mirror and saw a mass murderer, a creature guilty of enormous crimes. Warburg's Herculean effort to compile an atlas of images and words from the First World War led him to a psychotic break within a week of the end of that war, when he re-enacted the other side of the Herculean role by attempting to murder his whole family. John Nash's paranoid style of game theory led him to rationalize the strategic framework of Mutually Assured Destruction and the world-destroying system known as neoliberal capitalism.

Schizophrenia in this light would reveal itself as the extreme expression of the normal, baseline condition of the human animal, namely, the paradoxical position known as "sovereign subjectivity." This is a version of subjectivity that is routinely linked to the "bourgeois" subject, both abject and omnipotent, but it may have a broader application. Louis Sass describes schizophrenia in terms drawn from Wittgenstein's account of "solipsistic vacillation," which involves a sense of "swelling up to fill the world, yet of also being infinitesimal, only a negligible point at the center of the vastness."[20] "Schreber's feeling of being the conscious center of the world," Sass argues, "was continually transforming into its opposite."[21] Sass further suggests that Wittgenstein himself was tempted by solipsism in his early philosophy when he made remarks such as "the only reality is my present experience," or "As my idea is the world, in the same way my will is the world-will."[22] Sass thinks that Wittgenstein's later philosophy is a reaction against this sort of idealism, which verges on schizophrenic solipsism.

But there is something a bit unsatisfactory, in my view, about Sass's confident conclusion that Wittgenstein's later philosophy delivers us from "a form of life that is self-deceptive, futile, and ultimately absurd."[23] Of course all these adjectives apply very well to much of human life; but is philosophy the cure for them? Or would it be better to say, with Warburg, Blake, Elyn Saks, and perhaps (in a better reading of Wittgenstein) that we are *incurable*, and the problem is to recognize that and devise ways of dealing with it? If we were to learn that lesson from schizophrenia, it might lead us back to that moment at the outset of Foucault's *History of Madness,* when he describes the medieval institution known as the "Ship of Fools" on which the madmen and women were confined and sent off into exile to keep them away from normal healthy people. Suppose that we were to adjust the scale of this ancient metaphor for collective madness and associate it with the Spaceship Earth on which we find ourselves today? Certainly it would change our attitude toward gifted schizophrenics and lead us to recognize that we are all in the same boat. And that by any reasonable measure, Schreber was a relatively harmless guy, whereas we as a species meet the basic legal criterion for madness, namely, that we are a danger to ourselves and others.

NOTES

1 Schreber's life has been documented recently in a film, *Shock Head Soul* (Simon Pummell, 2012), and evoked in multimedia installations by Richard Crow, a novel by Alex Pheby, and curator/scholar Angela Woods, director of the "Hearing the Voice" Project. This trio performed recently at the Empty Shop, Durham, NC: http://hearingthevoice.org/2016/12/01/an-evening-with-daniel-paul-schreber-empty-shop-durham-13-january-2017-from-7-10pm/.

2 Kaczynski left elaborate writings that record his delusions. More typical, perhaps, is the case of Greg Bottoms, whose brother Michael "saw the face of God," but mainly left a trail of destruction that ruined his family, and continues to haunt Bottoms, who narrates Michael's numerous episodes of murderous rage. See *Angelhead: A Memoir* (New York: Three Rivers, 2005). Other notable first-person accounts of mental illness (not just schizophrenia) include John Perceval, Vaslav Nijinsky, William Styron (depression), Kay Redfield Jamison (bipolar disorder), and Andrew Solomon. Marguerite Sèchehaye's *Autobiography of a Schizophrenic Girl: The True Story of "Renee"* (New York: Grune & Stratton, 1951) is also crucial.

3 Angela Woods, *The Sublime Object of Psychiatry: Schizophrenia in Clinical and Cultural Theory* (Oxford: Oxford University Press, 2011).

4 The best "clinical" account of Blake is provided by literary scholar Andrew Cooper, "Blake and Madness: The World Turned Inside Out," *English Literary History* 57, no. 3 (1990): 585–642. Cooper discusses Blake's allegorical and mythological poems in terms of Melanie Klein's models of "projective identification."

5 Elyn Saks, *The Center Cannot Hold* (New York: Hyperion Books, 2007).

6 This is my interpretation, not Saks's. She tells the story of what strikes me as excessively harsh punishment by her parents for marijuana smoking as

a teenager. But she is silent about how this episode might have produced an affective foundation of self-loathing for her later illness.

7 Jacques Derrida, "The Law of Genre," *Critical Inquiry* 7, no. 1 (Autumn 1980): 55–81.

8 Sylvia Nasar, *A Beautiful Mind* (New York: Simon & Schuster, 1998).

9 Friedrich Kittler, *Discourse Networks 1800/1900*, trans. Michael Metteer with Chris Cullens (Stanford, CA: Stanford University Press, 1990).

10 Bettina Brand-Claussen, *Beyond Reason: Art and Psychosis* (Berkeley: University of California Press, 1998).

11 Kittler, *Discourse Networks 1800/1900*, 291.

12 For a detailed account of Gabriel Mitchell's life, see my memoir, *Mental Traveler: A Father, a Son, and a Journey through Schizophrenia* (Chicago: University of Chicago Press, 2020).

13 Zvi Lothane, *In Defense of Schreber: Soul Murder and Psychiatry* (Hillsdale, NJ: Analytic Press, 1992), 289; Sigmund Freud, "Notes on a Case of Paranoia," in *The Standard Edition of the Complete Psychoanalytic Works*, ed. James Strachey (London: Hogarth Press, 1958), 13:78–9.

14 See Lothane, *In Defense of Schreber.*

15 See Saks, *Center Cannot Hold*, chap. 3.

16 R.D. Laing, *Politics of Experience* (New York: Pantheon, 1968), 129.

17 Laing, *Politics of Experience*, 129. The Lacanian notion that the therapist must serve as "secretary to the insane." Jean Allouch, "Psychotic Transference," in *Lacan on Madness*, ed. Patricia Gherovici and Manya Steinkoler (New York: Routledge, 2015), 118.

18 Inserted as a footnote to Warburg's lecture on the Hopi Serpent Ritual. See Ernst Gombrich, *Aby Warburg: An Intellectual Biography* (Chicago: University of Chicago Press, 1986).

19 See Melanie Klein, "Notes on Some Schizoid Mechanisms," *International Journal of Psycho-Analysis* 27 (1946): 99–110, for the basic argument about the madness of early childhood.

20 Louis Sass, *The Paradoxes of Delusion: Wittgenstein, Schreber, and the Schizophrenic Mind* (Ithaca, NY: Cornell University Press, 1994), 69.

21 Sass, *Paradoxes of Delusion*, 72.

22 Sass, *Paradoxes of Delusion*, 73.

23 Sass, *Paradoxes of Delusion*, 73.

9 The Delusional Metaphor: On Schreber's Anathema

DAVIDE TARIZZO

He began to doubt whether he was mortal at all.

– Elias Canetti

In order to do justice, we must know the truth. We must know who we are talking about and what they truly did to each other. But can we do justice to ourselves? That is, can we truly know ourselves and what we did or suffered in the past? Can we judge ourselves? The story of Schreber is a case in point: Can a judge grasp the truth about himself and do justice to himself, as Schreber wished he could do by changing the Order of the World and transfiguring the Law?

What Is True?

As to the truth about the Schreber case, it remains largely unavailable. To be sure, Daniel Paul Schreber did not ignore the fact that his father, Daniel Gottlieb Moritz Schreber, and his suicidal brother, Daniel Gustav Schreber, had played some role in causing his suffering. As Daniel[1] remarks in his *Memoirs*, "There is something rotten in the state of Denmark."[2] And neither Freud nor Lacan misses the significance of these figures when they tackle the issue of "soul-murder," the assassination of Daniel's mind. Let us start with some passages taken from Freud's, Lacan's, and Daniel's writings, all of which focus on this abominable "crime."[3]

Freud

The patient was himself not clear as to the actual nature of that crime, but it was connected with matters of discretion which precluded their publication (as we see from the suppressed third chapter). From this point a single thread takes us further. Schreber illustrates the nature of soul-murder by referring to the legends embodied in Goethe's *Faust*, Byron's *Manfred*, Weber's *Freischütz*, etc., and one of these instances is further cited in another passage. In discussing the division of God into two persons, Schreber identifies his "lower God" and "upper God" with Ahriman and Ormuzd respectively; and a little later a casual footnote occurs: "Moreover, the name Ahriman also appears in connection with a soul-murder in, for example, Lord Byron's *Manfred*." In the play which is thus referred to there is scarcely anything comparable with the bartering of Faust's soul, and I have searched it in vain for the expression "soul-murder." But the essence and the secret of the whole work lies in an incestuous relation between a brother and a sister. And here our thread breaks off short.[4]

Lacan

It is clear that what we are presented with here is a disturbance that occurred at the inmost juncture of the subject's sense of life. The censorship, which mutilated the text of his *Memoirs* before the addition announced by Schreber to the rather roundabout explanations that he tried to give of the disturbance's process, inclines me to think that he associated facts that could not be published due to the conventions of the time with the names of people who were still alive. The following chapter [chapter 3] is thus missing in its entirety and, to exercise his perspicacity, Freud had to confine himself to the allusion to *Faust*, *Der Freischütz*, and Byron's *Manfred*, the latter work (from which he assumes Ahriman, the name of one of the manifestations of God in Schreber's delusion, was borrowed) seeming to him to derive its full value in this reference from its theme: the hero dies from the curse borne in him by the death of the object of fraternal incest.[5]

Daniel

I believe I may say that at that time and at that time *only*, I saw God's omnipotence in its complete purity. During the night – and as far as I can remember in one *single* night – the lower God (Ahriman) appeared. The radiant picture of his rays became visible to my inner eye, while I was lying in bed not sleeping but awake – that is to say he was reflected on my inner nervous system. Simultaneously I heard his voice; but it was not a soft whisper – as the talk of the voices always was before and after that time – it resounded in a mighty bass as if directly in front of my bedroom

> windows. The impression was intense, so that anybody not hardened to terrifying miraculous impressions as I was, would have been shaken to the core. Also what was spoken did not sound friendly by any means: everything seemed calculated to instill fright and terror into me and the word "wretch" [*Luder*] was frequently heard – an expression quite common in the basic language to denote a human being destined to be destroyed by God and to feel God's power and wrath. Yet everything that was spoken was genuine, not phrases learnt by rote as they later were, but the immediate expression of true feeling.[6]

One can hardly overstate the importance of this painful experience that Daniel had "in one *single* night," presumably in July 1894, a few days after his arrival at Sonnenstein. Following Lacan's lead, we can relate this episode to the beginning of Daniel's delusional reconstruction of the whole of reality. Freud too highlights this episode when he describes Daniel's cosmogonic and onto-theological lucubrations in terms of "an attempt at recovery."

> *The delusional formation, which we take to be the pathological product, is in reality an attempt at recovery, a process of reconstruction.* Such a reconstruction after the catastrophe is successful to a greater or lesser extent, but never wholly so; in Schreber's words, there has been a "profound internal change" in the world. But the human subject has recaptured a relation, and often a very intense one, to the people and things in the world, even though the relation is a hostile one now, where formerly it was hopefully affectionate.[7]

From Doctor Weber's medical report to the Court of 9 December 1899 we know that after the "profound internal change" of July 1894, Daniel began to see himself and the people around him differently, behaving in a rather uncanny way. At that moment, the report says, there emerged "undisguised, the fantastic delusional elaboration of his continual hallucinations." Step by step, Daniel was thus entering a new world, created by his disfigured mind.

> In November 1894 the patient's stiff posture loosened a little, he came out of himself more, became more mobile, started to speak coherently although in an abrupt and somewhat staccato manner; there now emerged undisguised, the fantastic delusional elaboration of his continual hallucinations; he felt himself adversely influenced by certain persons previously known to him (Flechsig, v. W...), who he believed to be present there, thought that the world had been changed by them, God's omnipotence destroyed, he himself struck by their curses; maintained that they pulled thoughts out of his body and suchlike.[8]

The fact that Daniel was a paranoiac was pretty clear to everyone around him. But how to decode his distorted behaviour and mental disease? As is widely known, Freud insists on Daniel's homosexuality and makes unspecified allusions to Daniel's relationship with his father and brother. The question of incest is mentioned en passant. In short, Freud's idea is that some "catastrophe" had occurred during Daniel's childhood. According to Freud, this "catastrophe" had first been abolished internally and had then returned from without, hitting Daniel in the form of a traumatic hallucination, the night when he saw "God's omnipotence in its complete purity."

> We may say, then, that the process of repression proper consists in a detachment of the libido from people – and things – that were previously loved. It happens silently; we receive no intelligence of it, but can only infer it from subsequent events. What forces itself so noisily upon our attention is the process of recovery, which undoes the work of repression and brings back the libido again on the people it had abandoned. It was incorrect to say that the perception which was suppressed internally is projected outwards; the truth is rather, as we now see, that what was abolished internally returns from without.[9]

We can pause here for a moment. My first point concerns the truth that Freud is so willing to tell us – the truth about Daniel's homosexuality, or the truth he alludes to in the opening lines of his "Postscript" to the Schreber case: "I feel confident that every reader with a knowledge of psycho-analysis will have learned from the material which I presented more than was explicitly stated by me, and that he will have found no difficulty in drawing the threads closer and in reaching conclusions at which I no more than hinted."[10] Are we really in a position to draw the threads closer? Here, as in other cases, Lacan helps us to refine Freud's analysis and deepen our understanding.

What Is Real?

Something went badly wrong in Daniel's childhood. Yet Freud's interpretation is far from convincing. Consider the issue of Daniel's homosexuality. After reading his *Memoirs*, it seems too simplistic to venture that Daniel was a homosexual. Undeniably, his book centres on the idea of being transformed into a woman. But it also revolves around a missing idea, on which Daniel himself places a strong emphasis. To cut a long story short, Daniel was not (or did not want to be) only a woman for God. At the same time, he identified with God, even though he could not make sense of such identification. At any rate, these were the two opposite poles of his delusional thoughts. On the one hand, Daniel thought of himself as a woman who attracts, and is attracted by, God. He was She, the beloved. On the other, Daniel thought of himself as God, the redeemer. He was He, the One. As a result, he thought of himself as being both man and woman. Hence the phantasy that gave him most pleasure – not a phantasy about homosexuality but one in which *he was having sexual intercourse with herself.*

> In order not to be misunderstood, I must point out that when I speak of my duty to cultivate voluptuousness, I *never mean any sexual desires towards other human beings (females) least of all sexual intercourse,* but that I have to imagine myself as man and woman in one person having intercourse with myself, or somehow have to achieve with myself a certain sexual excitement, etc. – which perhaps under other circumstances might be considered immoral – but which has nothing whatever to do with any idea of masturbation or anything like it.[11]

This passage is key to understanding Daniel's sexuality. As a matter of fact, Daniel felt no desire towards other human beings, whether males or females. Although he sometimes confessed to being excited by the view of women, he was neither a heterosexual nor a homosexual. Rather, in order to attain a certain degree of sexual arousal, Daniel was forced to play the woman's part in his phantasies and imagine that he – *viewed as a man* – was falling into a sexual embrace with herself – *viewed as a woman.*

> I believe that God would never attempt to withdraw (which always impairs my bodily well-being considerably) but would follow my attraction without resistance permanently and uninterruptedly, if only I could *always* be playing the woman's part in sexual embrace with myself, always rest my gaze on female beings, always look at female pictures, etc.[12]

Thus Daniel was "man and woman in one person." He embodied "*der einzige Mensch,*" or "*der Mensch schlechthin,*" the human being as such, the One who has survived the end of the world. Being the only specimen of humankind on Earth, *he is she,* in the sense that Daniel, the prophet, is the One human being who can finally abolish the difference between man and woman.

> Since God entered into nerve-contact with me exclusively, I became in a way for God the only human being, or simply the human being around

> whom everything turns, to whom everything that happens must be related and who therefore, from his own point of view, must also relate all things to himself.[13]

It would be worth analysing the use of gender pronouns in Daniel's *Memoirs*, but alas this would go beyond the scope of the present chapter. Let me just stress once again that Daniel's *Entmannung*, his eviration and transformation into a woman, has nothing to do with homosexuality, because such an emasculating transformation amounts to his simultaneous transformation into Him, into God.

> The crowning glory of the whole of creation, however, was the man; the plan of creation was to form him in the image of God, as a being who *after death is transformed again into God*. It is impossible for me to give a detailed scientific account of the cosmogenetic theory I have sketched roughly above.[14]

The last sentence is symptomatic of Daniel's disease. "It is impossible for me ..." What is impossible? As Daniel himself sometimes remarks, it is impossible for him not only to give a scientific account of his cosmogenetic theory but also to spell out the leading idea that hides behind it. "The leading idea is missing."[15] Despite the voices that bother him with the question, "Why do you not say it?,"[16] no answer follows. Why not? Why such a painful struggle with words? All of this becomes less mysterious when we realize that Daniel's pain was caused by the puzzle of how it is possible to be a man and a woman *at the same time*.

From the point of view of legal theory, this observation proves to be crucial. First of all, in light of the above, it becomes clear that Daniel was not a homosexual, for the simple reason that one cannot be a homosexual unless one makes a difference between males and females. To be a homosexual means to be a man who is attracted to men or else a woman who is attracted to women. Yet the problem with Daniel was that he saw himself as being both a man and a woman. He was the man who desired to have sex with herself. Shall we conclude, then, that Daniel was transgender? This conjecture would run into the same difficulty. Contrary to Goodrich's opinion,[17] Miss Schreber was not concerned with her *true* sexual orientation, nor was she dreaming of a third sex. The problem was that Daniel could not accept the *real* of sexuality, that is, the encounter of one human being with another. Hence his (or hir) refusal of the sexual difference, of *any* sexual difference between human beings, which is real before being true, and which usually prevents humans, whatever their gender, from thinking that all other people are nothing but "fleeting-improvised" beings.[18]

Indeed, what is real? A chair is real, or a table. I cannot say that the chair is *true*. Fortunately, the chair is real, and when I am sitting on it, I am able to ask, What is a chair? The answer to *that* question can be true or false, not the chair itself. The chair is real, as it is impossible for it to be a chair and a table *at the same time*. In other words, what is real is the difference between something and something else. According to Lacan, this difference, or differentiality, renders the chair and the table real.[19] But this difference was not obvious to Daniel. Where does a chair end? And where does a table begin? Where does a man end? And where does a woman begin? A question like this does not raise the problem of one's true sexual orientation. Moreover, Daniel is not an "idiot," as he says time and again. *He already knows the truth*. But the truth he has in mind is quite difficult to put into words. "The leading idea is missing."

Again, which idea? Unexpectedly, part of the answer can be found in Georg Cantor's theory of actual infinite sets. Adopting a mathematical approach to the Schreber case, we may say that Daniel, who spent a lot of time counting, was not able to count up to three. "I simply *count* 1, 2, 3, 4, etc."[20] But the point is that he did not count in the way that all other people do. In fact, by counting, he did nothing but shift from an odd number to an even number, and vice versa. For him, "1, 2, 3, 4, etc." meant: odd, even, odd, even, etc. As Cantor argues, the set of all natural numbers is infinite. This entails, as Cantor goes on to explain, that the subset of all odd numbers and the subset of all even numbers are equipotent, or equinumerous, with the set of all natural numbers – which represents the cardinality (the power) of the "countable," of the first transfinite number: aleph 0. Now, imagine that one replaces odd numbers with male numbers, and even numbers with female numbers. If the cardinality of each subset is equal to the cardinality of the set of all natural numbers, then the two subsets appear to be equinumerous, because each of them is equinumerous with the set of all natural numbers. And from this one can infer that odd numbers are equal to even numbers, that man is equal to woman, whenever they are counted by God, namely, from the point of view of the actual infinite set, which includes, and equates, males and females. Such is the mathematical rendering of Daniel's lucubrations. And therein lies the secret of the "leading idea" that pleased and at the same time tormented him so much. Daniel lived in a room at Cantor's hotel, the well-known Paradise, as David Hilbert called it. On the door of his room, he could read a number, aleph 0, the power of the countable, the number that names the divine identity between man and woman. But the fact is that a number is not a name. In order to become a name that could really identify him, this number had to be changed into a metaphor. Hence the words that Daniel heard in the air: "*Die Sonne ist eine Hure*" (The sun is a whore).[21] According to Lacan, these words conveyed a delusional metaphor: "God is a whore."[22]

> It is the lack of the Name-of-the-Father in that place which, by the hole that it opens up in the signified, sets off a cascade of reworkings of the signifier from which the growing disaster of the imaginary proceeds, until the level is reached at which signifier and signified stabilize in a delusional metaphor.[23]

The Delusional Metaphor

To recapitulate, Daniel was not homosexual or transgender. In reality, he was the herald of a divine *monosexuality* "that unites the delusional ego to the divine other" by way of "asymptote," as Lacan says.[24] Indeed, Daniel was the man who desired to have sexual intercourse with herself, which is clearly impossible. How to achieve this desire? Worse still, how to assume it? Before going into further detail on this point, let me recall Lacan's warning about "the catastrophic effect – which is, in fact, constantly found in work with psychotics – of any suggestion that goes in the direction of getting the subject to recognize his latent homosexuality."[25] In plain English, Freud's elaboration on Schreber's homosexuality must not lead us astray.

Rather, Lacan suggests, we should pay close attention to the formula "God is a whore," which is the delusional metaphor that identified Daniel as a monosexual being. But to begin with, why does Lacan consider this phrase to be a metaphor? And what is the difference between ordinary and delusional metaphors? Simply put, "God is a whore" is a metaphor because it establishes an identity between two entities (God on one side, a whore on the other), which makes no sense prima facie, when it is taken literally. "God is a whore" is ultimately a figure of speech, one that "is produced in nonmeaning," as Lacan explains about metaphors in general.[26] Moreover, "God is a whore" plays the role of a metaphor from a psychoanalytic point of view because it paves the way for the subject's identification, thus supplanting the "paternal metaphor" that usually leads to such identification (via the Oedipus complex).

However, "God is a whore" is not an ordinary but a delusional metaphor, Lacan avers, and this is due to Daniel's understanding of it. Indeed, Daniel identified himself with God – he was the man *who after death ("soul-murder") is transformed again into God* – but simultaneously identified with a whore – he was the man *who desired to fuck herself.* Daniel, therefore, could not take the metaphor "God is a whore" as a mere figure of speech (one that hints, for example, at the way in which the Catholic Church conceived of God in Luther's days). Daniel's divine monosexuality compelled him to literalize that metaphor. For him, God was a whore, literally, because Daniel himself was the two at the same time. In this case, Two equals One, and this is how an ordinary metaphor is transformed into a delusional figure of speech. By the way, this explains why Daniel was not in a position to articulate his new monosexual identity in the first person, *ego.* He could not do so because his new identity hinged on the untenable nonsense of a literalized metaphor that blatantly violated the law of identity, prescribing that *he is she.* As a result, he could not recognize the message *"Die Sonne ist eine Hure"* as coming from his own mouth. That message was not among Daniel's thoughts and never became one of *his* words. From the perspective of his devastated mind, that message had been whispered by the voices (we know about it, not from Daniel but from Doctor Weber, who heard Daniel uttering those words more than once) and that was the missing thought, "the leading idea" that should have secured Daniel's new identity but nonetheless contravened the law of identity, thereby destroying the possibility of any consistent and trustworthy identification. Due to the unaccountability of this delusional *he is she,* "the leading idea" remained unspeakable in the first person and gave Daniel no more than a clue about his potential (asymptotic) – not actual – identification. He was left with the hope, not the certainty, that "all nonsense cancels itself out" one day.[27]

In the aftermath of the revelation, *"Die Sonne ist eine Hure,"* Daniel went through the changes. He now loved dressing like a pretty woman, and he started to conceive of himself as a survivor and a redeemer, i.e., the messianic initiator of a new religion for a reborn humankind. Under the spell "God is a whore" that both dignified and mortified him, he began to worship two different Gods, but again Two equalled One in his eyes, and this was not without serious consequences. On the one side, Daniel's transformation into a whore could only increase God's masculinity, empowering the lower God, Ahriman, to the detriment of the upper God, Ormuzd. Ahriman, not Ormuzd, was the God that Daniel sought to seduce, for Ahriman represented the God of "voluptuousness" (Daniel's name for a sexuality without, or beyond, the sexual difference), Ahriman was the God who could have morphed into Daniel after penetrating him. On the other side, the penetration itself was bound to manifest and foster Daniel's femininity, thereby diverting him from his goal: to become God, to become Ahriman, to identify as "a being who after death is transformed again into God." He was thus stuck in a maddening contradiction: Two should have equalled One, but Two continued to be more than One.

Once more, we can cast further light on Daniel's impasse with the help of set theory. In an infinite set like aleph 0, the power set, namely the set of all subsets, is always more numerous than the set itself, aleph 0. For Daniel, this entails that if we mix together and sum the subset of male numbers and the subset of female numbers, the result does not confirm the equipotence between each of the two subsets and God's pansexual infinity, aleph 0. To the contrary, the result exceeds God and ends up dethroning him. Such is the destabilizing power of the delusional metaphor, "God is a whore."

All of this shows that we need not only reread Lacan's analysis of the Schreber case, but also develop it. For one thing, consideration should be given to the concept of *anathema*. In Greek, this word means the same as the German *Verwerfung*, but the concept of *Verwerfung*-anathema does not mean the same as "foreclosure" (Lacan's translation of *Verwerfung*). It means something like "malediction." In Daniel's view, the malediction falls on him, of course, but it falls on God, too. This idea runs throughout his *Memoirs*, which centre upon the anathema that strikes both him and God while unifying them through metaphor, "God is a whore," For Lacan, instead, the *Verwerfung*-foreclosure is what prevents the subject from activating the paternal metaphor. The notion of *Verwerfung*-foreclosure refers to the fact that the Name-of-the-Father is a priori excluded from the symbolic register. As a result, Lacan maintains, the subject cannot put the paternal metaphor into effect and enter into a process of identification monitored by the paternal metaphor. Psychosis will explode sooner or later.

In many respects, Lacan got it right. The collapse of the sexual difference between man and woman, which is the prelude to the end of the world, goes hand-in-hand with the collapse of God, the Father. There appears to be a strict and structural nexus between the two catastrophes: the apocalypse of the World and the debacle of the Father. When the Father is gone, nothing is possible, Lacan famously stated. Having said this, we should nonetheless ask ourselves whether Lacan's words accurately reflect the facts. When he talks about Daniel's *Verwerfung* in terms of foreclosure, *forclusion*, his argument seems to be insufficient in its accuracy. This is not to say that the notion of *Verwerfung* is meaningless. The point is that Lacan's understanding of this notion is not entirely convincing. As already indicated, the notion of *Verwerfung*-foreclosure basically means that the Name-of-the-Father has never been integrated into the symbolic register, with the result that the psychotic has never been affected by the paternal metaphor. The consequence is a "hole" in the Other (which is the "treasure trove" of signifiers).

> I will thus take *Verwerfung* to be "foreclosure" of the signifier. At the point at which the Name-of-the-Father is summoned – and we shall see how – a pure and simple hole may thus answer in the Other; due to the lack of the metaphoric effect, this hole will give rise to a corresponding hole in the place of phallic signification.[28]

However, the problem is this: if the Name-of-the-Father has never been integrated into the symbolic register and the paternal metaphor has never been put into effect, as Lacan argues, how can one perceive a "hole" in the Other? More properly, we should speak of "nothing" and confess that we do not see "nothing" that enables the psychotic to "summon" the Name-of-the-Father the day when psychosis explodes. Lacan himself notices that his line of reasoning is faulty:

> But how can the Name-of-the-Father be summoned by the subject to the only place from which it could have come into being for him and in which it has never been? By nothing other than a real father, not at all necessarily by the subject's own father, but by One-father [*Un-père*].[29]

This famous remark poses the same problem as before: If the *Verwerfung*-foreclosure of the Name-of-the-Father prevents the psychotic from putting the symbolic function of the Father into force, how can this subject recognize anyone as a "real father," as "One-father"? How can anyone see anyone else as a "real father" when that function is not at one's disposal and there is nothing but "a pure and simple hole" in its place? Again, Lacan tries to clear the air:

> Yet this One-father must still come to that place to which the subject could not summon him before. For this, the One-father need but situate himself in a tertiary position in any relationship that has as its base the imaginary couple *a-a'* – that is, ego-object or ideal-reality – involving the subject in the field of eroticized aggression that it induces. We should try to detect this dramatic conjuncture at the beginning of each case of psychosis.[30]

Still, the question remains: In the complete absence of the Name-of-the-Father, after the primal *Verwerfung*-foreclosure, how can anyone regard anyone else as being "in a tertiary position"? On the basis of

Lacan's theory of *Verwerfung*-foreclosure, there is no way to answer this question. We therefore need to slightly revise the theory. When it comes to Daniel, we should redefine *Verwerfung* as anathema. Daniel did not foreclose the Name-of-the-Father. For him, the Name-of-the-Father was cursed: "God is a whore." In other words, Daniel did not repel the Name-of-the Father from the very beginning. Rather, he put it to work in his early days, thus putting the paternal metaphor into effect. But then, *after some period of time*, things took a wrong turn, and at that moment Daniel disowned the paternal metaphor, leaving a "hole" in the symbolic register. At that point, not a moment before, his world fell to pieces.

As already noted, a veil is thrown over the truth. Nevertheless, what matters most is not the truth but the real. What was real for Daniel, and impossible to confront, was a Father that had become a chair or a table.[31] In one way or another, that Father had contravened his own fatherhood – we do not know exactly when or how. For this reason, the paternal metaphor had been *deactivated* ("soul-murder"), and it took years to reactivate it in a highly distorted and delusional form, which pushed Daniel into an equally distorted and delusional identification: "God is a whore." If this conjecture is valid, it follows that the delusional metaphor was not meant to *compensate* for the original foreclosure of the Name-of-the-Father, as Lacan says. Quite the contrary, the delusional metaphor served to *ratify*, on the symbolic level, the malediction of Name-of-the-Father, which had never been completely absent from Daniel's subjectivity.

Under this assumption, several aspects of his pathological condition can be explained. I shall limit myself to mentioning just two of them. First, the appearance of a split god, or Father, in the shape of Ormuzd and Ahriman, the wise Lord and the malign Spirit, whose conflict reflects the inner contradiction between the two poles of *Verwerfung*-anathema, the positive and the negative: the reactivation, and therefore the acknowledgment, of the Name-of-the-Father on the one hand; the malediction, and therefore the repulsion, of it on the other. Second, depersonalization and the hearing of voices. As a result of the initial deactivation of the paternal metaphor that had caused the loss of Daniel's identity, Daniel could not attribute the reactivation-via-malediction of the paternal metaphor to himself, because his own ego had been killed long before. The revelation could originate only from without, from the voices, from language itself, in a storming experience of invention that lasted years, until the day when the Word came to Daniel. *"Luder!"*

> Regarding the question that I am foregrounding here concerning the signifier's alienating impact, I will refer to the low point that came on a night in July of 1894 when Ahriman, the lower God, revealing himself to Schreber in the most impressive trappings of his power, addressed him with a simple and, according to the subject, common word of the basic language: *Luder!* To translate the word we must do more than simply look it up in the SachsVillatte dictionary, to which the French translator confined his efforts. Niederland's reference to "lewd" in English, meaning whore, does not seem acceptable to me as an attempt to convey the sense of spineless or slut, which is what it means when used as an obscene insult. But if we take into account the archaism indicated as characteristic of the basic language, I believe we can justifiably link this term to the root of the French leurre, and of the English "lure," which is certainly the best *ad hominem* address to be expected coming from the symbolic: the Other with a capital O can be awfully impertinent.[32]

"*Luder!*", rhyming with the name of the religious reformer, was the Word that Daniel received from the voices in July 1894, the night of his "profound internal change." After awhile, the anathema followed, "*Die Sonne ist eine Hure.*"[33] And once the anathema against the Name-of-the-Father was launched, the problem for Daniel was how to make it liveable, or at least tolerable. After great pain, he realized that to achieve this result he had to introduce – or better, witness – a change in the Order of the World, a kind of Nietzschean transvaluation of all values. The identification of blessedness with "voluptuousness" was the key to such a revolution, that led to the establishment of a reversed theological hierarchy between the wise Lord (the Persian God Ormuzd) and the malign Spirit (the Persian God Ahriman). In short, the entire ethical and onto-theological Order of the World had to be turned upside down in order to keep faith with the anathema that had damned, and yet revived, the Name-of-the-Father. *Luder* had to become Luther.[34]

To conclude, it would be misleading to think that the notion of *Verwerfung*-anathema and Daniel's experience can be generalized. The reactivation-via-malediction of the Name-of-the-Father – which we may term the Schreber complex – does not lie at the heart of all psychoses. Consider Joyce's "madness." As Lacan points out, Joyce suffered from a lack on the side of his father, not from the latter's intrusive presence.[35] Moreover, the Joyce complex, unlike the Schreber complex, revolves around a delusional metonymy, not a delusional metaphor.[36]

Regarding monosexuality, there would be lots to say. Today the proliferation of gender identities is deemed to be politically correct. *Vaste programme.* I wonder whether monosexuality too might be classified as a gender identity. Sometimes the truth, the true face of truth, the Sphynx, is not just unrecognizable; it is mocking.

NOTES

1 In the following, I will call Schreber by his first name, Daniel, for reasons that readers will understand by themselves. I am grateful to Henry Zvi Lothane (author of *In Defense of Schreber: Soul Murder and Psychiatry*, London: Analytic Press, 1992), who informed me that Daniel was actually called Paul by his relatives. In fact, Daniel was also Paul – and Luther, and Jesus Christ ...
2 Daniel Paul Schreber, *Memoirs of My Nervous Illness* (New York: The New York Review of Books, 2000), 186.
3 "Soul murder is a crime, not a diagnosis." Leonard Shengold, *Soul Murder Revisited: Thoughts about Therapy, Hate, Love, and Memory*, New Haven, CT: Yale University Press, 2000, 3.
4 Sigmund Freud, *Psycho-Analytic Notes on an Autobiographical Account of a Case of Paranoia*, in *Standard Edition* (London: Hogarth, 1958), 12:44.
5 Jacques Lacan, *On a Question prior to Any Possible Treatment of Psychosis*, in *Écrits* (New York: W.W. Norton, 2006), 466.
6 Schreber, *Memoirs*, 131.
7 Freud, *Psycho-Analytic Notes on an Autobiographical Account of a Case of Paranoia*, 71 (italics in the original).
8 Dr. Weber, *Medical Expert's Report to the Court*, in Schreber, *Memoirs*, 329.
9 Freud, *Psycho-Analytic Notes*, 71.
10 Freud, *Psycho-Analytic Notes*, 80.
11 Schreber, *Memoirs*, 250 (italics in the original).
12 Schreber, *Memoirs*, 252 (italics in the original).
13 Schreber, *Memoirs*, 233.
14 Schreber, *Memoirs*, 217 (italics in the original).
15 Schreber, *Memoirs*, 283.
16 Schreber, *Memoirs*, 286.
17 "If hell is other people, Schreber certainly has his share of the inferno. Exteriority constantly demands conformity, the appearance of his sexual offices, the sound of his genuflection. He has to fight himself, conduct an interior war, act the lawyer so as to be released, while inside he screams and bellows, howls and hallucinates, and hears voices mocking, insulting, provoking, cajoling and stringing him along as he nonetheless fearlessly pursues his inner imperative, his libidinal economy, which is perhaps always at some level a hidden force." Peter Goodrich, *Schreber's Law:*

Jurisprudence and Judgment in Transition (Edinburgh: Edinburgh University Press, 2018), 124.

18 To Goodrich and others who argue that Miss Schreber was "painfully and proleptically ahead of hir time" (Goodrich, *Schreber's Law*, 135), I am tempted to reply that Daniel would have probably considered their argument to be "fleeting-improvised." This is not to say, however, that I suggest pathologizing "transitional" desires (see Patricia Gherovici's contributions in chapter 7 of this volume, and elsewhere) for the simple reason that I do not see how to draw a line between pathology and normality. Any attempt to save Daniel from "pathologization" seems to restate, instead, such a distinction, just shifting it from one place to another. "Tout le monde est fou," not my words. Everybody is insane.

19 According to Lacan, the real is not an element but rather the *condition* of the symbolic register, what ensures that there is language and that language is a system of relations between discrete elements, the signifiers. Importantly, Lacan theorizes that no element of the symbolic register can symbolize that *condition*. And this explains why that *condition* is symbolized by an absent signifier, the phallus. Every time a signifier is elevated to the dignity of a metalinguistic condition of language, Lacan avers, it actually hints at the phallus (by way of metaphor or metonymy). But the fact is that "there is no metalanguage." That is to say, the phallus is absent by definition. In view of this, Lacan's "phallogocentrism" amounts to saying that one element of the symbolic register cannot be another. A chair is not a table. A man is not a woman. No totalization of language is possible from within language. For this reason, the speaking-being is affected by a lack. This lack, or partiality, or differentiality, or impossibility, is what Lacan calls the real.

20 Schreber, *Memoirs*, 273.

21 Schreber, *Memoirs*, 331.

22 Lacan, *On a Question*, 485.

23 Lacan, *On a Question*, 481.

24 Lacan, *On a Question*, 476–7.

25 Lacan, *On a Question*, 456.

26 Jacques Lacan, *The Instance of the Letter in the Unconscious*, in *Écrits*, 423.

27 Schreber, *Memoirs*, 273.

28 Lacan, *On a Question*, 465–6.

29 Lacan, *On a Question*, 481.

30 Lacan, *On a Question*, 481

31 For more details, see Morton Schatzman, *Soul Murder: Persecution in the Family* (New York: Random House, 1973), chap. 6.

32 Lacan, *On a Question*, 477–8.

33 It is worth noting that Luther had often used the word "*Hure*" in reference to the Roman Catholic Church and, more importantly, to "reason" (*Vernunft*). In light of this, Daniel's *Memoirs* may be defined as the nth *Kritik der reinen Hure*, which is a genre in modern literature (in his writing on Schreber, Lacan mentions, for instance, Georges Bataille's *Madame Edwarda*).

34 "Schreber may well have known that Martin Luther's family name had been 'Luder' before he himself changed it to 'Luther' in 1517, the year of his famous ninety-five theses." Eric L. Santner, *My Own Private Germany: Daniel Paul Schreber's Secret History of Modernity* (Princeton: Princeton University Press, 1996), 162n48.

35 Jacques Lacan, *The Sinthome: The Seminar of Jacques Lacan, Book XXIII* (Cambridge: Polity Press, 2016).

36 Davide Tarizzo, "La metonimia delirante: sull'inesistenza di Joyce," *La Psicoanalisi* 62 (2017): 132–56.

Appendix: Judge Schreber's Last Case

August und vom 16. September 1893 (Bl. 73 und bez. Bl.
75 derselben Beilageakten) sowie vom 10. Oktober dessel-
ben Jahres (Bl. 15 flg. der Sachakten) ganz unzweifel-
haft ergiebt, nicht der Fall. Unter diesen Umstän-
den wäre die vom Wagner beantragte Beiordnung
eines Rechtsanwalts behufs der Erhebung einer Kla-
ge im Sinne von § 620, Abs. 1, der C.P.O. eine völ-
lig zwecklose Maßregel und ist daher durch den an-
gefochtenen Beschluß mit vollem Rechte abgelehnt
worden.

Von dem gegenwärtigen Beschlusse ist von Amtswe-
gen dem Beschwerdeführer eine Ausfertigung zuzu-
stellen und eine weitere Ausfertigung zu den Sach-
akten zu bringen.

Dr Schreber

3/10 Entscheid. Gebr. von einem
Beschwerdegegenstande im Wer-
the von 2000 M.

Sch

G.L. III. C. 198/93
Ruling by the Third Civil Senate of the k.S.O.C.G
from 11 November 1893
on III. C. 198/93

The appeal raised in Reinsdorf on 18 October 1893 by former miner Karl Louis Wagner against the ruling by the President of the IV. Civil Chamber of the Landgericht Zwickau is dismissed as unfounded. In accordance with §45, Section 1 of the German Court Fees Law (*Gerichtskostengesetz*) and in conjunction with §92, Section 1 of the Code of Civil Procedure (*Zivilprozessordnung*), the complainant also bears the costs of his unsuccessful appeal.

The Amtsgericht Zwickau – following page 62[a], which since 1888 determined Wagner's mental illness–related incapacitation, and files submitted through W. 16/88 via the ruling from 17 March 1893, which ordered his tutelage – advised that Wagner's request to lift his incapacitation be considered. The annulment could now be requested by way of a lawsuit, which the complainant's appointed legal guardian and the public prosecutor were permitted to file (§620, Section 2 of the Code of Civil Procedure).

Wagner's legal guardian solely rejected seeking legal redress in accordance with Page 77[b] of the previously enclosed records, and Wagner, as per page 78 of the same documents, is informed of this. In accordance with page 15 of these papers, which is pursuant to a provision in §620, Section 3 of the Code of Civil Procedure, Wagner subsequently petitions the Landgericht Zwickau, the appropriate trial court, to assign him legal representation to raise his appeal. The president of the trial court, who was called upon to make a decision in this case, however, rejected this request, likely due to the hopelessness of the intended legal proceedings. The filed complaint was directed at this.

It could not have been successful.

The opposite presupposed that [Insert] the reason for his legal incapacitation had in the meantime ceased, meaning that his mental state had returned to normal. This, however, is not the case, as can undoubtedly be deduced not only from the omissions in assessments by the community doctor, Dr. Barth, in Zwickau from 20 February to 16 March 1893, who also served as an expert witness in the case, but also from the written submissions by Wagner dated 21 August, 28 August, 16 September (pages 73 and 75 of the same records), and 10 October 1893 (page 15ff of the same records).

[Insert:] the intended lawsuit would not have any chance of success, meaning that there were few clues to support Wagner's claim.

Under these circumstances, the appointment of a lawyer to raise an appeal, as requested by Wagner in accordance with §620, Section 1 of the Code of Civil Procedure, would have been an entirely pointless measure and was thus rightly rejected by the disputed ruling.

A copy of the current ruling shall be delivered to the complainant through official channels and a further copy shall be added to the files.

[Signature] Dr. Schreber
[Note:]
3/10 decision; Subject of complaint valued at 2,000 M.
[signed] Sch.

G. L. III. C. 198/93

Beschluß
des dritten Civilsenats des k.S.O.C.Gs.
vom 11. November 1893
zu III. C. 198/93
Die von dem vormaligen Bergarbeiter Karl Louis Wagner in Reinsdorf gegen den Beschluß des Vorsitzenden der IV. Civilkammer des Landgerichts Zwickau vom 18. Oktober 1893 eingelegte Beschwerde, als welche die von Wagner unter dem 1. November 1893 an das O.L.G. gerichtete schriftliche Eingabe ihrem Inhalte und Zweck nach sich darstellt, wird als unbegründet zurückgewiesen, der Beschwerdeführer hat auch in Gemäßheit von § 45, Abs. 1, des Ger. Kost. Ges. in Verbindung mit § 92, Abs. 1, der C.P.O. die Kosten seines erfolglosen Rechtsmittels zu tragen.
Das Amtsgericht Zwickau hat nach Blt. 62[a] der vor demselben seit dem Jahre 1888 über die wegen Geisteskrankheit erfolgte Entmündigung Wagners und angeordnete Bevormundung desselben unter W. 16/88. ergangenen Akten mittelst Beschlußes vom 17. März 1893 den Antrag Wagners auf Wiederaufhebung seiner Entmündigung nahegelegt. Diese Wiederaufhebung könnte zwar nunmehr im Wege der Klage beantragt werden, zu deren Erhebung sowohl der dem Beschwerdeführer bestellte Vormund, als auch der Staatsanwalt Befugt wäre (§ 620, Abs. 2, der C.P.O.). Allein der Vormund Wagners hat nach Blt. 77[b] der voran-

gezogenen Beilagsakten die Erhebung der Klage
abgelehnt und Wagner ist nach Blt. 78 derselben
Akten hiervon in Kenntniß gesetzt worden. Hie-
rauf hat sich der letztere nach Blt. 15 der Sach-
akten gemäß der Vorschrift in § 620, Abs. 3,
der C.P.O. an das Landgericht Zwickau als das
zuständige Prozeßgericht mit dem Antrage ge-
wendet, ihm zur Erhebung der Klage einen
Rechtsanwalt als Vertreter beizuordnen.
Der insoweit zur Entscheidung berufene Vorsit-
zende des Prozeßgerichts hat aber diesen An-
trag, und zwar, wie man annehmen muß, we-
gen Aussichtslosigkeit der beabsichtigten Rechts-
verfolgung abgelehnt und hiergegen richtet sich
die eingelegte Beschwerde.
Einen Erfolg konnte dieselbe nicht haben.
Das Gegentheil setzte voraus, daß der [*Einschub*]
Grund ~~der~~ seiner Entmündigung ~~Wagners~~ inzwischen
weggefallen d.h. ~~daß dessen~~ sein Geisteszustand wie-
der in normaler geworden sein solle. Dies ist aber,
wie sich sowohl aus den gutachtlichen Auslaßungen
des als Sachverständigen gehörten Bezirksarztes
Dr. Barth in Zwickau vom 20. Februar und 16. März
1893 (Blt. 55ff und 61[b] jener Beilagsakten), als
auch aus den schriftlichen Eingaben Wagners vom 21./28.
[Einschub:] beabsichtigten Klage mindestens einige Aussicht auf Erfolg nicht abzusprechen
wäre, daß also irgend welcher Anhalt für die Behauptung Wagners gegeben wäre, nach welcher der
August und vom 16. September 1893 (Blt. 73 und bez. Blt.
75 derselben Beilagsakten) sowie vom 10. Oktober dessel-
ben Jahres (Blt. 15ff der Sachakten) ganz unzweifel-
haft ergibt, nicht der Fall. Unter diesen Umstän-
den wäre die von Wagner beantragte Beiordnung
eines Rechtsanwalts behufs der Erhebung einer Kla-
ge im Sinne von § 620, Abs. 1, der C.P.O. eine völ-
lig zwecklose Maßregel und ist daher durch den an-
gefachtenen Beschluß mit vollem Rechte abgelehnt
worden.
Von dem gegenwärtigen Beschluße ist von Amtswe-
gen dem Beschwerdeführer eine Ausfertigung zuzu-
stellen und eine weitere Ausfertigung zu den Sach-

akten zu bringen.
[Unterschrift] Dr. Schreber
[Notiz:]
3/10 Entscheid. Gebr. von einem Beschwerdegegenstand im Werthe von 2000 M.
[gez.] Sch.

Contributors

Daniela Gandorfer holds a PhD in comparative literature from Princeton University. She is the co-founder of the research agency Logische Phantasie Lab (Loφ Lab) and is a postdoctoral researcher at University of California, Santa Cruz. Her work lies at the intersection of science and technology studies, law, and philosophy and focuses on the ethics of sensing and sense-making in technological and scientific "frontier spaces." In addition to her various articles, book chapters, and essay publications, Daniela co-edited the notable "Matterphorical" special issue of *Theory and Event* (Johns Hopkins Press, January 2021) and, most recently, the *Research Handbook in Law and Literature and Literature* ((Edward Elgar Publishing, forthcoming 2022). Her book *Matterphorics: On the Laws of Theory* is forthcoming with Duke University Press.

Werner Gephart is a jurist, a sociologist, and an artist; he is a senior professor of sociology at the University of Bonn, founding director of the Käte Hamburger Center for Advanced Study of "Law as Culture," editor of Max Weber's writings on the law (*MWG* I/22–3), author, co-author, and editor of more than fifty books in law, culture, religion, and art. He has been awarded an honorary doctorate in philosophy by the University of Turin, and he was honorary artist at King's College London, 2017, as well as being Senior Villey Fellow at Paris II (Panthéon Assas) in 2021/2.

Patricia Gherovici, PhD, is a recipient of the 2020 Sigourney Award for her clinical and scholarly work with Latinx and gender-variant communities. She is co-founder and director of the Philadelphia Lacan Group and Associate Faculty, Psychoanalytic Studies Minor, University of Pennsylvania, honorary member at IPTAR, and founding member of Das Unbehagen. Her single-authored books include *The Puerto Rican Syndrome* (Other Press, 2003), winner of the Gradiva Award; *Please Select Your Gender: From the Invention of Hysteria to the Democratizing of*

Transgenderism (Routledge, 2010), winner of the Boyer Prize; and *Transgender Psychoanalysis: A Lacanian Perspective on Sexual Difference* (Routledge, 2017). Most recently, with Chris Christian she published *Psychoanalysis in the Barrios: Race, Class, and the Unconscious* (Routledge, 2019), winner of the Gradiva Award, and the American Board and Academy of Psychoanalysis Book Prize.

Peter Goodrich is an ardent advocate of argute alliterations and the habile silent *p*, as in "ptomaine," "raspberry," and "rhubarb." Peter perturbs the Panglossian portals and protocols of pandectian legalities and other plagiarisms with the pataphysical portents of posthuman sciences and their paromoion postulates. A practitioner of widdershins in the *circulus disciplinarum*, he is author, recently and most compositely, of *Advanced Introduction to Law and Literature* (Edward Elgar) and the forthcoming *Vision and Decision: On the Judicial Uses of Images* (Oxford University Press). Chef, filmmaker, and olericulturalist, he is working on a project entitled "Laugh and Critique."

W.J.T. (Tom) Mitchell is a peripatetic professor of art, literature, media, and sandcastling at the University of Chicago where he has been editor of *Critical Inquiry* for forty years. Demonstrating the continuing triumph of hope over experience, he continues to write books like *Iconology, Picture Theory, Image Science,* and *What Do Pictures Want?* That last question is still awaiting a clear and unequivocal answer. Meanwhile his recent exhibition (Metapictures) in Chicago was entirely given away to the public on its closing, and his memoir, *Mental Traveler: A Father, a Son, and a Journey through Schizophrenia* has been making the rounds of bookstore readings.

Rajgopal Saikumar is a doctoral candidate in English at New York University. His writings have appeared in *South Asia: Journal of South Asian Studies, Cambridge Journal of Postcolonial Literary Inquiry,* and *Routledge Human Rights in India.*

Mark Sanders is professor of comparative literature and English at New York University and Extraordinary Professor of Afrikaans and Dutch at Stellenbosch University. He is the author of several books, including *Learning Zulu: A Secret History of Language in South Africa, Ambiguities of Witnessing: Law and Literature in the Time of a Truth Commission,* and *Complicities: The Intellectual and Apartheid.* His essay "Psychoanalysis, Mourning, and the Law: Schreber's Paranoia as Crisis of Judging" appeared in *Law and Mourning,* a volume edited by Austin Sarat and Martha Merrill Umphrey.

Ludwig Schmitz is a PhD candidate in the department of Comparative Literature at New York University. He is writing a book on the Swedish social democratic intellectual Gunnar Myrdal's contacts with Afro-American and South Asian writers, tracing the emergence of a certain concept of the social in these mid-twentieth century conversations on equality, race, and development. He is translating fiction from Swahili to Swedish and occasionally contributes with essays and op-eds to Swedish newspapers.

Davide Tarizzo is associate professor of moral philosophy at the University of Salerno, Italy. He has written extensively on psychoanalysis and political theory. Among his publications are *Introduzione a Lacan* (2003); *Giochi di potere. Sulla paranoia politica* (2007); *La vita, un'invenzione recente* (2010; English translation as *Life: A Modern Invention*, Minnesota University Press, 2017); *Political Grammars: The Unconscious Foundations of Modern Democracy* (2021). He is working on project provisionally entitled *The Morals of Life: Biology, Biopolitics, Bioethics.*

Katrin Trüstedt is research associate with the project "Politics of Appearing" and head of the program area "History of Theory" at the Leibniz Center for Literary and Cultural Studies in Berlin. Her research is situated at the intersection of literature, philosophy, and law. She is the author of *The Comedy of Tragedy* (Konstanz University Press, 2011), and co-editor of *Happy Days: Life and Knowledge in Cavell* (Fink, 2009), *Pure Joke: The Comedy of Theater since Brecht* (special issue of the Brecht Yearbook, 2019), and *Representing Agency* (special issue of *Law and Literature*, 2020). Katrin is a general editor of the journal *Law and Literature.* Her latest book on "Stellvertretung" (advocacy, agency, representation, substitution) (Konstanz University Press, 2021), unfolds the notion of speaking and acting for others in theatre, theology, law, and literature.

Index

www.ingramcontent.com/pod-product-compliance
Lightning Source LLC
LaVergne TN
LVHW090158080826
844660LV00013B/862/J

* 9 7 8 1 4 8 7 5 0 9 1 5 6 *